SONORAN DESERT

Wildflowers

A Field Guide to Common Species of the Sonoran Desert,
including Anza-Borrego Desert State Park,
Saguaro National Park, Organ Pipe Cactus National
Monument, Ironwood Forest National Monument, and the
Sonoran Portion of Joshua Tree National Park

by Richard Spellenberg

FALCON®

GUILFORD, CONNECTICUT
HELENA, MONTANA

AN IMPRINT OF THE GLOBE PEQUOT

Text design: Sue Cary
Photo credits: All photos by the author unless otherwise indicated.

Library of Congress Cataloging-in-Publication Data is available.

ISBN 0-7627-1136-1

Manufactured in Korea
First Edition/First Printing

CAUTION
Ingesting plants or plant parts poses a potentially extreme health hazard and could result in sickness or even death. No one should attempt to use any wild plant for food or medicine without adequate training by a fully qualified professional. The author, publisher, and all others associated with the production and distribution of this book assume no liability for the actions of the reader.

All participants in the recreational activities suggested by this book must assume responsibility for their own actions and safety. The information contained in this guidebook cannot replace sound judgment and good decision-making skills, which help reduce risk exposure; nor does the scope of this book allow for disclosure of all the potential hazards and risks involved in such activities.

Learn as much as possible about the recreational activities in which you participate, prepare for the unexpected, and be cautious. The reward will be a safer and more enjoyable experience.

EDICATION

This book is dedicated to Carol, whose capacity to appreciate each day as a wonderful opportunity to enjoy and to see beauty in a multitude of circumstances sets a marvelous example for us all.

ACKNOWLEDGMENTS

No complex project is ever completed without the generous help and encouragement of many people. To single out one person from others, I would like to express my sincere appreciation to my wife, Naida Zucker, for her extraordinary patience as I spent long hours in the field or at the computer; her help with technical aspects of computer software; her reviews of manuscript; her assistance in the field with notes and photographic paraphernalia; and her tolerance of my frustration stemming from wind, drought, heat, annoying insects, and long distances traveled. In so many ways, this book is a product of her efforts as well as mine. I also extend sincere gratitude to Mary Brunt, who assisted in the care of my aged mother during my wife's and my field excursions.

Numerous individuals directly helped with identifying or locating plants. On numerous occasions I contacted Phil Jenkins of the University of Arizona for help with plant identifications and locations of hard-to-find species. He and colleagues Richard Felger and Steve McLaughlin provided invaluable help. Ross Zimmerman helped in locating cacti in the Tucson area, and with his father, Jim, my longtime good friend and colleague, we spent enjoyable hours in mesquite thickets searching out the marvelous Queen-of-the-Night cactus. Many others provided expert assistance, among them: Dan Austin and Richard Miller, Convolvulaceae (Florida Atlantic University and Duke University, respectively); Peter Hoch, *Oenothera* (Missouri Botanical Garden); John MacDougal, *Passiflora* (Cornell University); Bruce Parfitt, *Echinocereus* (University of Michigan–Flint); Mark Porter, Polemoniaceae (Rancho Santa Ana Botanical Garden); John Strother, Asteraceae (University of California, Berkeley); Kelly Allred, grasses, Chris Stubben, *Aquilegia* (New Mexico State University); John Weins, *Passiflora mexicana* (Arizona–Sonora Desert Museum); and George Yatskievych, *Orobanche* (Missouri Botanical Garden).

Jim and Rachel Zimmerman, Tom and Eleanor Wootten, and John and Beverly Smith and their daughter Julia provided hospitality and lodging during field work. Russ Buhrow, Sallie Herman, and April Bourie (Tohono Chul Park, Tucson), Joanie Cahill (Anza-Borrego Desert State Park), Arnie

Sealove and Officer C. Stevens (Hoover Dam Visitor Center), and Sandi Williams (Arizona–Sonora Desert Museum) all provided assistance in various ways. My son, Michael, cured some baffling technical problems involving modern cameras. Finally, Susan Hettinga and Paula Gonzalez from the Camera Shop, and Lisa Morales of Leo's Images, all in Las Cruces, and Carl's Darkroom Film Processing in Albuquerque provided excellent, consistent, and friendly service.

To each, thanks so much.

The Sonoran Desert

About 40 percent of the Sonoran Desert is in the United States and 60 percent is in Mexico. Unique to North American deserts, it has a sea coast of 2,360 miles (3,800 km) situated practically in the middle of the desert. Its southern third lies beneath descending, dry, warm air, part of the worldwide atmospheric circulation. Its northern portion is in rain shadows caused by high mountain ranges to the east and west. The northern and eastern edges are marked by occasional complete days of freezing. The southern limit is defined by average penetration of frost from the north. The west edge is either limited by the sea or by rainfall sufficient to sustain chaparral (a dense shrub vegetation type). Generally northwest–southeast trending mountain ranges, with valleys between, dot the interior. Elevation of the desert ranges from about 100 feet below sea level west of the Colorado River in the United States to about 3,000 feet, or up to nearly 3,500 feet along its eastern edge in Arizona. Much of the desert is geologically igneous, some areas basaltic, others andesitic or of closely related rock. Limestone occurs sporadically. The desert's proximity to the sea, its low elevation, its varied topography and geology, and its latitude make it a subtropical desert where freezes are uncommon and rarely severe. All contribute to its biological diversity, the greatest of any North American desert.

Further contributing to the Sonoran Desert's diversity is its rainfall pattern. Less than 2–3 inches of rain falls per year, on average, in the low areas in California and northern Baja California. Most or all is in winter. In the vicinity of Phoenix and Tucson, rains fall in winter and in summer. Near Tucson there is about 13 inches per year. In the southern parts of the desert in Sonora, most rain falls in summer.

The Sonoran Desert is divided into six subdivisions, based on vegetation, which reflects the climate. Relationships of plants suggest that the Mojave Desert might be considered part of the system, but freezing excludes most trees of the Bean Family (Fabaceae) and large cacti. The two subdivisions north of the international boundary, the low, hot, very dry, winter-rainfall Lower Colorado River Valley and the comparatively lush, higher and colder, bi-seasonal–rainfall Arizona Upland, are strongly contrasting. The former has large barren areas, few trees, and no large cacti—it is too hot and dry. The latter has trees and columnar cacti related to the dry forests of Mexico, but only those that can withstand winter frosts. Those that cannot are restricted to the southern subdivisions.

EVOLUTION OF THE SONORAN DESERT

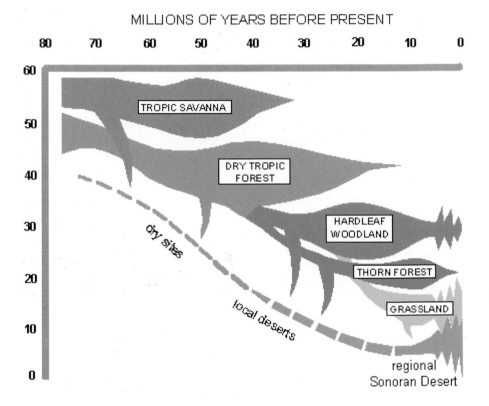

MILLIONS OF YEARS BEFORE PRESENT

The Origin of the Sonoran Desert

The Sonoran Desert, as a major assemblage of dry-adapted plants similar to those of today, formed 15–8 million years ago, as one vegetation type replaced another during a long-term drying trend in western North America. Rain shadows from the rather young Sierra Madre Occidental to the east and the newly forming mountains of Baja California to the west contributed to the drying trend. The tectonic stretching and tearing of southwestern North America as the continent ground against the Pacific Plate caused low valleys where little rain falls and the Gulf of California to form. In the last 2 million years, the desert has fluctuated, moving north and south, and up and down mountains, as glaciers to the north and in high mountains advanced and retreated. In its present composition of plant species, the Sonoran Desert is estimated to be only about 4,500 years old, when Foothills Palo Verde *(Cercidium microphyllum),* Desert Ironwood *(Olneya tesota),* Organpipe Cactus *(Stenocereous thurberi),* and other plants arrived from southern retreats.

Arizona Upland vegetation

Characteristics of vegetation of the Arizona Upland subdivison of the Sonoran Desert: North of the international boundary, the Arizona Upland subdivision forms the eastern half of the Sonoran Desert. It is the highest, coldest part, receiving 12–15 inches of rain per year, with slightly more than half falling in summer. This is a very rich association of plants with trees, shrubs, large and small cacti, and many kinds of herbaceous plants, perennial and annual. In the valleys, where colder air collects, there may be extensive stands of Velvet Mesquite *(Prosopis velutina)*. Saguaro *(Carnegia gigantea)* grows on warmer slopes above the valleys. Freezing events restrict northward expansion of less hardy southern species.

Some of the major plant species can be seen in the photo above from the south slopes of the Tucson Mountains. The yellow flowering tree is Foothills Palo Verde *(Cercidium microphyllum)*. To its right is an Ocotillo *(Fouquieria splendens)* with red flowers. A Saguaro near the center is just beginning to flower; numerous others dot the slopes. In front of the Palo Verde is Jojoba *(Simmondsia chinensis)*, a shrub with opposite, evergreen leaves. With its flat pads bright with reflection of the morning sun, Tulip Prickly-Pear *(Opuntia phaeacantha)* can be seen sprawling in the foreground. Creosotebush *(Larrea tridentata)* is common throughout.

Transition vegetation

Vegetation of the transition region from the Arizona Upland to the Lower Colorado River Valley subdivisions of the Sonoran Desert: The transition from the Arizona Upland subdivision to the hotter, drier Colorado River Valley subdivision occurs along a band that begins north of Parker in western Arizona, trends southeastward to near Phoenix, then south to the international border near Organ Pipe Cactus National Monument. This transition occurs at 1,000–1,500 feet, in an area receiving 7–8 inches of rain a year, about equally divided between winter and summer. From east to west across the transition, vegetation becomes sparser, and trees are more often restricted to watercourses. The photograph above is from the upper elevations of the transition area in Organ Pipe Cactus National Monument, the Ajo Mountain Range forming the background.

The evergreen Creosotebush *(Larrea tridentata),* with opposite, pinnately divided leaves, each with only two leaflets, is at lower left and lower right. Three large cacti are in midground, the columnar Saguaro *(Carnegia gigantea)* at left center, Jumping Cholla *(Opuntia fulgida)* in middle, and at right center, the many-stemmed Organpipe Cactus *(Stenocereus thurberi).* Triangleleaf Bursage *(Ambrosia deltoidea),* very common on the Arizona Upland, is the gray shrublet in center foreground, now mostly leafless. Foothills Palo Verde *(Cercidium microphyllum)* is scattered behind the cacti.

Colorado River Valley vegetation

Vegetation of the Lower Colorado River Valley Subdivision of the Sonoran Desert: This subdivision is low, hot, and dry, with summer temperatures occasionally exceeding 120 degrees F. Rainfall is primarily in the winter, at the driest sites sometimes less than 3 inches per year. Vegetation density and diversity steadily decrease from the transition between the two subdivisions as elevation and rainfall decrease westward. Trees are sparse, restricted to watercourses, and on harsher sites almost all vegetation is restricted to places where water gathers after rain. The Saguaro *(Carnegia gigantea)* (left and right of photo) is smaller and less frequent. In California, too hot and dry for columnar cacti, Saguaro is found only in a few small populations near the Colorado River. Desert pavement, a layer of pebbles resulting from wind and water action, is common. The photo above looks west to the Gila Mountains east of Yuma.

Scattered shrubs of Ironwood *(Olneya tesota)*, Foothills Palo Verde *(Cercidium microphyllum)*, and Creosotebush *(Larrea tridentata)* are seen in the water channels. The small gray shrub in left mid-ground is White Bursage *(Ambrosia dumosa)*, very common in this subdivision. An Ocotillo *(Fouquieria splendens)* is seen near front center. In larger washes, Smoketree *(Psorothamnus spinosus)*, not shown in this photo, will occur.

Plant form on Sonoran Desert vegetation

How Plants Do It on the Desert

The water problem. Cellular activity requires water; life depends on it. In a desert, water, a scarce resource, is often central to adaptations that promote its efficient, even miserly, use.

Plants are between the proverbial "rock and a hard place." Once a seedling germinates, it cannot get up and move to a preferable, perhaps gentler, site. If it is a green plant, it must produce (by photosynthesis) its sugars (its "food") from the sun's energy, water from the soil, and carbon dioxide from the air by extraordinarily complex chemical reactions in the cell. The carbon dioxide must enter ("the rock") the plant through tiny pores in leaves and green stems, but when carbon dioxide enters, water can escape ("the hard place"). Desert plants must minimize water loss, or avoid completely dry conditions.

The photograph on page 8 from the Castle Dome Mountains in western Arizona shows plants with different strategies for coping with the photosynthesis versus water-loss problem. The paragraph below reviews these plants, and the following pages detail the strategies in general, and relate them to some of the wildflowers in this book.

The yellow bush in the foreground is Brittlebush *(Encelia farinosa);* its leaf number changes with soil moisture. Silvery leaves help reflect heat, keeping the leaves cool. Barely visible in front of the rock is Notch-Leaf Scorpion-Weed *(Phacelia crenulata),* and the green haze on the hillside is Blond Plantain *(Plantago ovata).* Both are annuals, growing when there is adequate moisture, avoiding drought by way of dormant seeds. The green tufts to the left of Brittlebush are California Fagonia (*Fagonia laevis*), a perennial that persists during drought, putting up green stems from its deep, dormant roots when there is soil moisture. Ocotillo *(Fouquieria splendens),* in the center, is similar in this respect, producing leaves after rains, but in this case the stems are persistent and very drought resistant. The two cacti, the Saguaro *(Carnegia gigantea)* in the background, and Beavertail Cactus *(Opuntia basilaris)* in left foreground, store water and conserve it by opening their pores in the cool of the night, letting in carbon dioxide and storing it, and closing the pores and photosynthesizing during the day when it is hot.

Beating the water problem—plant form on the Sonoran Desert. The Sonoran Desert is the richest of deserts with regard to diversity of plant form, much of which is involved with water conservation. The major strategies for meeting the demands of growth and reproduction, which require photosynthesis and conservation of water, are many. Examples are provided from plants included in this book.

Annual plants. Annual plants germinate, grow, and produce seeds within one year. They "avoid" drought through seed dormancy. Those on the Sonoran Desert that germinate in winter or early spring, maturing by summer, often have their closest relatives on the Mojave Desert. Examples are suncups *(Camissonia)*, poppies *(Eschscholzia)*, lupines *(Lupinus)*, various mustards *(Brassica, Dithyrea,* some *Draba)*, Indian-Wheats *(Plantago)*, fiddlenecks *(Amsinckia)*. Summer annuals germinate after the summer rains begin. Closest relatives usually are from the east or south. Examples are Devil's Claw *(Proboscidea parviflora)*, some sunflowers *(Helianthus petiolaris)*, and many morning glories *(Ipomoea purpurea, I. barbatisepala)*.

Facultative perennials. "Facultative" means that an organism may adopt one of two or more strategies depending upon environmental conditions. In this case the same species may function either as annual or a perennial. Perennial plants can get a "jump" on those that are strictly annual, growing rapidly when conditions are right, perhaps claiming more resources and producing more seed. Desert Marigold *(Baileya multiradiata)*, trailing four o'clocks *(Allionia)*, and many globemallows *(Sphaeralcea)* are examples.

Root and bulb perennials. The underground portion persists through cold or drought, the top dying back. Some root perennials are thorn-apples *(Datura)*, Desert Anemone *(Anemone tuberosa)*, Parish's Larkspur *(Delphinium parishii)*, Colorado Four O'Clock *(Mirabilis multiflora)*, and Desert Rhubarb *(Rumex hymenosepalus)*. Bulbs are enlarged, food-storing, subterranean buds. On the Sonoran Desert all bulb perennials, such as Blue Dicks *(Dichelostemma capitatum)*, Desert Lily *(Hesperocallis undulata)*, and Mariposa Lilies *(Calochortus)*, are stimulated only by winter rains.

Succulent rosettes. Leaves are crowded together on a stem, and by their arrangement may funnel water to the roots. Roots are shallow and readily absorb any water, which is stored in the leaf where it is immediately available for cellular activities. Leaves have a waxy covering to retard water loss. Photosynthesis is as described in the section "Stem succulents." Examples are Desert Century Plant *(Agave deserti)*, Yucca, and Gila Live-Forever *(Dudleya collomae)*.

Succulent leaves, not in rosettes. Not as massive as most of those above, and without the funneling capacity to direct water to roots, these plants are also shallow rooted, store water in the leaves, and probably have photosynthesis as in cacti. Most are short-lived. They survive short periods of drought by relying on water stored in leaves. Examples here in the Purslane Family *(Portulacaceae)* are Purslane *(Portulaca oleracea),* Copper Purslane, *(P. suffrutescens),* and Red Maids *(Calandrinia ciliata).*

Stem succulents. Stem succulents may be bulky and unbranched or branched, or slender and shrubby. On the Sonoran Desert in the United States, almost all are cacti (for example, *Ferocactus, Opuntia).* A few are milkweeds *(Asclepias),* although these may just as easily be considered as part of the next group. The cylindrical or spherical shape reduces surface area relative to volume, reducing water loss. Nocturnal absorption and storage of carbon dioxide occurs through open pores (stomates) at night when it is cooler and less water is evaporated; during the day they are closed and photosynthesis takes place. Water loss is reduced.

Small-leaved green-stemmed leafy perennials. Green leaves are produced on green stems. Photosynthesis occurs in both. A balance between sugar production and water loss is achieved by minimizing surface area for evaporation and for heating. As drought progresses, leaves may be dropped, the stems continuing photosynthesis. Palo Verdes *(Cercidium),* Sweetbush *(Bebbia juncea),* and Turpentine Broom *(Thamnosma montana)* are examples.

Drought-deciduous thin-leaved plants. Persistent above-ground stems produce thin, water-consuming leaves, which during "good times" photosynthesize rapidly. When water is unavailable, leaves are dropped. Some species may continue lower rates of photosynthesis in their stems; others will be dormant. The classic is Ocotillo *(Fouquieria splendens),* which may produce several flushes of leaves a season after good rains. Other examples are Chuparosa *(Justicia californica)* and Western Coral-Bean *(Erythrina flabelliformis).*

Low leafy softwood semi-shrubs. Flexibility is the key here. This is the most common plant form on the Sonoran Desert. These are neither shrubs, with hard wood and relatively permanent branches, nor soft, fleshy, easily wilted herbs. They can rapidly alter structure, numbers of branches, and numbers of leaves. By such means they are constantly adjusting to degree of drought. Examples are Desert Holly *(Atriplex hymenelytra),* Bastard Sage *(Eriogonum wrightii),* and Brittlebush *(Encelia farinosa).*

Evergreen hardwood shrubs. These remarkable, deep-rooted plants withstand severe drought and still maintain photosynthesis. Most have leaves modified to withstand heat and retard water loss (small, can be rotated to minimize surface exposed to sun, waxy coating, very small pores, etc.). One is Creosotebush *(Larrea tridentata)*, pictured in some of the introductory photos. When fully charged with water it is a deep, "healthy" green. When drought stricken it is a brownish olive-green, and may even drop its leaves bit by bit. It can recover quickly. A small, drenching summer storm may leave a bright green swath of well-watered Creosotebush across miles of otherwise brown, drought-weary shrubs.

Winter-deciduous perennials. None of these plants is sufficiently showy to be included in this book. They are woody plants that lose their leaves when it is cold, as does Velvet Mesquite *(Prosopis velutina)*. The woody, hard tissues are more resistant. They can grow near the northern edges of the Sonoran Desert where winters are dry and freezing occurs.

Parasites. Parasites live at the expense of another organism, their host, and are dependent upon its ability to withstand the rigors of the desert. Parasites do not necessarily show specific adaptations to the desert environment. Flat-Globe Dodder *(Cuscuta umbellata)*, Purple Pop-Ups *(Pholisma arenarium)* and Desert Broomrape *(Orobanche cooperi)* are examples.

Halophytes. These plants grow in habitats with high salt and alkalinity, habitats common on deserts where water drains, stands, and evaporates. The plants must use salty water. Their "reward" is to occupy areas where "ordinary" plants do not grow. Western Sea-Purslane *(Sesuvium verrucosum)* is an example.

Keeping Cool on the Desert

The water-saving nature of various life forms on the desert is enhanced by other features, some serving more than one purpose. If a plant can keep its surfaces cool, less water will evaporate. As important, life-sustaining processes in plants operate at optimal temperatures. When temperatures are too high (also too low), cell activity simply slows to a crawl or ceases. Death can result. In honeysweet *(Tidestromia)* species photosynthesis is most efficient at high temperatures. To develop molecular processes to accommodate extremes, however, is not simple because of the complexity of interactions within cells. It is often simpler to develop mechanisms that reduce heating in the desert sun. Many desert plants show degrees of both, adjustment of molecular processes and mechanisms to retard heating.

Edge effect and the boundary layer. Air moves more slowly near a surface (there is "drag") than it does farther away. This layer of air against an organism is the boundary layer, and it acts as insulation, retarding heat loss through convective cooling. Where moving air strikes an edge, the boundary layer is considerably thinner and heat is carried away; the edges are cooler. Small leaves have more edge relative to expanse of surface than do large leaves, and their tissues can more easily be kept cooler. Small, divided leaves have more edges, and cooling is enhanced.

Cacti, especially when large, are not smoothly cylindrical or spherical. The folds, ribs, and nipples serve to increase surface relative to volume and may act like fins on a radiator. Moving air tumbles, twists, and turns across the surface, perhaps scouring the boundary layer to thinness, increasing convective cooling. The folds and undulations of a cactus's surface also serve another function. As a cactus absorbs water, the surface can stretch, accommodating the expanding volume.

Cooling through reflection. Why are so many desert plants covered with pale hairs or a pale, waxy surface? Why not dark brown, or black? Because pale colors reflect light and heat; dark colors absorb both. Pale hairs may be combined with divided leaves, as in Scarlet Milkvetch *(Astragalus coccineus)*, or on a plant that adjusts to drought as in Brittlebush *(Encelia farinosa)*. Waxes also form a layer impervious to water, thus retarding water loss. A layer of hairs can also retard water loss by keeping a moist layer of air against the plant, in effect increasing the boundary layer, but this then may increase heating. A balance must be found between heat retention and avoiding water loss. Spines may also serve similar functions. Those of Teddy-Bear Cholla *(Opuntia bigelovii)* are pale and dense. Their pale color reflects heat; their density shades the surface.

The angle of exposure. Large succulents can absorb and hold considerable heat. When they are erect, as is the case for chollas and beavertail cacti *(Opuntia)*, they are less exposed to the overhead summer sun. If you have a pad-forming *Opuntia (O. basilaris, O. engelmannii, O. violacea,* or any other) and wish to experiment, very carefully bend and anchor a branch so one or more pads face up directly to the noontime sun. It may soon develop burned patches on its surface.

Plants with leaves often have great flexibility in leaf orientation, and those with compound leaves show particularly fine adjustment. In the base of the leaf stalk, often as a swollen patch called a "pulvinus," are cells that absorb and release water. Similar cells may also occur along the midrib of folded leaves. When cells are full of water they expand; when they lose water they are flabby. The expansion and softening of adjacent cells in the stalk of a leaf allow it to twist, turn, or fold the leaf blade or leaflet.

Watch a lupine during a day. Arizona Lupine *(Lupinus arizonicus)* and Arroyo Lupine *(L. sparsiflorus)* are both excellent practitioners of leaf control. These annual species are drought avoiders, growing when it is cooler and moist. At the base of each leaflet is a pulvinus, and at the leaf stalk base is a larger pulvinus. In the morning and evening all the leaves face the sun, and leaflets are expanded. In the middle of the day, depending on whether it is hot or dry or there is ample water, leaflets may be partially folded and partially drooping or they may be fully expanded. These plants balance maximum potential for photosynthesis against the need for water conservation. Numerous plants, including many desert shrubs, also continuously orient their leaves to minimize heating.

Protecting That Tasty Morsel

Plants support nearly all life on earth through photosynthesis. That is, they use energy from the sun to take small, low-energy molecules such as carbon dioxide and water, break them apart, and rearrange the parts into high-energy sugars, thereby storing the sun's energy. From those sugars and other smaller molecules, through myriad cellular processes, starches, fats, and proteins are built. Plants use these molecules to live and grow; animals that eat plants use them to live and grow, and animals that eat animals ultimately depend on the productivity of plants. So do the fungi and many of the bacteria that break down dead matter, releasing for their use the energy still stored in complex molecules, returning low energy molecules back to the air and soil.

Under many circumstances plants protect the energy they store from being taken by animals, including insects. In the desert, where plants struggle against odds for survival, protection of their hard-earned body tissues becomes paramount. There are several ways plants do this: They may hide in time and space, mount a mechanical defense, or enter into chemical warfare. Animals respond through time and develop adaptations that overcome a particular defense, but by this time the plant species may have developed new ones. Many plants employ more than one defense system.

"Hiding" in space and time. An otherwise defenseless plant that grows upon an inaccessible cliff has pretty well secluded itself in space from animals that might eat it. A less obvious means of "escaping" animals that eat plants, especially insects, is to appear suddenly and briefly in one area, and then disappear. Another population may appear at another time elsewhere when environmental conditions are just right. By the time insects find a population and begin to ravage it, the plants may have produced seed and withered. Many desert annuals are protected in this manner.

Mechanical defenses. Using the equivalents of swords, knives, and needles are obvious defenses against animals. There is a matter of scale involved, also. The stout spines of the Desert Century Plant *(Agave deserti)* might protect against large animals, but small ones are unaffected. Some cacti seem truly diabolical. One can only imagine a small animal poking its nose into the spines of Graham's Nipple Cactus *(Mammiliaria grahamii)*, being stabbed by a spine, pulling back, and being snagged and held by one of the longer hooked spines. Species of *Opuntia* have large spines and clusters of minute, irritating bristles called glochids that, under a microscope, look like harpoons with barbs. Packrats, however, seem oblivious to even the spiniest of *Opuntia* species. Filling leaves full of tough fibers, or even microscopic grains of silicates (glass), as in grasses, reduces animal use of plants. Even insect use of plants can be stayed by mechanical defenses. A thick covering of hairs reduces an insect's ability to munch on softer tissues. Hooked hairs, such as in Adonis Blazingstar *(Mentzelia multiflora)*, might snag and hold the legs of small insects, especially of larvae, exposing them to predators or holding them to dry and die in the heat. Gummy secretions, such as those from the glandular hairs of Devil's Claw *(Proboscidea parviflora)* or Desert Sand Verbena *(Abronia villosa)*, may also have the same effect on small insects.

Chemical warfare. Plants are masters at chemical warfare, using a diverse array of toxic chemicals to protect their flesh and seeds. For this reason, and also because of unpredictable, severe allergic reactions, we warn readers to always be trained by an expert as to which wild plant is safe to eat and touch and which is not. All too often the difference between a beneficial medicine and a dangerous toxin is simply one of dosage. Ordinarily, plants that are toxic also taste bad and may also have a strong odor; they are often bitter or very resinous. Domestic livestock tend to leave such plants alone except under the most severe range conditions. Then such plants tend to increase in numbers on the ranges as the more palatable plants are removed.

Plant toxins number in the thousands and are diverse. Many still are chemically uncharacterized. Most are dose-dependent; severity of reaction may depend on body mass or individual sensitivity. One species eating a plant may be affected; another is not fazed. Particularly in insects, a species may develop the ability to detoxify a compound, such as mustard oil, and then this species is able to exploit a resource unavailable to others. The toxin becomes an attractant, as are mustard compounds for cabbage moths. Toxins are usually distributed throughout the plant, but true to nature's efficiency, they are most often concentrated in the more valuable tissues, the leaves, food storage organs such as roots and tubers, and in seeds.

The following is a quick review of major categories of toxins in plants, their general effect, and examples from genera found in this book. **Alkaloids,** such as nicotine, most often act through the nervous system, but they can severely affect other organs. Among numerous genera, alkaloids occur in *Argemone, Corydalis, Datura, Delphinium, Heliotropium, Lupinus, Nicotiana,* and *Senecio.* **Glycosides** are even more widespread than alkaloids. Glycosides combine various sugars and other compounds—the latter may be dangerous when released from the glycoside. Species of *Bahia, Linum, Manihot,* and *Phaseolus,* and may yield cyanide. *Brassica* and *Linum* may produce a glycoside that prevents iodine uptake, affecting the thyroid. Irritant oils, which we relish in mustard, are produced in *Brassica, Erysimum,* and the species of *Anemone.* Glycosides that profoundly affect the heart are found in various lilies and members of the Figwort and Dogbane Families (Scrophulariaceae and Apocynaceae, respectively). Saponins, which form a foamy froth in water (which may be used as a shampoo), enter the body through wounded tissue and cause destruction of red blood cells. Species of flax *(Linum)* contain saponins, as do leaves of Agave, perhaps contributing to the severe pain of a puncture from Century Plant. **Oxalates** are found in many plants and in high concentrations clog the tiny tubules of the kidney with crystals, causing painful kidney failure. *Rumex* and *Portulaca* have oxalates. **Resins** and **resinoids** are widespread and diverse. They directly affect nervous or muscle tissue. Species of milkweed *(Asclepias)* produce toxic resins. **Phytotoxins** are proteins with very high toxicity. They may cause severe allergic reactions, or they may break down other proteins critical to cell function. Species of *Jatropha* and other members of the Spurge Family (Euphorbiaceae) contain phytotoxins. **Mineral poisons** abound, compounds that are at least in part or wholly absorbed from soil. In the American West, nitrate poisoning is common, causing severe debilitation or death to cattle and sheep. Species of *Amsinckia, Cirsium, Datura, Euphorbia, Rafinesquia, Rumex, Salvia, Solanum, Sonchus, Tribulus,* and *Verbesina,* among numerous others, cause nitrate poisoning. Plants may accumulate selenium if it is in the soil. Animals that ingest selenium-bearing plants may wander aimlessly, bumping into obvious obstacles, or they may become emaciated and die. Many species of *Astragalus* and all of *Stanleya* and *Xylorhiza* grow on selenium-bearing soils and accumulate the mineral. Some species of *Machaeranthera* may or may not grow on such soils, but when they do they are toxic.

From Seedling to Seed

For an organism that cannot get up and move to another place, it is a real trick to predict that "now is the time to go for it." How does a seed in the soil "know" that it should germinate, grow, and have a reasonable chance of producing more seed? This question has been asked over and over, for one species and another, by plant biologists for generations. Answers are only partial. The annuals that form such spectacular spring displays on the Sonoran Desert must have winter rains in sufficient amounts at the right time in late fall or early winter for germination, and then rain must come about once per month to ensure survival and flowering. Plants that live in washes often require a scouring of the seed coat so that water may enter the seed—a signal that there is enough soil moisture to establish a seedling. Other seeds, sitting in moist soil, have their seed coats weakened by bacterial or fungal action during prolonged moist times and then can germinate. Some require a long, cold period, and warming soil is then a signal that suitable weather has arrived. Others, somehow, respond only to summer rains—they will not germinate during the cool of winter. A number of desert species will germinate almost anytime there is sufficient rain, winter or summer.

Adapt or Lose the Race

An important biological measure of success is the ability to contribute progeny to the next generation; those individuals that contribute more are the more successful. The ability to contribute to the next generation is enhanced or reduced by factors of the environment, both physical (rain, temperature, soil, etc.) and biological (other organisms). Adaptations that deal with aspects of the environment contribute to success.

On the one hand, plants in a stable, predictable environment need to change little over time and can accomplish that by mating with close relatives or even pollinating themselves, thus preserving combinations of genes that work so well in the current, stable environment. These plants are less likely to produce showy flowers since they need not attract pollinators from far away. On the other hand, plants living in changing environments or environments that are patchy and unpredictable to their seeds do best by mixing up genes each generation and trying out new combinations. Some of the progeny, the seeds and seedlings, should do well in environments slightly different from that experienced by the parents. These plants often tend to be showy to attract pollinators that may carry pollen from distant sources, perhaps where the environment slightly differs.

You Are Invited . . .

. . . to find a pleasant stretch of Sonoran Desert and visit it repeatedly several times a day, several days in a season, and observe the plants and what they are doing. Some plants will have long-lived flowers; others are open for only a few hours. There is a progression of flowers blooming across the sunflower head, from periphery to center, and stamens and pistils of each flower mature at different times. Yellow Suncups *(Camissonia)* open on a spring morning and close in the afternoon, whereas the white ones open in the evening, closing in the early morning. The *Portulaca* flower winks on and off on a summer morning. Cactus-Apple *(Opuntia engelmannii)* opens in morning, closes in afternoon; Desert Christmas Cactus *(O. leptocaulis)* opens in afternoon, closing in early evening; Jumping Cholla *(O. fulgida)* opens in late afternoon and closes . . . ? Bees visit daisies and penstemons, hummingbirds visit Ocotillo and penstemons, small moths visit nocturnal *Siphonoglossa*, large moths visit thorn-apples *(Datura)*, bats agaves, bees and bats the Saguaro, little flies the Dutchman's Pipe. The lupine starts blooming early in the season and, by changing the color of the white patch of the banner, sends a message to pollinating insects that its flowers are spent. Early in the season the ragworts *(Senecio)* bloom, late in the season it is Turpentine Bush's turn *(Ericameria laricifolia);* both are Asteraceae. Leaves burst from bud, expand, and wither or, on other plants, they change ever so slowly. Stems swell and shrink. It is continuous change, each species "doing its thing," during its time, dealing with the water problem, beating the heat, fending off animals that would eat it, attracting pollinators, sharing resources, moving genes through the population. The desert, dry, sere, inhospitable to many, is vibrantly alive and exciting. Take a while to pause and watch it.

How to Use This Guide

The book is designed for anyone with an interest in the plants that grow on the Sonoran Desert north of the Mexican border. The user will find it useful also 100 miles or more to the south. Specialized knowledge is not needed. Technical terms have been avoided except where they lend such efficiency that to avoid them becomes cumbersome. Perhaps 3,500 species of plants occur on the Sonoran Desert in its total extent. Maybe half are found north of the border. Of those 1,500 or so, this book covers more than 300 of the most conspicuous, most characteristic, or otherwise curious or interesting plants that might be showy enough to earn "wildflower" status.

In this book, plants are grouped according to color. As imperfect as this system is (when is yellow not yellow, but orange?), it seems the best method for rapid and accurate identification of conspicuous flowers. Color categories are: **white, green, yellow, orange to red, pink to purple, and blue.** Within each color category plants are arranged in alphabetical order by Latin family name and then alphabetically by Latin scientific name (genus). This most often places similar-looking plants together. If there are several species treated within a genus, these too are alphabetical.

Within any one species, flower color may vary, as do characteristics of any organism. White variants are common among pink, blue, and purple species. Species most commonly with orange flowers may have yellow-flowered variants; red flowers may have orange or yellow variants. Some plants are spectacularly multicolored, such as Mexican Passion Flower *(Passiflora mexicana),* which could be equally placed in "green" (where you will find it) or in "pink and purple." Variations in shades of lavender to violet are difficult for many observers to distinguish, and these are often simply seen as "pink" or "blue" by them. We have grouped plants in their most prevalent color. Thus, occasionally, if a person cannot find a conspicuous flower in one color section, he or she should try a related color.

Flower structure may also occasionally vary. Sometimes plants that normally have 5-lobed flowers will have some flowers with 4 or 6, or even 7 lobes. If you have a flower that seems to match, but number of lobes is not as described, look around to see if the flower you have is the "normal" condition.

Each entry begins with a **common name(s)** appropriate for the Sonoran Desert, the **scientific name,** and the **family** to which the species belongs. Next comes a brief **description.** The first sentence or series of phrases in the description attempts to give a "mind's eye" picture of the plant, so the user, with the use of the photograph, can immediately say "yes" or "no" regarding identification. Next are characteristics of various parts of the plant. Measurements given are of two kinds, those that give general size, and those that give a range. Often, only relative size is important, and a single measurement, for example ½", is given. Variation may be a few small fractions of an inch around this figure, but greater precision is not important for identification. Where ranges are given, as in ½–2", the variation that the range includes becomes important in describing the species for the user.

The next part of the entry summarizes **flowering season.** This is necessarily very general, for flowering period for any one species varies with elevation and with latitude and in the desert with the timing of rainfall. Next follows **habitat/range,** where the user will find information about general characteristics of the plant's habitat, at what elevations to expect the species, and generally where in the Sonoran Desert region (and beyond) the species occurs. Finally the section on **comments** provides information about the plant, such as use, peculiar features, toxicity, the meaning of a name, and the like.

Classifying and Naming Plants

This guide gives common names and scientific names of plants and the plant family to which the plant belongs. Common names may be those used by people living within an area for a common plant, such as Cresosotebush for the widespread shrub of the hot deserts, *Larrea tridentata.* Or a common name may be recently contrived for use in a book for the general public, such as Interior Goldenbush for the flowering shrub *Ericameria linearifolia.* Such names often become adopted as a widespread common name. Common names are not precise. A plant may have several common names, and a single common name may apply to one or more species, especially when they are similar in appearance.

The structure of the more precise scientific name traces back to the work of a Swedish botanist, Carl Linnaeus (1707–1778). In 1753 he published *Species Plantarum,* in which he employed two-part names for the first time, creating the scientific binomial. The first part of the name is the genus name (plural is "genera"). The genus contains one or more related species. The second part of the name is the specific epithet and refers to a species in question. The two parts, genus name + specific epithet, form the species name. Thus, *Larrea tridentata,* with its two parts, refers to the species of shrub so common on the Sonoran Desert. There are other species in the genus *Larrea* in southern South America. When there is no chance of confusion, the genus name is often abbreviated with the first letter *(L. tridentata).* The scientific name is unique to a single species and is international in use.

Scientific names for a species may change in a highly regulated manner as botanists learn more about the relationships of that species or the history of its technical nomenclature. In this guide we have attempted to use up-to-date scientific names. In addition to numerous highly technical references, the following botanical summaries have been very useful: *Arizona Flora* by T. H. Kearney and R. H. Peebles (2nd ed. with supplement, 1960), *A California Flora* by P. A. Munz and D. D. Keck (1959), *Vegetation and Flora of the Sonoran Desert* by F. Shreve and I. L. Wiggins (1964), *The Jepson Manual–Higher Plants of California* edited by J. C. Hickman (1993), and *Flora of the Gran Desierto and Río Colorado of Northwestern Mexico* by R. S. Felger (2000). Scientific names are drawn from the latter two modern references and from *Synthesis of the North America Flora,* version 1.0, by J. T. Kartesz and C. A. Meacham (1999), which is available on compact disk.

The "family" is a level of classification above that of genus. In it are placed genera that are believed to be more closely related among themselves than they are to other genera. The family name has a standardized ending, "-aceae." A family usually has a suite of readily seen features that apply to most species within it. For the avid naturalist, the learning of characteristics of families is very useful. There are about 400 plant families in the world, but around 350,000 plant species. With some effort we can learn the characteristics of 100–150 families, the number of families in the American West, and thus we can have some familiarity with plants anywhere in this region. Even easier, most areas have only 10–20 common families—learning their characteristics makes much of the flora familiar at this level. For example, many members of the Bean Family (Fabaceae) have a flower type we illustrate in the introductory material and call the "pea" flower. The fruit in the family, the bean pod, is distinctive. Learning such features helps one to recognize families, which then makes identification of species much easier in the field.

Examining the Plant for Identification

First of all, caution! Desert plants often defend themselves. Spines are obvious; the tiny bristles (glochids) of *Opuntia* (chollas and beavertails) are not. Many species have stiff, bristly hairs that irritate soft skin. Some fill the hairs with an irritant and inject it into the skin, as might a little hypodermic needle. More insidious are chemicals that cause dermatitis, which may affect everyone, or often just those who are sensitive. In some plants only the sap is irritating. If a plant is bristly or clearly glandular, it is best to use gloves or a piece of paper to protect one's self until you know you are not bothered by this plant.

A small magnifying glass of about 10x, which can be purchased for a few dollars, adds tremendous enjoyment to plant study. Small flowers may be elaborately formed and colored. Surface features, such as protective hairs, are amazingly diverse.

Diagrams and descriptions that will help you see critical plant features useful for identification follow this section. When attempting to identify a plant, note features of the flower (color, size, petals joined or separate, symmetry, number of stamens, and in some instances position of ovary relative to other parts). Note whether the stems are woody or soft and herbaceous. Look at the leaves. Are they opposite or alternate, simple or divided, and if divided are they completely so, and in which manner—pinnately or palmately? Examine the edge of the leaf—is it smooth, wavy, scalloped, or toothed? Such features, in total, characterize a particular species and are used in describing flowers in this guide.

The photo of the flower and the description should serve to identify species correctly. In some instances a plant under consideration may look somewhat like the photo and nearly fit the description but seems not quite the same. You are very likely to have found a close relative to one in this book, perhaps even another species in the same genus. The "comments" section in the descriptions often guides the reader to other similar species.

Important leaf features to note. First look at position—are leaves all at the base (basal), in a rosette, or spread along the stem? Next determine arrangement. The point at which leaves attach to the stem is the node. Is there only one leaf at a node (alternate), two leaves opposite one another at a node (opposite), or several at a node (whorled)? The part of the plant that is at the angle formed by the stalk of the leaf where it attaches to the stem at the node is called the axil.

A leaf usually has two parts. The stalk (technically "petiole") attaches the expanded portion, the blade, to the stem. It is in the blade that most photosynthesis takes place, that is, the production of sugars using carbon dioxide and water, driven by the sun's energy. In this book, to save space and reduce technical words, we have often used "leaf" instead of blade when characteristics of the stalk are not important. When both parts are important, a distinction is made.

Several characteristics of the leaf blade are important. What is the general size and shape? Size and shape may vary with drought and also with position on the plant. Is the blade thin or thick and succulent? Is the tip pointed, blunt, or round? Is the base tapered or indented like the top of a heart? Is the edge smooth (entire), wavy, or toothed? Illustrations of leaf characteristics are provided in this section.

A leaf may also be unlobed or variously lobed or divided. If unlobed or if lobed, but the lobes do not extend to the midrib and divide the leaf into separate leaflike parts, the leaf is said to be simple. The nature of the lobing and the presence or absence of teeth on the edges can be important in identification. Degree of lobing often varies with leaf position on the plant. Often lower leaves are lobed and upper are not, or vice versa.

If the leaf is divided completely to the midrib into several leaflike segments, the leaf is said to be compound. Each segment is a leaflet. This sometimes is a difficult distinction for an inexperienced individual. A leaf, compound or simple, will have a bud (sometimes very small) in the axil; there are no buds in the angle the leaflet makes with the midrib or stalk of a leaf. In addition, leaflets of compound leaves are often arranged in the same plane. There are two kinds of compound leaves, those that have the arrangement of a feather (pinnately compound—see a photo of *Astragalus*), and those that have the symmetry of a hand (palmately compound—see a photo of *Lupinus*). Particularly in the case of pinnately compound leaves, the leaflets may be divided one or more times. In this book we call the major division a "segment" (it is actually a pinna), with the final leaflike divisions called the leaflets. Compound leaves are common in tropical and in hot-desert plants. Leaves that are pinnately two or three times divided are especially common in the Bean Family (Fabaceae—see a photo of *Mimosa*).

Bracts are small, leaflike structures, sometimes scalelike, that are often present on the stem in plants with underground stems or near and among the flowers in many species of plants. They may appear as small versions of the plant's leaves, or they may more closely resemble scales. They may be green or brightly colored, or they may be thin, papery, and translucent.

A picture is, indeed, worth a thousand words. The pictures in this section of leaf variation will help to clarify points about leaf structure and variation, as will the illustrations of flower structure help clarify terms associated with flowers and flower clusters. The glossary also helps to define terms used here.

Structure of the flower. Flowers are the most complicated part of the plant. For a plant to reproduce sexually generation after generation, the flower must function reliably. There are many ways to successfully reproduce, and, thus, flowers come in many shapes, sizes, and colors. Because precision is required in this complex process, the flowers of a species cannot be changed easily when the season is dry or wet, or from one generation to the next, and be expected to function properly. Thus, in a species, flowers are all similar. In most genera, flowers differ but little. In a family, flowers provide most of the consistent characteristics that distinguish the family. Therefore, we need to pay attention to them in classification and in identification.

Flowers have two different functions that require precise interaction of various processes within the plant and in the environment in which the plant grows. The first is to effect pollination, that is, the transfer of pollen (which bears the sperm) from an anther on the same plant or different plants to the stigma at the top of the pistil. The pollen then grows through the stigma and style to the ovary, which contains from one to many eggs. Fertilization of the egg by sperm occurs. This begins the second function, the development of the seed and fruit. The seed is essentially a little survival packet, containing an embryo, nutritive tissue in or around the embryo, and usually an outer casing that retards water loss. As the seed matures, so does the ovary, which becomes the fruit. Whether dry or fleshy, the fruit is often involved in dispersal of the seed.

Flowers that use insects in the process of pollination are usually showy, often fragrant, and they may provide nectar as a reward to the visitor. Flowers that depend upon birds are brightly colored (often red), usually are odorless, but provide nectar. Flowers that depend upon wind pollination are small, not colorful, and may be lacking petals or sepals. Flowers that regularly self-pollinate, that is, move pollen from an anther within the flower to the stigma of the same flower, are often small and colorful (they may also attract small insects).

A diagram of a generalized flower is given in Figure 4. Overall shape may vary from platelike to bowl-like, bell-shaped, tubular and trumpet-shaped, or simply tubular. A complete flower has four series of parts. Beginning at the base and proceeding upward, the series of parts are sepals, petals, stamens, and pistil. In each series the parts may be separate from one another, or they may be partly or completely united. Thus, for the sepals and petals, two other terms are useful. Sepals, separate or united but considered collectively, form the calyx. Petals collectively form the corolla. The sepals (or calyx) are usually green and form the outer covering of the bud. The petals (or corolla) are usually colored or white and attract pollinators. Some plants have no petals, but the sepals are petal-like and joined (Nyctaginaceae). Others have sepals and petals both petal-like and separate (Agavaceae, Liliaceae). In still others separate sepals may intergrade so perfectly into separate petals that there is poor, or no, distinction (Cactaceae). We use the term "petal-like parts" to express these conditions.

As a flower is examined "face on," that is, looking directly into the center of the flower, it is seen to have one of two common kinds of symmetry. It may be divided into equal or nearly equal halves by lines through the center in many directions and, if so, it is radially symmetrical. In the text in this guide, we have reduced this to "radial," a term we do not often use because this is the "typical" condition. If, however, the flower can be divided into two equal halves, essentially mirror images, in only one way, by only one line through the center, then the flower is bilaterally symmetrical (bilateral). Because this is such a useful characteristic in identification, we always mention it. Bilateral symmetry, by the way, is associated with pollination by fast, efficient insects.

We do not necessarily describe the next two series of parts because they are not always important in identification of the species (in genera and families, certainly). They are important to the flower, for these are the sexually functional parts. The stamens consist of a slender stalk, the filament, which ends in the pollen-producing sac, the anther. Pollen is released when the anther opens. Stamens may be few *(Veronica)* or many (*Mentzelia,* Cactaceae). Stamens are many and united by their filaments in Malvaceae. In *Penstemon* one stamen of the five has lost its anther and probably functions somehow in assisting in transfer of pollen.

Stamens, by comparison to animals, are functionally the male part of the flower. By similar analogy, the pistil is the female part of the flower. It consists of a pollen-receiving stigma, a sperm-transmitting style, and the egg-containing ovary. It develops into the fruit. All the other parts (stamens, petals, sepals) may attach below the ovary, a common condition, or they may attach at the top of the ovary (an important family characteristic for the Evening Primrose Family, Onagraceae).

To this point, bisexual flowers, the most common occurrence, have been described. In situations where outcrossing has been enforced, plants may have unisexual flowers on the same plant or male flowers on one plant, female flowers on another. Where either of these more specialized situations occurs in a wildflower included in this guide, we have noted it for the reader.

A family that is very well represented on the Sonoran Desert is the Bean Family (Fabaceae). The unifying feature in this family is the fruit, basically a pea pod variously modified. There are three great groups in the family. *Mimosa* and relatives have small radial flowers with long showy stamens, often making "pufflike" clusters. Palo Verde *(Cercidium)* and relatives have somewhat bilateral flowers with the upper petal positioned slightly inner-most relative to the other four petals. Relatives of *Astragalus, Lupinus,* and *Psorothamnus* have a specialized, easily recognizable, bilateral flower of a form that we refer to as a "pea" flower (see the figure on page 32) because sweet peas *(Lathyrus)* and garden peas *(Pisum)* have such a flower. This bilateral flower has a large upper (and outer) petal called the standard or banner, two petals at the side called wings, and two petals in the center joined together like the prow of a boat, called the keel. The stamens, at first held inside the keel, usually are united by their filaments; curiously, in most cases only nine of them are united, the tenth is separate.

The flower cluster, and when a "flower" is not a flower. Flowers may be borne one to many on a plant. When there are many they are often in some kind of arrangement distinct from the leafy portion. We have called this the "flower cluster" (technically it is the inflorescence). We describe flower clusters as long and slender, branched, open and few-flowered, and so forth.

In some families the flower cluster has been modified to resemble a single flower. This is the case in the Sunflower Family (Asteraceae), the second largest family (in terms of species) in the world, after orchids (Orchidaceae). On the Sonoran Desert the Sunflower Family is the largest family, with hundreds of species, many of them showy. A glance through the white and yellow sections of this book show that the family cannot be avoided if a wildflower enthusiast wishes to know the desert wildflowers well. The flower cluster so much resembles a single flower that we see the "sunflower" as a plant with a huge "flower" with yellow "petals." Actually what we are seeing is a compact flower cluster of small flowers, a structure commonly called a flower head, or simply "head," the term used here.

The head in the Sunflower Family (Asteraceae) is understandably confusing, but its structure is very simple to interpret. See figure on page 32. It consists of a few to several hundred tiny flowers held on a central disk (it may be dome-shaped) surrounded by green bracts. As might be imagined, such a structure in a large and important plant family has generated many terms by botanists. We can understand the structure and avoid most of the terms, but not all. The bracts, usually green, beneath the head serve in the manner of a calyx, protecting the head when it is a bud. Once the head blooms, one or two kinds of flowers are evident.

The flower of the Sunflower Family is small. It consists of an ovary with all other parts attached on top. The calyx, if present, is represented by bristles, hairs, or scales (called the "pappus"). The corolla is basically trumpet-shaped, with a tubular base and with five lobes, or it may be all developed to one side resembling a single petal. In the center are five stamens, usually sort of stuck together by their anthers. In most flowers of this family, two branches of the style can be seen protruding through the ring of anthers.

These tiny flowers are aggregated in the flower head. For many species in the family, the flowers in the center of the head are radially symmetrical—these are the disk flowers. Those around the outside of the head often are long and narrow, expanded toward the periphery. They are showy, oriented like rays of a star, and are called ray flowers. These are the yellow parts of the "sunflower." Some other members of this family present a third situation. All their flowers are strap-shaped, much like an old time razor strop. In the center they are smaller; near the periphery they are larger and are then much like ray flowers. We call all these flowers "strap-shaped flowers" to distinguish them from true ray flowers. Desert Chicory *(Rafinesquia neomexicana)* is an example of a species with a head containing only strap-shaped flowers. This is a well-defined group within the Sunflower Family. In addition to having strap-shaped flowers, these plants also have milky sap. Finally, a very few species of the Sunflower Family on the Sonoran Desert have only bilateral flowers in the head, those near the periphery larger. Each flower has two upper lobes and three lower lobes. An example is Desert Holly *(Acourtia nana)*.

In the Sunflower Family the base of the flower, when mature, resembles a seed. Keep in mind the sunflower "seed," which is really a fruit. It consists of the ovary, other parts of the flower so tightly united with the ovary that to distinguish them by ordinary means is impossible, and the true seed within. Characteristics of this "seedlike fruit," as we have called it, are important in accurate identification of species, particularly the characteristics of the modified calyx (pappus) that sits atop the fruit. Most of us have seen these structures. In your mind's eye recall the dandelion; its seedlike fruit is slender and dark, and on top of it is a parachute made of feathery white bristles (pappus). In descriptions we draw your attention to this, for it is important and interesting, but we avoid the term pappus.

Warning

Plants have developed defenses against being eaten. It is chemical warfare. Even the leaf blade of rhubarb *(Rheum rhabarbum)* is toxic to us, though we enjoy the sour leaf stalk in pies. To eat a plant or plant part collected in the wild, in vacant lots, along roads, anywhere, is inviting trouble. Many plants are severely toxic to all; others cause horrible allergic reactions to some. Painful sickness, permanent damage, and ghastly death are all possible. Do not attempt to use any wild plant for food, medicine, or cosmetic until you have been thoroughly trained by a fully qualified professional. Although this book mentions human uses of plants, this is for interest only and not to encourage use or to suggest that such practices are safe. Indigenous people experimented over generations to learn how to use wild plants, and certainly serious mistakes were made. The author, publisher, and all others associated with the production and distribution of this book assume no liability for the actions of the user.

Enjoy!

Learning about native plants is a very enjoyable pastime. It takes one outdoors, and it brings the kaleidoscope world of wildflowers to attention. The diversity on the Sonoran Desert is truly remarkable, and among all the wildflowers, sometimes the smallest are among the most beautiful. Please practice responsible wildflower study, leaving the plants as you found them for others to enjoy. Have fun exploring with a camera and a close-up lens among the flats, mountainsides, canyons, and occasional springs and rivers of this remarkable part of the world.

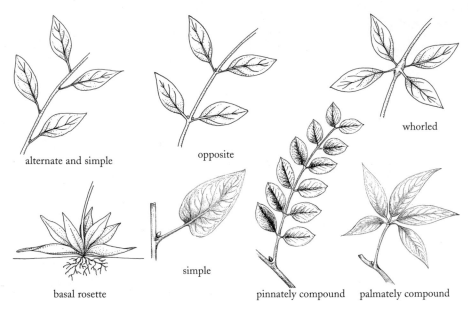

alternate and simple

opposite

whorled

basal rosette

simple

pinnately compound

palmately compound

Figure 1. Leaf type and arrangement

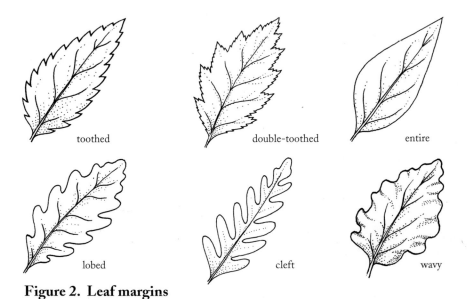

toothed

double-toothed

entire

lobed

cleft

wavy

Figure 2. Leaf margins

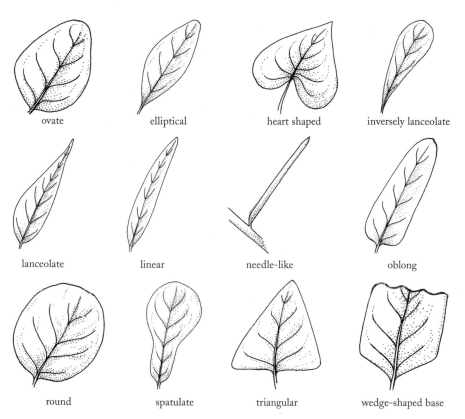

ovate   elliptical   heart shaped   inversely lanceolate

lanceolate   linear   needle-like   oblong

round   spatulate   triangular   wedge-shaped base

Figure 3. Leaf shapes

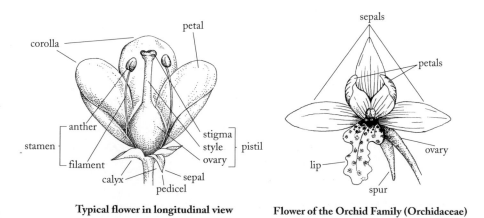

corolla

petal

anther

stamen

filament

calyx

pedicel

sepal

stigma
style
ovary

pistil

Typical flower in longitudinal view

sepals

petals

lip

ovary

spur

Flower of the Orchid Family (Orchidaceae)

Figure 4. Flower parts

Figure 5. Flowers of the Sunflower Family (Asteraceae)

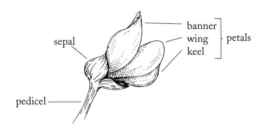

Figure 6. "Pea" Flower of the Bean Family (Fabaceae), side view

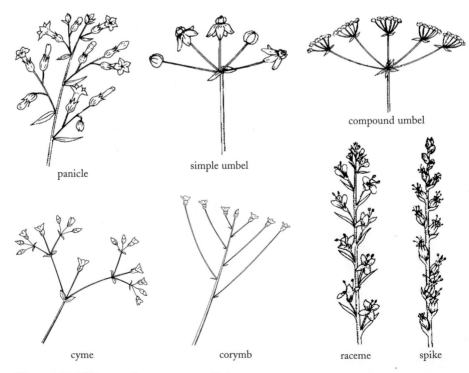

Figure 7. Flower clusters, or inflorescence

WHITE FLOWERS

White Prickly Poppy

This section includes white or cream flowers and those that grade into very pale, nearly white shades of pink, blue, yellow, or green.

Dwarf White Honeysuckle

DWARF WHITE HONEYSUCKLE
Siphonoglossa longiflora
Acanthus Family (Acanthaceae)

Description: Slightly woody plants with slender, white or pale cream flowers at bases of upper leaves. Corollas with a very slender tube 1¼–1½" long, flared to an arching, notched upper lip and a deeply 3-lobed lower lip. Leaves opposite, lanceolate, ¾–2½" long. Stems up to 14" tall.

Flowering Season: April–October.

Habitat/Range: Rocky slopes, 3,000–4,000', southern Arizona and northwestern Mexico.

Comments: Flowers bloom in the evening, and each flower lasts only 1 night, the white corollas falling from the plant in early morning and littering the ground beneath it. The long, slender, pale nocturnal flower and the tube, with nectar, oriented upward for easy access suggest moth pollination. The plants are heavily browsed by desert wildlife and domestic animals.

BANANA YUCCA, DÁTIL
Yucca baccata
Agave Family (Agavaceae)

Description: Stout plants up to 6' tall, with a rosette of long, daggerlike leaves near the ground and hanging cream-white flowers in a dense, slender cluster. Flowers with 6 broadly lanceolate, waxy, petal-like parts 2–4" long. Pod cylindrical, 3–9" long, 1–2" in diameter. Leaves 1–2½' long, rigid, concave on upper side, 1–2" wide, tapered to a fierce point, with curled, whitish fibers on margin.

Flowering Season: April–July.

Habitat/Range: Arid hills and flats, 3,000-8,000', southeastern Arizona, much of the American Southwest beyond the Sonoran Desert.

Comments: Young pods may be boiled or roasted and eaten and resemble sweet potato in taste. When baked and mashed, the resultant paste may be dried and stored to be used later as a sweetener.

Banana Yucca, Dátil

SOAPTREE YUCCA, PALMILLA
Yucca elata
Agave Family (Agavaceae)

Description: Large plants up to 23' tall, with numerous coarse, narrow leaves in rosettes at top of stem and numerous hanging cream-white flowers in long, large clusters. Flowers with 6 waxy, narrowly elliptical to ovate, petal-like parts 1½–2¼" long. Pod oblong, 1½–2½" long. Leaves 1–3' long, ¼–1" wide at base, tapered to pointed tip.

Flowering Season: May–July.

Habitat/Range: Arid flats and low hills, 1,500–6,000', southern Arizona to Texas, northern Mexico.

Comments: The Tohono O'odham harvested young leaves for weaving fine baskets. The roots, known as *amole,* may be pounded in water, yielding a detergent and a fine rinse for hair. Numerous other Native Americans ate the flowers of species of *Yucca.* Chopped stems may be fed to livestock in times of shortage of forage.

Soaptree Yucca, Palmilla

Mojave Yucca, Spanish Dagger, Datillo

MOJAVE YUCCA, SPANISH DAGGER, DATILLO
Yucca schidigera
Agave Family (Agavaceae)

Description: Treelike plants to 15' tall with stout, daggerlike leaves in a rosette at end of stem and with dense, oval clusters of cream-white flowers. Flowers with 6 widely lanceolate, waxy, petal-like parts 1–2" long. Pod oblong, 2–3" long. Leaves rigid, concave on upper side, 1–5' long, 1–1½" wide, tapered to a stout point, the margins with curled, whitish fibers.

Flowering Season: March–April.

Habitat/Range: Rocky slopes, mostly below 5,000', extreme western and northern edge of Sonoran Desert in California; also southern Nevada, northwestern Arizona and northwestern Mexico.

Comments: Yuccas depend on nocturnal moths for seed set. The moths gather pollen and tamp it into the stigma, then lay eggs in the ovary. Larvae eat some but not all of the seeds. Pupae develop in soil near the yucca.

Sonoran Globe-Amaranth

SONORAN GLOBE-AMARANTH
Gomphrena sonorae
Amaranth Family (Amaranthaceae)

Description: Slender plants with white, salmon, or pinkish flower heads ½" wide, in clusters formed by densely packed, translucent, scalelike bracts. Bracts ⅛–¼" long, overlapping, concealing among their bases tiny flowers with long, tapering sepals almost as long as the bracts; no petals. Leaves opposite, a pair always just beneath the terminal heads on stem, ¾–3½" long, more or less oval or oblong, with short stalks, or no stalks. Stems unbranched or with branches ascending at a very narrow angle, 8–24" tall.

Flowering Season: August–September.

Habitat/Range: Stony hills or rocky, grassy slopes, 3,000—5,500', southeastern Arizona and northwestern Mexico.

Comments: Plants may be dried, the translucent heads adding accent to dried flower arrangements.

WOOLLY BLUESTAR
Amsonia tomentosa
Dogbane Family (Apocynaceae)

Description: Flowers in loose clusters, the corolla whitish or pale purplish, with 5 pointed lobes ⅜" long, spreading from the top of a slender tube. Corolla lobes darker on back. Tube ½" long, usually pale leaden purple or blue, swollen at top. Stamens 5, hidden inside swelling of tube. Fruit 2 slender pods 1¼–3" long, at first joined at tip, later free, often breaking apart at constrictions between seeds. Leaves broadly lanceolate, ascending, ¾–1½" long, hairless or woolly-hairy. Stems in a clump, 5–14" tall.

Flowering Season: April–June.

Habitat/Range: Rocky ground, 100–5,000', southeastern California to southwestern Utah and western Arizona.

Comments: The presence or absence of hairs is apparently an inherited trait. Flowers have a delicate jasmine scent, attracting nocturnal insects.

Woolly Bluestar

Parachute Plant, Gravel Ghost, Tobacco Weed

PARACHUTE PLANT, GRAVEL GHOST, TOBACCO WEED
Atrichoseris platyphylla
Sunflower Family (Asteraceae)

Description: Branched, wiry plants with leaves at base and white flowers in heads at ends of stems. Flower heads ¾–1¼" wide, consisting only of strap-shaped flowers, those in center shorter, all blunt at tip and ending in 5 tiny teeth. Seedlike fruit ⅛" long, whitish, with 5 thick, corky ribs; no scales or bristles at top. Leaves all at base, broad, 1¼–3" long, grayish green, often tinged with purple, finely toothed on edges, lying flat on ground. Stems 1–6' tall, widely and openly branched in robust plants.

Flowering Season: March–April.

Habitat/Range: Gravelly washes and slopes, below 4,200', southeastern California to southwestern Utah and western Arizona.

Comments: Flower heads open as the day warms, appearing as little parachutes suspended above the desert floor on inconspicuous stems.

White Tackstem, White Cupfruit

WHITE TACKSTEM, WHITE CUPFRUIT

Calycoseris wrightii
Sunflower Family (Asteraceae)

Description: Bluish green plants 2–8" tall, branched from base, with bright white flower heads 1–1½" across, the underside of the flowers often with a rosy blush. Upper parts of plant with many dark, tack-shaped hairs, each with a stalk and a glandular head. Flower heads only with strap-shaped flowers, those in center much shorter than those on periphery. Inner bracts on head about ½" long, with translucent margins; outer bracts very short, in 2–3 series at base of head. Seedlike fruits slender, dark, shallowly grooved, with a long, slender tip that ends in a minute cup to which many fine white bristles are attached. Leaves mostly at base, 1½–5" long, pinnately divided into linear lobes.

Flowering Season: March–May.

Habitat/Range: Gravelly places, 500–4,000', southeastern California to Utah, western Texas, northwestern Mexico.

Comments: This is one of the most conspicuous of spring wildflowers, but like so many winter annuals, it requires good winter rains to flourish. It is very similar to Desert Chicory *(Rafinesquia neomexicana),* but that species has no tacklike stalked glands.

DESERT PINCUSHION
Chaenactis stevioides
Sunflower Family (Asteraceae)

Description: White, pincushion-like flower heads ½–1" across in open clusters at tips of stems 4–18" tall. Flowers all of disk type, ¼" long in center of head, larger and bilateral at edge of head. Bracts around head narrowly lanceolate, ⅜" long, cobwebby-hairy, all about same length, tips erect and blunt. Seedlike fruit club-shaped, stiffly hairy, ³⁄₁₆" long, topped by 4–5 lanceolate scales (if in 2 series, outer scales much shorter than inner). Leaves 1–5" long, pinnately lobed, cobwebby-hairy, lobes linear, tips often curled; leaves in basal rosette usually withering by flowering time.

Flowering Season: February–May.

Habitat/Range: Open ground, 1,000–6,000', much of western United States.

Comments: There are several species of pincushions, all with similar appearances.

Desert Pincushion

Spiny Aster, Mexican Devilweed

SPINY ASTER, MEXICAN DEVILWEED
Chloracantha spinosa
Sunflower Family (Asteraceae)

Description: Plants form broomlike clumps of sharply pointed, 2–9' tall stems, often with slender thorns near base. Flower heads ¼" high, less than ½" wide, each with 15–30 white ray flowers ⅛–¼" long and yellow disk flowers. Bracts of head hairless, pointed, in 3–5 series, the edges thin, translucent. Seedlike fruits with many pale tan, very fine bristles at top. Leaves at base linear, up to 1½" long, those higher on stem mere bracts.

Flowering Season: May–October.

Habitat/Range: Alkaline clay soil, 100–4,000', southeastern California to southern Utah and western Texas, south to Central America.

Comments: This is an aggressive weed in agricultural areas, often in hedgelike thickets along canals. The one species in this genus was once considered part of the huge genus *Aster.*

Spreading Fleabane

SPREADING FLEABANE
Erigeron divergens
Sunflower Family (Asteraceae)

Description: Well-branched, softly hairy, grayish plants 4–18" tall, having flower heads with 75–150 slender white or purplish rays ¼–½" long. Disk yellow, less than ½" wide. Bracts of head all about ¼" long. Leaves narrow, widest above middle, sometimes with lobes; leaves near base ¾–2½" long, those higher on stem smaller. Hairs on stem minute, directed downward or straight out. Seedlike fruit with 6–12 fragile bristles at top, surrounded by minute bristles or scales.

Flowering Season: February–October.

Habitat/Range: Dry places, common on roadsides, 1,000–9,000', throughout western North America.

Comments: The numerous slender rays and the bracts around the head nearly all of same length serve to help recognize the many species of *Erigeron*. Few occur in the Sonoran Desert.

WHITE EASTER-BONNET
Eriophyllum lanosum
Sunflower Family (Asteraceae)

Description: Dwarf, woolly plants, branched mostly from base, branches each ending with single head of white rays surrounding a yellow disk ⅛–¼" wide. Rays 8–10, ⅛–¼" long, oblong, usually slightly to strongly drooping. Bracts around head 8–10, in 1 series, ¼" long, tapered to a slender tip, woolly. Seedlike fruit slender, club-shaped, ⅛" long, hairless or nearly so, topped by several narrow, bristlelike scales ⅒" long. Leaves inversely narrowly lanceolate, ¼–¾" long, often pressed against stem. Stems ½–6" long.

Flowering Season: February–May.

Habitat/Range: Open ground, below 4,500', southeastern California to Utah, southwestern New Mexico, and Baja California.

Comments: Plants may carpet ground if rains are sufficient or be uncommon and tiny in dry years.

White Easter-Bonnet

PLAINS BLACKFOOT, BLACKFOOT DAISY
Melampodium leucanthum
Sunflower Family (Asteraceae)

Description: Rays 8–10, broad, oblong, usually about ½" long, surrounding a yellow disk of 25–50 flowers. Outer bracts of head 5, broadly ovate, the base of each bract united with that of adjacent bract. Inner bracts enfold seedlike fruit of ray flowers. Seedlike fruit without scales or bristles at top. Leaves opposite, oblong, ¾–1¾" long, less than ½" wide. Stems 6–20" tall.

Flowering Season: March–November.

Habitat/Range: Rocky slopes and flats, commonly on limestone, 2,000–5,000' in Arizona, southeastern Arizona to Texas and the southern Plains states; also northern Mexico.

Comments: This is a showy plant that has a long blooming season, particularly where it receives a little extra water. It now is used as an attractive ornamental in semi-dry landscaping, living for several years.

Plains Blackfoot, Blackfoot Daisy

Mojave Desertstar

MOJAVE DESERTSTAR
Monoptilon bellioides
Sunflower Family (Asteraceae)

Description: Ground-hugging plants with conspicuous, narrow white rays surrounding a yellow disk. Rays 9–20, ¼–⅜" long; disk less than ¼" across. Bracts around head many, narrow, more or less folded, ¼" long. Seedlike fruit broader near top, somewhat flattened, finely hairy, with several tiny bristles and scales at top. Leaves linear, ¼–½" long. Stems less than 10" long, usually lying on ground.

Flowering Season: February–April.

Habitat/Range: Gravelly ground, -100–3,500', southeastern California to southwestern Utah, western Arizona and northwestern Mexico.

Comments: Plants are often very small, the heads seeming to sit right upon the barren ground. Daisy Desertstar *(M. bellidiforme)* is very similar but has a tiny crown and only 1 bristle atop the seedlike fruit.

Desert Rockdaisy

DESERT ROCKDAISY
Perityle emoryi
Sunflower Family (Asteraceae)

Description: Glandular-hairy plants ¾–24" tall, bearing flower heads with yellow disks surrounded by white rays. Heads ½–¾" across, the 8–13 rays about ³⁄₁₆" long. Bracts on head numerous, narrow, ¼" long. Leaves ¾–4" long, heart-shaped to triangular in outline, deeply toothed or lobed. Seedlike fruits slender, flat, ⅛" long, edges densely stiff-hairy, top with a crown of tiny scales, often also with a single bristle.

Flowering Season: December–October.

Habitat/Range: Crevices of cliffs, among boulders, on rocky slopes, and in washes, below 3,000', southeastern California, southern Nevada, southwestern Arizona, northwestern Mexico.

Comments: As is true for so many desert annuals, plants may be very small in dry years, large and bushy following sufficient rain.

DESERT CHICORY
Rafinesquia neomexicana
Sunflower Family (Asteraceae)

Description: Smooth, grayish green plants 4–20" tall, the branches ending in heads with only white strap-shaped flowers, which are ½–¾" long, blunt at end, with 5 tiny teeth, usually blushed with maroon on back. Bracts around head tapering to a long point, the inner ones much longer than the very short outer ones. Seedlike fruit nearly ½" long, tapering at top to a stalk that bears fine, white, feathery bristles. Leaves pinnately lobed, 2–6" long, the upper ones much smaller than lower.

Flowering Season: February–July.

Habitat/Range: Open desert, 500–4,500', southern California to southwestern Utah, western Texas, and northwestern Mexico.

Comments: Very similar to White Tackstem *(Calycoseris wrightii),* but without the tacklike glands on upper stem and bracts of head. Both exude milky sap when picked.

Desert Chicory

White Zinnia

WHITE ZINNIA
Zinnia acerosa
Sunflower Family (Asteraceae)

Description: Low, rounded, semi-shrubby plants with opposite, linear leaves and with heads bearing broad white rays surrounding a small yellow disk. Rays 4–6, ⅜" long, indefinitely 3-toothed at tip. Disk flowers 8–13, protruding above rays. Bracts around head overlapping in several series, blunt-tipped. Seedlike fruit flattish, broader near tip, ⅛" long, with 2–3 unequal bristles at top. Leaves ½–¾" long, sharp-tipped. Stems many, 4–12" tall.

Flowering Season: April–October.

Habitat/Range: Rocky, often calcareous soil, 2,000–5,000', southern Arizona to western Texas and northern Mexico.

Comments: *Zinnia,* which contains our domestic Zinnia, is named for the German botanist Dr. Johann Gottfried Zinn (1727–1759), who collected the first zinnias known to Europeans in the mountains of Mexico. While collecting he is reputed to have been set upon by bandits, who when about to murder him, opened his pack and discovered it stuffed with flowers. Only an idiot would do such, and to kill the feeble-minded would bring bad luck. He was let go.

Panamint Cat's Eye

PANAMINT CAT'S EYE
Cryptantha angustifolia
Borage Family (Boraginaceae)

Description: Well-branched, bristly-hairy plants with tiny white flowers in coiled clusters. Corolla less than ⅛" across, 5-lobed, with tiny entrance to tube surrounded by 5 yellow pads. Fruit divides into 4 narrowly ovate segments ⅛" long, 1 slightly longer, all minutely grainy on back, each with a groove on angle of central face. Leaves linear or oblong, ½–1½" long. Stems 2–24" long.

Flowering Season: February–June.

Habitat/Range: Sandy or rocky soil, below 5,000', much of Southwest.

Comments: The many cat's eyes are easy to recognize by their tiny white flowers in coiled clusters but difficult to identify as to species. One must note the number of mature segments of fruit, patterns of granulation on surface of fruit, and whether all fruit segments are similar.

QUAIL PLANT, COLA DE MICO
Heliotropium curassavicum
Borage Family (Boraginaceae)

Description: Smooth, grayish blue-green plants with small white flowers in "fiddleneck" clusters. Corolla funnel-shaped, 5-lobed, about ¼" across, white, with a yellow center that becomes brown-maroon with age. Leaves inversely lanceolate, up to 1½" long, almost ½" wide, thick and fleshy. Stems usually growing in patches, up to 16" long.

Flowering Season: Most vigorously March–October, but throughout the year.

Habitat/Range: Clay, usually where moist, often where salty, 0–5,000', throughout the Southwest, widely ranging in the Western Hemisphere.

Comments: The youngest buds are well inside the tight coil of the flower cluster, the cluster uncoiling as the flowers bloom. The coil gives the name Cola de Mico, "monkey's tail." The seedlike fruits are eaten by seed-eating birds, giving the other common name.

Quail Plant, Cola de Mico

Southwestern Spectacle-Pod

SOUTHWESTERN SPECTACLE-POD
Dimorphocarpa wislizenii
Mustard Family (Brassicaceae)

Description: Grayish green, erect plants 1–3' tall, unbranched or branched near the base, with white flowers and tiny pods that resemble eyeglasses. Petals 4, ¼–⅜" long. Stalks beneath individual flowers usually about ½" long. Pods flat, angled sharply upward at tip of stalk, ½–⅝" wide, deeply notched at bottom where stalk attaches, much less deeply notched at top. Leaves narrowly lanceolate to oblong, usually with prominent teeth or lobes along edges.

Flowering Season: February–October.

Habitat/Range: Sandy soil, 1,000–6,000', from southern Nevada to southern Arizona, eastward to the southern Great Plains, southward into Mexico.

Comments: Southwestern Spectacle-Pod is common along roadsides, flowering in spring after winter rains and later in the year after summer rains.

California Spectacle-Pod

CALIFORNIA SPECTACLE-POD
Dithyrea californica
Mustard Family (Brassicaceae)

Description: Lightly grayish hairy plants with spreading or reclining stems arising from a basal rosette, bearing white or very light lavender cross-shaped flowers and pods resembling greenish spectacles. Petals 4, narrow, ½" long, prominently 3-veined. Pods spreading, flat, 2-chambered, ⅜–½" wide, notched more or less equally at base and tip. Leaves 1¼–6" long, stalked, lanceolate or wider, broader in upper half, the leaves on stem smaller, without stalks. Stems 4–30" long.

Flowering Season: February–May, sometimes again in October–November.

Habitat/Range: Sandy places, below 4,500', southeastern California and southern Nevada to western Arizona and northwestern Mexico.

Comments: "Spectacle-Pod" applies both to *Dithyrea* and *Dimorphocarpa,* once all in *Dithyrea,* but which differ in the orientation of the pod.

WEDGE-LEAF WHITLOW-GRASS
Draba cuneifolia
Mustard Family (Brassicaceae)

Description: Small plants, 1–4" tall, rarely more, with most leaves near base, and with small white flowers in clusters at step tip. Petals 4, ⅛" long. Leaves broadly, inversely lanceolate, coarsely toothed, the base wedge-shaped, ¼–2½" long. Pods spreading, lanceolate, ⅛–½" long. Foliage, stems, and sometimes pods with minute, branched hairs.

Flowering Season: February–May.

Habitat/Range: Open areas, usually where sandy, 1,000–7,000', much of North America.

Comments: This is a harbinger of spring everywhere, blooming before most plants are getting started. As the days warm, it quickly matures, bears fruit, and then withers.

Wedge-Leaf Whitlow-Grass

GARDEN ROCKET, SALAD ROCKET
Eruca vesicaria ssp. *sativa*
Mustard Family (Brassicaceae)

Description: Coarse, branched plants 1–3' tall, with deeply pinnately lobed leaves and white or cream, cross-shaped flowers in long, open clusters. Petals 4, sharply bent above sepals, veined with dark maroon, the broad portion above sepals almost ½" long. Fruit a 4-ribbed, nearly cylindrical pod ½–1" long, with a more or less flattened, beaklike tip half as long as the pod to equally long. Leaves 2–6" long, with a few hairs on midrib on lower side, the terminal lobe the largest.

Flowering Season: March–July.

Habitat/Range: Disturbed areas such as roadsides and fields, mostly below 3,000', introduced from Europe and now common in the American Southwest.

Comments: The leaves may be used as a pungent addition to salads, or they may be cooked in a manner similar to mustard greens.

Garden Rocket, Salad Rocket

Bush Pepperwort

BUSH PEPPERWORT
Lepidium fremontii var. *fremontii*
Mustard Family (Brassicaceae)

Description: Rounded, many-branched plants up to 3' tall, somewhat woody at base, with pinnately cleft leaves, tiny white flowers, and flat, purselike pods. Petals 4, ⅛" long. Fruits oval or broader in upper half, ¼" long, slightly notched at tip, the style in notch equaling or exceeding top of fruit. Leaves near base of plant 1–4" long, cleft into 3–9 linear lobes; leaves near top of plant shorter, often linear.

Flowering Season: February–May.

Habitat/Range: Rocky and sandy places below 5,000', southeastern California to Utah and western Arizona.

Comments: A second variety, *L. fremontii* var. *stipitatum,* rare on rocky slopes on the Sonoran Desert, has a very short stalk at the base of the pod, above a joint on the stalk that connects to main stem. In Bush Pepperwort, the stalk from the stem joins directly to the pod without an intervening joint.

Western White Bladderpod

WESTERN WHITE BLADDERPOD
Lesquerella purpurea
Mustard Family (Brassicaceae)

Description: Grayish green plants with few stems, 4-petaled white flowers in loose clusters, and small, spherical pods on slender, spreading or down-curved stalks. Petals ⅜" long. Pods ¼" in diameter, green, often blushed with purple. Leaves oval to more or less inversely lanceolate, 1–5" long, edges uneven and wavy or deeply lobed. Stems 4–16" long.

Flowering Season: January–May.

Habitat/Range: Open slopes and washes, 1,500–5,000', southern Arizona to western Texas and northwestern Mexico.

Comments: Other bladderpods in the region have yellow flowers. The gray hue of the foliage is imparted by dense, minute, starlike hairs that have many rays, easily visible with a lens.

ARIZONA JEWELFLOWER
Streptanthus carinatus ssp. *arizonicus*
Mustard Family (Brassicaceae)

Description: Smooth, grayish green plants 8–24" tall, with long, open clusters of whitish, flask-shaped flowers ½" long. Sepals 4, ⅜" long, whitish, swollen at base, folded lengthwise. Petals 4, narrow, dull pale yellowish, veined with maroon, curled outward beyond sepal tips. Fruit a strongly flattened, erect pod ³⁄₁₆" wide, 2–3" long. Leaves slightly wider above middle, ½–2" wide, 1½–10" long, upper leaves indented at base, without a stalk, seeming to clasp the stem.

Flowering Season: January–April.

Habitat/Range: Rocky hillsides, 1,500–4,500', southern Arizona and New Mexico, northwestern Mexico.

Comments: In the western part of the range, flowers are whitish or cream. Eastward they become more strongly yellow. Plants of the subspecies *carinatus,* uncommon in Arizona, have purple flowers.

Arizona Jewelflower

Desert Night-Blooming Cereus, Queen-of-the-Night, Reina de la Noche

DESERT NIGHT-BLOOMING CEREUS, QUEEN-OF-THE-NIGHT, REINA DE LA NOCHE

Peniocereus greggii var. *transmontanus*
Cactus Family (Cactaceae)

Description: Gray-green, erect or sprawling, 4- to 6-sided stems 1–7' long bear large, funnel-shaped, nocturnal white flowers. Flowers 2½–3½" in diameter, 6–8" long, with many narrowly lanceolate, petal-like segments and several hundred stamens. Stems ½–¾" thick, with 4–6 ribs, bearing clusters of 11–13 mostly dark spines ⅛" long or less, mostly lying parallel to the stem. Fruit broadly football shaped, 2–3" long, red, and fleshy.

Flowering Season: June–July.

Habitat/Range: Under desert trees and in shrubs, 1,000–3,500', southern Arizona and northern Sonora.

Comments: This is one of the best-known, fairly common, but least seen, of the Sonoran Desert wildflowers. The stems of this cactus mimic dead stems and branches and are very difficult to see among brush. All the plants within an area bloom simultaneously, filling the air with sweet scent to attract moths, the flowers easily seen from a distance in the twilight. The massive turniplike root should not be dug; plants grown from seed may now be purchased in nurseries.

Redtip Threadstem

REDTIP THREADSTEM
Nemacladus glanduliferus
Bellflower Family (Campanulaceae)

Description: Dainty plants 2–10" tall, with stiff, threadlike stems and tiny white bilateral flowers. Corolla ⅛" across, 3 upper lobes bent upwards and red tipped, 2 lower lobes curved forward and with an indefinite violet band near base when young. Leaves in basal rosette, ½–1" long, inversely lanceolate, with teeth or divided.

Flowering Season: March–May.

Habitat/Range: Open, sandy places, below 7,000', southeastern California to Utah, New Mexico, and northwestern Mexico.

Comments: A hand lens aids appreciation of this remarkable, hard-to-see plant. On the ovary are 3 yellow-green glands, between stamen filaments. On the filaments are glistening, transparent, rodlike cells. Near the anthers filaments are fused. During development, the flowers rotate 180° and the top becomes the bottom. How or for what purpose this happens is unknown. There are 13 species in this peculiar genus, all restricted to southwestern North America.

CLAMMYWEED
Polanisia dodecandra
Caper Family (Capparaceae)

Description: Strongly resin scented plants 4–32" tall, covered with sticky, glandular hairs. Flowers many, in elongate clusters at top of stems. Petals 4, white, the ¼–½" long blade tapered to a long, slender base. Stamens purple, 10–20, longer than petals. Leaves palmately compound; leaflets 3, lanceolate, ¾–2" long. Fruit a pod 1½–2½" long, splitting open in upper portion.

Flowering Season: May–October.

Habitat/Range: Open sandy areas, 1,000–6,500', throughout most of Sonoran Desert; much of western North America.

Comments: The surface of this plant is sufficiently glandular that it feels cool and moist, or "clammy." The glands probably inhibit plant-eating insects and larger animals. The genus name refers to the many stamens, which are unequal in length.

Clammyweed

Frostmat, Sandmat, Onyx Flower

FROSTMAT, SANDMAT, ONYX FLOWER
Achyronychia cooperi
Carnation Family (Caryophyllaceae)

Description: Several branch systems radiating from top of root, broad at base, tapering to tip, the entire plant resembling a flat, irregular, greenish star. Flowers numerous, tiny, whitish, ⅛" long, in tight clusters in leaf axils. Each flower with 5 green, fleshy sepals, and each sepal with wide, white, translucent edges. Petals absent. Leaves ⅛–¾" long, broader in their upper halves. Stems 1–8" long.

Flowering Season: January–May.

Habitat/Range: Sandy flats and washes, below 3,000', southern California, western Arizona, northwestern Mexico.

Comments: Frostmat, so named because of the frosty appearance imparted by the numerous translucent white flowers, is common after winters with sufficient rain. As plants mature and dry, the stems bend upward from the base, becoming erect or nearly so.

Field Bindweed, Orchard Morning Glory

FIELD BINDWEED, ORCHARD MORNING GLORY
Convolvulus arvensis
Morning Glory Family (Convolvulaceae)

Description: Vines or ground-hugging patches with white or pinkish ¾–1" long, funnel-shaped flowers. Stigma with 2 linear, not flattened, branches. Leaves ½–4" long, arrowhead-shaped or narrowly heart-shaped. Stems branched, up to 2' long.

Flowering Season: May–October.

Habitat/Range: Roadsides, disturbed places, and agricultural areas, mostly below 5,000', throughout much of North America.

Comments: This attractive European immigrant is one of the worst of agricultural weeds, designated "noxious weed" in a number of states. Its deep roots and underground stems make it difficult and expensive to eradicate. Recently the host-specific Bindweed Gall Mite from southern Europe has been released in the Southwest in an attempt to control the plant.

RAGGED ROCKFLOWER
Crossosoma bigelovii
Rockflower Family (Crossosomataceae)

Description: Erect, open, irregularly branched shrubs 3–6' tall, with white flowers borne singly in axils. Petals 5, narrowly inversely lanceolate, ½" long. Stems 15–30, yellow. Ovaries 1–6 in center of flower, yellow-green, shaped like little pea pods, curved outward, ½" long. Leaves broadly inversely lanceolate to elliptic, borne singly on young stems, in clusters on older stems, ¼–¾" long.

Flowering Season: December–May, sometimes also in September.

Habitat/Range: Rocky slopes, 1,500–4,000', southeastern California to southern Arizona and northwestern Mexico.

Comments: Ragged Rockflower has a sweet, delicate fragrance. Crossosomataceae has only 9 species and is restricted to arid and semi-arid southwestern North America.

Ragged Rockflower

Flat-Globe Dodder

FLAT-GLOBE DODDER
Cuscuta umbellata
Dodder Family (Cuscutaceae)

Description: Stems like tangled, yellow-orange string less than ¹⁄₁₀" thick, up to 3' long, bear tiny whitish flowers. Flowers in groups of 3–7, the groups gathered into many-flowered clusters. Corolla ⅛" across, with a bowl-like base and 5 narrowly triangular lobes bent back from rim. Between each pair of the 5 stamens are oblong, fringed scales. The fruit is a round capsule opening by an irregular lid.

Flowering Season: August–October.

Habitat/Range: Open areas, mostly below 5,000', southern Arizona to western Texas, south into Mexico.

Comments: Flat-Globe Dodder is a parasite that appears after summer rains fall, spreading over and wrapping around newly sprouted green plants. Dodder *(Cuscuta),* in general, is easy to recognize, but species are distinguished by technical characteristics of the tiny flowers and fruit.

Rattlesnake Weed, White-Margin Sandmat, Golondrina

RATTLESNAKE WEED, WHITE-MARGIN SANDMAT, GOLONDRINA

Chamaesyce albomarginata
Spurge Family (Euphorbiaceae)

Description: Matted plants with opposite oval or oblong leaves and tiny white flower clusters, each cluster mimicking a single flower. Flower cluster ⅛–¼" across; the cuplike base has 4 white, petal-like lobes, each with a reddish pad at the base. In the center of the cup are many tiny stamens and a single 3-lobed ovary on a stalk that extends out of the cup, through a gap between the lobes on the rim. The leaves are up to ¼" long. On each side of stem between the leaf bases is a triangular bit of white tissue. The stems are up to 16" long and bleed with white sap when broken.

Flowering Season: February–October.

Habitat/Range: Open, sandy to clay soils, 1,000–6,000', southern California to Utah and Oklahoma, south into northern Mexico.

Comments: The tiny flap of white tissue between leaf bases distinguishes this species from similar ones.

Chiricahua Milk-Spurge

CHIRICAHUA MILK-SPURGE
Chamaesyce florida
Spurge Family (Euphorbiaceae)

Description: Open, delicate, spindly plants with linear leaves, milky sap, and small, bright white flower clusters, each of which resembles a single flower. Flower clusters consist of a green cup ⅒" tall with 4 white, petal-like lobes ⅛" long on rim, each lobe with a green gland at base. As lobes age they become pink. Ovary green, spherical, on a stalk that droops through a gap between lobes. Leaves ¼–2½" long, with tiny, well-spaced teeth on edges. Stems repeatedly forked, 4–24" tall.

Flowering Season: August–October.

Habitat/Range: Open, arid areas, 2,000–5,000', southern Arizona and northwestern Mexico.

Comments: The flowering structure is deceptive, resembling 1 true flower. Each stamen, however, is a minute male flower with no other parts, and the ovary on the stalk is the single female flower of the cluster.

Mala Mujer

MALA MUJER
Cnidoscolus angustidens
Spurge Family (Euphorbiaceae)

Description: Robust plants 6–48" tall, with palmate, 3- to 5-lobed leaves that have stout, stinging hairs. The flowers have no petals, but the white, papery, 5-lobed, funnel-shaped calyx is petal-like, ½–¾" across, and armed with stinging hairs. The female flower is found at base flower clusters; male flowers are scattered in the upper parts. Leaves are dark green, 3–8" wide, the stinging hairs about ¼" long, erect from a swollen white base.

Flowering Season: May–September.

Habitat/Range: Rocky slopes, 2,500–5,000', southeastern Arizona to northwestern Mexico.

Comments: This is a handsome plant with large, shiny, dark green, maplelike leaves accented by the conspicuous white bases of the stinging hairs. It beauty belies its nature; the common name means "bad woman," and refers to its sting.

DOWNY PRAIRIE-CLOVER
Dalea neomexicana
Bean Family (Fabaceae)

Description: Sprawling plants with grayish, hairy, pinnately compound leaves and shaggy spikes of tiny whitish "pea" flowers. Petals are yellowish white, drying pink or rose, the broad, flat portion of the banner ⅛" long, the inner margins of keel petals wrinkled. Calyx 10-ribbed, its narrow, pointed lobes nearly ¼" long, silky-hairy. Leaves with 7–11 leaflets, each wider near notched tip, gland-dotted near flat or wrinkled margins. Stems 1–14" long.

Flowering Season: December–August.

Habitat/Range: Deserts and arid grasslands, 2,100–5,300', southeastern Arizona to western Texas, south into Mexico.

Comments: This species, common along the eastern margins of the Sonoran Desert, is similar to Hairy Prairie-Clover *(D. mollis)* and Soft Prairie-Clover *(D. mollissima),* two species found farther west in the Sonoran Desert.

Downy Prairie-Clover

Arizona Mariposa

ARIZONA MARIPOSA
Calochortus ambiguus
Lily Family (Liliaceae)

Description: White, bell-shaped flowers, usually several in a loose cluster, are held erect on smooth, 1–2' tall, grayish green stems. Petals 3, fan-shaped, 1–1½" long, yellow, and hairy near the base, with a maroon gland at base surrounded by fringed membrane. Leaves linear, grayish green, those at base up to 1' long and usually withered by flowering time; upper leaves shorter.

Flowering Season: April on the Sonoran Desert, to as late as August at higher elevations to the north.

Habitat/Range: Dry slopes in brush, 3,000–8,000', Arizona and southwestern New Mexico.

Comments: This abundant species occurs at the upper edge of the Sonoran Desert in Arizona and higher and northward. *Mariposa* is "butterfly" in Spanish, a reference to the patterned, winglike petals. For some time, the distinction of the Arizona plants from those of the Rocky Mountain region was ambiguous, thus the specific name.

Desert Lily

DESERT LILY
Hesperocallis undulata
Lily Family (Liliaceae)

Description: Erect plants 1–8' tall, with white, funnel-shaped flowers spreading from central stalk. Flowers 2–2½" long, with 3 lanceolate petals that curve outward and 3 similar petal-like sepals, all with a broad greenish gray mid-stripe on back. Leaves linear, mostly all at base, folded lengthwise so upper surface is channeled, 8–20" long, the margins wavy.

Flowering Season: February–May.

Habitat/Range: Sandy flats, below 2,500', southeastern California and southwestern Arizona.

Comments: This plant, resembling a small Easter Lily (*Lilium longiflorum*), is unexpected and seems out of place in its harsh habitat. Deep bulbs, once eaten by Native Americans, may remain dormant for years, "awakening" only after deep, soaking rain.

THURBER'S COTTON, ALGODONCILLO
Gossypium thurberi
Mallow Family (Malvaceae)

Description: An openly branched shrub to 12' tall with palmately lobed leaves and deeply cup-shaped white flowers. Petals 5, round, ¾–1¼" long, sometimes with a purplish blush at base. Leaves with 3 to 5 narrow, lanceolate lobes ½–1¼" wide, 1½–4" long. Fruit a capsule splitting into 3–5 sections, interior of capsule and seeds with a few cotton hairs.

Flowering Season: August–October.

Habitat/Range: Rocky slopes, 2,500–5,000', southern Arizona and northern Mexico.

Comments: Plants are frequent at upper elevations of the eastern part of the Sonoran Desert, occurring along roads and highways. A native boll weevil breeds in the capsules, also infecting nearby commercial cotton crops. Attempts have been made to eradicate the plant near cotton fields, but elsewhere it is common.

Thurber's Cotton, Algodoncillo

Dollarweed, Alkali Mallow

DOLLARWEED, ALKALI MALLOW
Malvella leprosa
Mallow Family (Malvaceae)

Description: Low, grayish, almost matted plants with bowl-shaped, white to cream-colored, occasionally rose, flowers borne singly in axils of leaves. Petals 5, ½" long, roundish. Stamens many, filaments joined, forming a tube. Leaves round, kidney-shaped or roundish triangular, ½–1½" long, irregularly toothed on edges, covered with minute, scaly, starlike hairs. Stems 2–18" long.

Flowering Season: March–October.

Habitat/Range: Moist clay soil, 100–5,000', throughout Sonoran Desert; much of western United States and Mexico.

Comments: Two other species have white, bowl-shaped flowers very similar to those of this troublesome weed: Arrowleaf Mallow (*M. sagittifolia*—leaves narrowly arrowhead-shaped, 1–3 large teeth at base) and Scurfy Mallow (*M. lepidota*—leaves triangular, coarse teeth on edges).

Desert Wishbone-Bush

DESERT WISHBONE-BUSH

Mirabilis laevis var. *villosa*

Four O'Clock Family (Nyctaginaceae)

Description: Glandular-hairy plants with opposite leaves and white, broadly funnel-shaped flowers borne in green 5-toothed cups. Corolla-like part ½" long, 5-lobed, the lobes notched. Leaves broadly ovate, ½–1½" long, those of a pair unequal in size. Fruit hard and seedlike, football-shaped to almost spherical, brownish or blackish, sometimes striped, ⅛–¼" long. Stems forked, 12–30" long.

Flowering Season: March–October.

Habitat/Range: Rocky places, below 7,000', much of the Sonoran Desert.

Comments: Flowers open in evening, close in morning, each lasting only 1 night. Stems from the previous year, forked and bleached white, give the common name. Nevada Wishbone-Bush *(M. laevis* var. *retrorsa),* much less glandular, has small hairs pointing downward.

BROWNEYES

Camissonia claviformis ssp. *claviformis*

Evening Primrose Family (Onagraceae)

Description: Plants with a basal rosette of leaves and with flowers in 1-sided, nodding clusters. Petals 4, white, round, ⅛–⅜" long, attached to a tube ⅛–⅜" long situated at top of stalklike ovary. Interior of tube brownish maroon. Fruit an ascending or spreading, gently curved pod ⅛" wide, slightly wider toward tip, ½–1½" long. Leaves up to 8" long, often red-spotted, irregularly pinnately divided, the terminal lobe largest. Stems 4–16" tall.

Flowering Season: February–April, sometimes also October–November.

Habitat/Range: Sandy areas, below 5,500', much of arid western United States and northwestern Mexico.

Comments: Subspecies differ in hairiness, division of leaves, and flower color, some having pale yellow petals. All have a brown-maroon tube (the "brown eye"), and reddish petals in wilted flowers.

Browneyes

NARROWLEAF SUNCUP
Camissonia refracta
Evening Primrose Family (Onagraceae)

Description: White flowers and reddish buds nod in loose clusters at ends of stems. Petals ⅛–⅜" long, at first white, fading reddish, attached at end of a tube ¼" long located on top of a slender, stalklike ovary. Stigma extending beyond stamens. Fruit a slender pod ¾–2" long, less than ¹⁄₁₆" wide, without a stalk between its base and stem. Leaves narrowly lanceolate, 1–2½" long. Stems 2–10" tall, the surface peeling.

Flowering Season: March–May.

Habitat/Range: Sandy soil, -100–4,000', southeastern California to southwestern Utah and western Arizona.

Comments: Flowers open at dusk and close the next morning. Suncups *(Camissonia)* can be distinguished as a genus by the 4 petals and knoblike stigma. Pollen grains adhere in long strings, sticking to insects (and shoes and clothing).

Narrowleaf Suncup

California Evening Primrose

CALIFORNIA EVENING PRIMROSE
Oenothera californica ssp. *avita*
Evening Primrose Family (Onagraceae)

Description: Large white flowers with 4 petals bloom on grayish green plants with pinnately lobed leaves. Petals heart-shaped, ⅝–1½" long, attached at the top of a tube ¾–1½" long, which sits atop the ovary. Buds hanging at end of stem. Leaves oblong or lanceolate in outline, ¾–3" long. Pod cylindrical, ⅛" wide, ¾–3" long. Stems usually reclining, 4–32" long, the surface usually peeling.

Flowering Season: February–May.

Habitat/Range: Sandy soil in desert scrub or pinyon-juniper woodland, 1,800–7,500', southern California to Utah, Arizona, and northwestern Mexico.

Comments: Flowers open in the evening, an entire patch of this evening primrose "exploding" into flower in a half hour or so. Each flower closes forever before the heat of the next day.

Dune Evening Primrose

DUNE EVENING PRIMROSE
Oenothera deltoides ssp. *deltoides*
Evening Primrose Family (Onagraceae)

Description: Robust plants with large white flowers developing from nodding buds. Petals 4, ½–1½" long, each heart-shaped and attached by its tip to top of a tube ¾–1½" long, which is located at top of ovary. Leaves lanceolate to diamond-shaped, the upper leaves with teeth on edges, the surface with fine, erect hairs. Pods more or less cylindrical, ¾–2½" long, ⅛" wide at base and tapering to narrower tip. Usually 1 central, erect stem, and several stems spreading from the base, turning upwards at tips, the outer surface peeling as the stem ages.

Flowering Season: February–June.

Habitat/Range: Sandy areas, 100–3,500', southeastern California to southern Nevada and western Arizona, south in northwestern Mexico.

Comments: In a spring after a wet winter, this popular desert wildflower is common in sandy areas. It has a number of common names, including Devil's Lantern, Lion-in-a-Cage, and Basket Evening Primrose, all referring to the dead and dried plant. In the heat of the coming summer, the branches dry out and curl upward, forming the characteristic "cage" that may last 1 or 2 seasons.

WHITE PRICKLY POPPY
Argemone polyanthemos
Poppy Family (Papaveraceae)

Description: Prickly, grayish green plants with large, bowl-shaped white flowers. Petals usually 6, fan-shaped, 1½–2" long. Sepals 3, each with a stout horn up to ½" long at tip. Sepals fall as buds open. Leaves deeply pinnately divided, 4–8" long, prickly almost exclusively on larger veins. Stems 2–5' tall, bleeding with yellow sap when broken.

Flowering Season: Most vigorously July–September, but flowering much of the year.

Habitat/Range: Dry soil, 1,500–8,000', most of the American Southwest.

Comments: These plants are distasteful to livestock and therefore tend to increase in number on heavily grazed rangeland. If an animal overcomes the formidable prickly defense, the acrid taste is a warning—plants are poisonous. The yellow sap has been used to treat diseases of the skin. Plants were also boiled for baths in the treatment of rheumatism.

White Prickly Poppy

Creamcups

CREAMCUPS
Platystemon californicus
Poppy Family (Papaveraceae)

Description: Stems and leaves shaggy-hairy; flowers pale cream, borne singly at top of stalks. Sepals 3, petals 6. Petals spoon-shaped, ⅜–½" long. Stamens many, filaments flattened. Fruit at first a cylindrical head ½" high, then breaking into 6–25 segments, each of which breaks into several 1-seeded joints. Leaves mostly near base, narrowly lanceolate, ¾–3" long. Flowers stalks few to many, arising among leaves, 3–12" tall.

Flowering Season: March–May.

Habitat/Range: Moist, gravelly ground, especially in washes in deserts, 1,500–4,500', California to southwestern Utah and southern Arizona.

Comments: The general appearance of the peculiar fruit segments has been compared to tiny ears of corn. Hairiness varies, especially that of fruit. The genus name refers to the flat stamen filaments.

Desert Snow

DESERT SNOW
Linanthus demissus
Phlox Family (Polemoniaceae)

Description: Very low, wiry plants with white, bell-shaped flowers. Corolla ¼–⅜" long, 5-lobed, the opening of the tube yellow, the base of each lobe marked with 2 maroon lines. Stamens 5, included within tube. Leaves ¼–⅜" long, with 3–5 very narrow, sharply pointed lobes, or leaves undivided, linear. Stems repeatedly branched, often lying on ground, ¾–4" long.

Flowering Season: March–May.

Habitat/Range: Coarse sand, often in desert washes, below 2,000' in the Sonoran Desert, up to 4,000' elsewhere; southeastern California to southwestern Utah and southern Arizona.

Comments: The white, speckled flowers of this species sometimes make it difficult to spot in a wash with pale, gravelly sand.

SCHOTT'S CALICO
Loeseliastrum schottii
Phlox Family (Polemoniaceae)

Description: Low plants, generally less than 4" tall and 8" wide, with prickly leaves at end of stems, and small white or pale lavender bilateral flowers. Corolla ⅜" long, the upper lip 3-lobed, the lower lip with 2 lobes spreading to sides. At base of upper 3 lobes are maroon arches filled with yellow. Leaves ½–1¼" long, narrow, broader in upper half, with 3–5 prominent, bristle-tipped teeth.

Flowering Season: March to May.

Habitat/Range: Dry, sandy or gravelly areas, below 5,000', southeastern California to southwestern Utah, western Arizona and northwestern Mexico.

Comments: Schott's Calico is common on sand dunes. The maroon and yellow flower pattern forms a target so that visiting insects may quickly locate the nectar-bearing tube. Plants with weakly bilateral flowers tend to be self-pollinated.

Schott's Calico

SANTA CATALINA MOUNTAIN PHLOX
Phlox tenuifolia
Phlox Family (Polemoniaceae)

Description: Dark green, straggling plants 1–7' tall with bright white, trumpet-shaped flowers ¾" long. Flowers 6–18 in a loose cluster. Lobes of corolla flared outward, rounded, ⅜–½" long. Sepals 5, linear, sharply pointed, united about half their length with a translucent, flat membrane. Leaves opposite, well-spaced along the stem, linear to narrowly lanceolate, 1–2" long.

Flowering Season: March–April, sometimes also in October.

Habitat/Range: Among shrubs on rocky slopes, 1,500–5,000', south-central Arizona.

Comments: This unusual phlox has petal-lobes that gradually flare from the tube, rather than abruptly spreading at 90°. Flowers rarely are cream or blushed with lavender. Stems may climb through other vegetation, the plants making spectacular displays on supporting shrubs.

Santa Catalina Mountain Phlox

Abert's Wild Buckwheat

ABERT'S WILD BUCKWHEAT
Eriogonum abertianum var. *abertianum*
Buckwheat Family (Polygonaceae)

Description: Hairy plants branched in an open, forked manner, with round clusters of small whitish flowers. Within clusters, flowers are borne in bell-shaped cups nearly ⅛" long, with 5 teeth nearly ¼" long that bend outward and back as flowers mature. Each flower ⅛" long, with 6 petal-like segments, the 3 inner segments lanceolate, the 3 outer segments nearly round, the bases indented, all segments usually with a dull rose midvein. Leaves ovate or oblong, ½–1½" long. Stems 4–20" tall.

Flowering Season: March–September.

Habitat/Range: Sandy or gravelly flats or banks, 1,500–7,000', southern Arizona to western Texas and northern Mexico.

Comments: Wright's Wild Buckwheat *(E. wrightii)*, is very similar to this plant. It has many wiry stems in a bushy clump 1–2' tall and many white flowers in tiny rounded clusters.

Flat-Topped Skeleton-Weed, Flat-Topped Buckwheat

FLAT-TOPPED SKELETON-WEED, FLAT-TOPPED BUCKWHEAT
Eriogonum deflexum
Buckwheat Family (Polygonaceae)

Description: Wiry, dark green, more or less flat-topped, intricately branched, nearly leafless plants with tiny whitish flowers. Flowers ¹⁄₂₀–⅛" long, several in green, inversely conical, hairless, unribbed 5-toothed cups less than ⅛" long. Cups borne on downward-bent stalks less than ⅛" long. Each flower with 6 whitish or pinkish petal-like parts, the midrib of each part greenish, the bases of outer 3 parts each shaped like the top of a heart. Leaves at base of plant on long stalks, blades round to rather kidney shaped, ½–1½" long, densely white woolly on lower side, less densely hairy on upper side. Stems hairless, 4–18" tall, sometimes taller.

Flowering Season: Most vigorously July–September, but flowering most of the year.

Habitat/Range: Sandy areas, below 7,000', southeastern California to western Utah and western New Mexico, to northwestern Mexico.

Comments: The genus name, from Greek, means "woolly knees," referring to the hairy, swollen nodes on the stems of some species. The russet skeletons of Flat-Topped Skeleton-Weed may ornament roadsides for a full season after flowering.

CALIFORNIA BUCKWHEAT
Eriogonum fasciculatum var. *polifolium*
Buckwheat Family (Polygonaceae)

Description: Grayish-hairy shrubs with tiny white flowers in round heads. Several tapered, hairy, cuplike structures, 5-toothed, ⅛" long, compose each head, each cup holding several flowers on tiny stalks. Each flower ⅛" long or less, whitish or pinkish, with 5 petal-like parts, hairy. Leaves inversely lanceolate, ¼–¾" long, velvety-hairy, margins rolled under. Stems 1–2½" tall.

Flowering Season: April–December.

Habitat/Range: Dry slopes and washes, 200–7,500', southern California to southwestern Utah, western Arizona, and northwestern Mexico.

Comments: This widespead species has several varieties. Also in the Sonoran Desert region is the variety *flavoviride,* with light green leaves hairless on top. The cups that hold the flowers are also usually hairless.

California Buckwheat

WILLOWWEED
Polygonum lapathifolium
Buckwheat Family (Polygonaceae)

Description: Slender spikes of numerous, dense, whitish or pinkish flowers droop on plants with dark green, lanceolate leaves. Spikes up to 4" long. Flowers ¹⁄₁₀" long, with 5 petal-like parts, the outer ones with veins in shape of an anchor. Seedlike fruit round, ¹⁄₁₀" long, shiny, flat, indented on both sides. Leaves 2–8" long. At base of short leaf stalk, where it joins stem, is a brown, veiny sheath ½" long. Stems 2–7' tall.

Flowering Season: April–October.

Habitat/Range: Low areas where water stands, or along streams and river margins, 1,000–6,000' in Sonoran Desert region, much of northern hemisphere.

Comments: This weedy plant usually grows in dense patches. The anchorlike veins on petal-like parts of flowers, easily seen with a lens, are characteristic of this species.

Willowweed

Desert Anemone

DESERT ANEMONE
Anemone tuberosa var. *tuberosa*
Buttercup Family (Ranunculaceae)

Description: Slender plants 4–16" tall, with divided leaves and whitish flowers at tips of long stalks. Flowers without petals, but sepals petal-like, narrowly elliptic, ½" long, whitish or very pale lavender or pink on face, darker and hairy on back. Stamens many. Fruits seed-like, many in a woolly, cylindrical head ½–1¼" long. Leaves 1–2½" long, divided into 3 main segments, those again divided into narrow segments.

Flowering Season: February–April.

Habitat/Range: Among rocks on slopes, often where partly shaded, 2,500–5,000', southeastern California to southwestern Utah and southern New Mexico.

Comments: This is one of the earliest blooming wildflowers. By the time one is exploring for spring wildflowers, often all that is left of this species are woolly heads on long stalks.

TEXAS VIRGIN'S BOWER, BARBA DE CHIVATO
Clematis drummondii
Buttercup Family (Ranunculaceae)

Description: Clambering vines with pinnately compound leaves and white flowers. Petal-like sepals 4, narrow, ½" long, silky-hairy on outer surface; no petals. Male flowers with many stamens, those at center fertile, those on periphery sterile; female flowers with pistils in center surrounded by a few sterile stamens. Leaves with 5–7 leaflets, or upper leaves merely 3-cleft; leaflets ½–1" long, each usually 3-cleft into tapered, pointed, diverging lobes. Fruits in glistening white, feathery spheres, each fruit with a seedlike base and a feathery tail 2–4" long.

Flowering Season: March–September.

Habitat/Range: Among shrubs, below 4,000', from southern Arizona to western Texas and northern Mexico.

Comments: The 2 upper flowers in the photo are on a male plant; the single flower below is on a female plant.

Texas Virgin's Bower, Barba de Chivato

YERBA MANSA

Anemopsis californica
Lizard's-Tail Family (Saururaceae)

Description: Smooth plants in patches, with elliptic or oblong leaves and white, starlike flower heads with a conelike center. White structures in head are bracts, the lowest 5–8 resembling petals, ovate, ½–1¼" long, those on central cone only about ¼" long. Each bract is below a small greenish flower with 6 stamens. Leaf blades 2–6" long, on stalks about as long. Stems 6–20" tall.

Flowering Season: May–August.

Habitat/Range: Moist alkaline soil, 2,000–5,000', throughout the American Southwest and northern Mexico.

Comments: This is a valued medicinal plant among indigenous people. The creeping, aromatic, powdered rhizome may be used in teas for stomach problems, in poultices for wounds, in salves for skin problems, and mixed with leather ashes, tobacco, and fat for hemorrhoids.

Yerba Mansa

Green-Leaf Five-Eyes

GREEN-LEAF FIVE-EYES

Chamaesaracha coronopus
Nightshade Family (Solanaceae)

Description: Round or bluntly 5-angled, flat, dingy white flowers, each with a pale brownish green star pattern. Corolla ⅜–½" wide, the center with 5 white, hairy pads that fill the throat of the short tube. Hairs on plant sparse, some branched or starlike with several arms. Leaves narrow, often with a few lobes on edges, ¾–2½" long. Fruit a round, purplish berry ¼" wide, tightly contained by calyx. Stems, often in patches, 4–20" long.

Flowering Season: April–September.

Habitat/Range: Dry, open flats, 2,500–7,500', from southeastern California across the American Southwest to Kansas and western Texas, south into Mexico.

Comments: The tiny berries were eaten by Native Americans. Hairy Five-Eyes *(C. sordida)* has broadly lanceolate or diamond-shaped leaves, the hairy pads in center of flower not filling throat.

Sacred Thorn-Apple, Toloache

SACRED THORN-APPLE, TOLOACHE
Datura wrightii
Nightshade Family (Solanaceae)

Description: Robust plants 1–5' tall, with white, funnel-shaped corollas 6–8" long with 5 slender teeth on rim. Calyx cylindrical, with 5 unequal teeth, 5-ribbed near base; base forms a reflexed rim beneath fruit. Leaves 4–8" long, ovate, finely grayish-velvety, especially beneath, not glandular. Fruit bent down on stout stalk, round, 1¼–1½" wide, finely hairy, not glandular, covered with slender spines less than ½" long. Seeds light brown when ripe.

Flowering Season: May–October.

Habitat/Range: Open, disturbed areas, 700–6,500', throughout the Sonoran Desert and much of southern North America.

Comments: Desert Thorn-Apple (*D. discolor*), an annual, has a corolla with a purplish tube and 10 teeth on the rim. Seeds are black. It grows below 2,200'. Species of *Datura* are toxic and should not be ingested in any form, for there are periodic reports in the American Southwest of individuals dying from eating parts of the plant or drinking teas made from it. Indigenous people through generations of testing, and probably tragedy, learned to use the plant medicinally to cure many ailments. Hernán Cortés discovered Aztecs using it medicinally, then called *toloatzin*, which became *toloache*.

DESERT TOBACCO
Nicotiana obtusifolia var. *obtusifolia*
Nightshade Family (Solanaceae)

Description: Glandular-hairy, strongly odorous plants 8–30" tall. Corolla white or greenish white, tubular, ½–1" long, the abruptly flared end ¼–⅜" wide, with 5 round lobes. Calyx lobes 5, very narrowly triangular, ⅜–½" long, about as long as the fruit capsule. Leaves ovate to narrowly ovate, the bases surrounding the stem as if clasping it.

Flowering Season: Most vigorously March–April and August–October, but flowering throughout the year.

Habitat/Range: Rocky areas, mostly below 6,000', most of the American Southwest.

Comments: The genus is named for J. Nicot, who is reputed to have introduced tobacco to Europe. Desert Tobacco has 2 varieties; the variety *palmeri* has flowers ⅜–½" across and sepals longer than the fruit capsule. This and similar native species, called *punche* by early Spanish, were smoked by indigenous people and early settlers.

Desert Tobacco

Sharp-Leaf Ground Cherry

SHARP-LEAF GROUND CHERRY
Physalis acutifolia
Nightshade Family (Solanaceae)

Description: Flat, white flowers with yellow-green centers face downward, hanging from slender stalks on leafy plants. Corolla ¾–1" in diameter, with 5 blunt lobes, and with 5 hairy pads in the center alternating with the stamens. Stamens 5, erect in the center of the flower, the yellow or faintly bluish pollen sacs ⅛" long. Calyx enlarging as the berry within matures, ultimately becoming translucent and lantern-like, almost round, with 10 fine ribs. Leaves lanceolate, 1½–5" long, the margins irregularly toothed. Stems 8–36" tall.

Flowering Season: June–September.

Habitat/Range: Roadsides, stream margins, and agricultural areas, 100–4,000', southern California to western Texas and northern Mexico.

Comments: This is a close relative of the Mexican vegetable "tomatillo."

Turkey Tangle, Common Frog-Fruit, Hierba de la Virgen Maria

TURKEY TANGLE, COMMON FROG-FRUIT, HIERBA DE LA VIRGEN MARIA
Phyla nodiflora
Vervain Family (Verbenaceae)

Description: Matted plants with toothed leaves and dense, buttonlike heads of whitish flowers around a center of maroon buds. Heads ¼–½" across, at tip of erect stalk ½–3½" long. Corolla bilateral, with 2 upper lobes and 3 lower lobes. Leaves green, ovate or wedge-shaped, widest above middle, toothed from tip to middle or slightly below. Stems lying on ground, 2–4' long.

Flowering Season: June–September.

Habitat/Range: Low clay ground, 0–4,000', much of southern North America.

Comments: Often found in lawns, this is sometimes called lippia, its old genus name. Northern Frog-Fruit *(P. lanceolata)* has leaves broader below middle. Wedgeleaf Frog-Fruit *(P. cuneifolia)* is grayish-hairy, the leaves with teeth well above middle. All are in the Sonoran Desert in heavy soil.

COULTER'S WRINKLE-FRUIT
Tetraclea coulteri
Vervain Family (Verbenaceae)

Description: Grayish green plants with toothed leaves and slightly bilateral, pale cream flowers with long, protruding stamens and style. Corolla with a narrow tube about twice the length of the calyx, the flat, flared end of the corolla ½" wide, with 5 round lobes. Stamens 4. Leaves ovate to lanceolate, ½–1½" long, sharply pointed, with 2–4 irregular teeth on each edge, or the lower leaves without teeth. Fruit divided into 4 round lobes about ⅛" in diameter, the surface wrinkled and pitted.

Flowering Season: April–August.

Habitat/Range: Sandy flats and gravelly slopes, 2,000–4,500', southern Arizona to western Texas and northern Mexico.

Comments: Flowers open in the night and close quickly as the day warms.

Coulter's Wrinkle-Fruit

Pink and Purple Flowers

Graham's Nipple Cactus, Cabeza de Viejo

This section includes flowers ranging from pink to purple and plants with conspicuous purple fruits. Some bluish-flowered plants may be in this section, and plants with very pale pink or purple flowers may also have white or nearly white forms, so be sure to also check in the white and blue flower sections for the plant you are trying to identify.

Arizona Foldwing

ARIZONA FOLDWING
Dicliptera resupinata
Acanthus Family (Acanthaceae)

Description: Branched, leafy plants with rose-pink flowers protruding from between pairs of heart-shaped bracts. Bracts ¼–½" long, flat, closely pressed together. Flowers ½–¾" long, the petals joined as short tube that flares to upper and lower lips, the lower lip sometimes notched at tip, upper lip with a white area spotted with rose. Leaves lanceolate or ovate in outline, ¾–3½" long. Stems 1–2' long.

Flowering Season: April–October.

Habitat/Range: Rocky slopes and washes, among desert shrubs, and in grassland, 3,000–6,000', southeastern Arizona south into Mexico.

Comments: The pairs of bracts commonly are arranged in sets of 3 in open clusters at the ends of stems.

VIOLET WILD PETUNIA
Ruellia nudiflora
Acanthus Family (Acanthaceae)

Description: Purple, bilateral flowers tip upward from axils of opposite leaves and bracts. Corolla 1½–2½" long, with a long, gradually widening tube that abruptly flares at end to form a 2-lobed upper lip and a 3-lobed lower lip. Calyx ½–¾" long, with a short, tubular base and 5 long, narrow lobes. Stamens 4. Leaves ovate or oblong, ¾–5" long. Stems erect, more or less 4-sided, 2–12" tall.

Flowering Season: May–October.

Habitat/Range: Among rocks or shrubs, usually where moist, 2,500–4,000', southern Arizona, Texas, and Louisiana, to Mexico.

Comments: The common name describes the flower, but technical features indicate true relationships; it is not at all a petunia (Solanaceae), but is more closely related to Desert Honeysuckle *(Anisacanthus)* and Chuparosa *(Justicia)*.

Violet Wild Petunia

Western Sea-Purslane

WESTERN SEA-PURSLANE
Sesuvium verrucosum
Fig-Marigold Family (Aizoaceae)

Description: Flowers resemble bright reddish pink, 5-pointed stars borne at leafy tips of smooth, succulent plants. Sepals red-pink on inside, greenish on back, pointed, ¼–⅜" long. There are no true petals. Stamens many. Leaves opposite, linear or spatulate, ¼–1½" long. Stems many, branched, up to ½–3' long, reclining on ground, forming thick, matlike clumps up to 6' across.

Flowering Season: March–November.

Habitat/Range: Moist, heavy, often saline soil, 0–1,500' on Sonoran Desert, to 4,000' elsewhere, much of the American Southwest and southern Great Plains, tropical America.

Comments: This peculiar family is primarily subtropical, especially well developed in Africa. Ornamental iceplants (species of *Mesembryanthemum* and relatives) are in this family.

Narrowleaf Climbing Milkweed

NARROWLEAF CLIMBING MILKWEED
Funastrum cynanchoides var. *hartwegii*
Milkweed Family (Asclepiadaceae)

Description: Dense vines that smell like hot rubber and have round clusters about 1½" across with up to 20 pale purplish or whitish flowers. Flowers with 5 spreading, ovate petals ¼" long, usually blushed with pale violet. Center of flower with 5 white, inflated sacs ⅛" long. Leaves linear or very narrowly lanceolate, 1–3" long. Stems many, 3–6' long, bleeding with white sap when broken.

Flowering Season: May–September.

Habitat/Range: Gravelly or clay areas, often where disturbed, sometimes a weed in landscaped areas, 100–5,500', southeastern California to southern Utah, western Texas and northern Mexico.

Comments: Broadleaf Climbing Milkweed *(F. cynanchoides* var. *cynanchoides)*, from about the same area, has triangular or heart-shaped leaves up to 1½" wide.

DESERT HOLLY
Acourtia nana
Sunflower Family (Asteraceae)

Description: Colonial plants 1–8" tall with hollylike leaves, sometimes occurring in extensive patches. A single narrow head ¾–1" high at tip of stem, with 15–25 lavender-pink, tubular, 2-lipped flowers. Bracts around head stiff, lanceolate, tinged with maroon. Leaves stiff and leathery, oval or nearly round, coarsely spiny-toothed, ¾–2" long. Seedlike fruit brown, ribbed, topped by silky white or pale tan hairs about ½" long.

Flowering Season: March–June, often again in October.

Habitat/Range: Rocky or clay soils, often under bushes, below 6,000', southeastern Arizona to Texas and northern Mexico.

Comments: Plants are frequent in the eastern Sonoran Desert but are not commonly seen in flower. Flowers have a delicate odor of jasmine or violets. The species is often placed in the genus *Perezia*.

Desert Holly

BROWNFOOT
Acourtia wrightii
Sunflower Family (Asteraceae)

Description: Erect, leafy plants 2–4' tall with broad clusters of narrow heads with 8–11 honey-scented, pale pink flowers. Heads narrow, ½" high, the bracts bluntly pointed, without stalked glands. Corolla 2-lipped, the lower lip straplike and 3-toothed at tip, upper lip deeply divided into 2 lobes. Anthers joined in a tube beneath the 2-lobed style. Leaves leathery, narrowly oval or oblong, ¾–3" long, pointed at tip and toothed on edges.

Flowering Season: January–June.

Habitat/Range: Among trees and shrubs in rocky soil, below 6,000', most of Arizona to western Texas, south into northern Mexico.

Comments: The common name refers to the dense brown hairs at soil level where the stem joins the root. The root was used as a styptic by Native Americans. Leaves were used as a poultice.

Brownfoot

New Mexico Thistle

NEW MEXICO THISTLE
Cirsium neomexicanum
Sunflower Family (Asteracee)

Description: Spiny, slender plants 3–7' tall, covered with thin, white wool, the long, wandlike branches ending in round, lavender or creamy-white flower heads 2½–3" across. Heads with only disk flowers. Bracts around head spine-tipped, the middle and lower ones sharply bent downward, upper bracts erect and often twisted, all covered with cobwebby hairs. Leaves pinnately lobed, spiny, those at base up to 16" long, those on stem shorter, with their edges continuing down the stem from point of attachment. Seedlike fruit oval, more or less flattened, dark brown, with fine, white bristles (thistledown) 1" long at top.

Flowering Season: Mostly March–April; at higher elevations beyond the Sonoran Desert flowering into September.

Habitat/Range: Gravelly places, 2,500–6,000', southeastern California to Utah, Colorado, and New Mexico.

Comments: In western populations creamy-white flowers are more common.

Hoary Tansey-Aster

HOARY TANSEY-ASTER
Machaeranthera canescens
Sunflower Family (Asteraceae)

Description: Plants 2–4' tall, branched in upper parts and often bushy, gray-hairy, with flowers heads of narrow red-purple rays surrounding a yellow disk. Rays ½–¾" long. Bracts around head overlapping in 3–10 series, lanceolate, tapered to a fine point that curves outward. Seedlike fruit ⅛" long, brownish, club-shaped, slightly flattened, with 5–7 veins on each face, topped by a tuft of fine, tan hairs ¼" long. Leaves linear or broader, wider in upper half, 1–4" long, sometimes with small teeth.

Flowering Season: June–November.

Habitat/Range: Open areas, 150–7,000', much of western United States.

Comments: Hoary Tansey-Aster is a weedy plant often found in vacant lots, river bottoms, and along roadsides, blooming whenever there is sufficient soil moisture.

TAHOKA DAISY, TANSEY-ASTER
Machaeranthera tanacetifolia
Sunflower Family (Asteraceae)

Description: Flower heads with many narrow, red- to blue-violet (rarely white) rays ½–¾" long around a ½–1" wide yellow disk. Bracts of head ⅓–½" high. Leaves elaborately pinnately divided, ovate in outline, up to 3" long, glandular and lightly hairy, each segment tipped by a tiny spine. Seedlike fruits ⅛" long, covered by hairs lying against surface, topped with pale tan bristles ¼" long. Plants well-branched, 4–20" tall.

Flowering Season: June–October.

Habitat/Range: Dry, sandy, often disturbed areas, 1,000–6,000', widespread in western North America.

Comments: This species is sometimes cultivated as an ornamental. The similar Small-flower Tansey-Aster *(M. parviflora)* has paler rays; smaller, less divided leaves; and bracts around head only ¼" high.

Tahoka Daisy, Tansey-Aster

Spanish Needles

SPANISH NEEDLES
Palafoxia arida var. *arida*
Sunflower Family (Asteraceae)

Description: Branched plants 6–30" tall, glandular in upper parts, with slender, rayless heads of 10–20 dull pink flowers. Bracts around head ½–¾" long, aligned side by side, narrowly lanceolate. Seedlike fruit ½" long, slender, 4-sided, black. Fruits of peripheral flowers with no scales or 3–8 stiff, pale scales of varying lengths; fruits of central flowers with 4 short scales exterior to 4 longer scales ¼–⅜" long. Leaves linear to narrowly lanceolate, ¾–5" long.

Flowering Season: January–September.

Habitat/Range: Sandy flats, slopes and washes, -100–2,500', southeastern California to southwestern Utah, western Arizona and northwestern Mexico.

Comments: In sand of southeastern California and southwestern Arizona is *P. arida* var. *gigantea,* with plants 3–7' tall, the bracts around the head ¾–1" long.

Odora, Yerba del Venado, Slender Poreleaf

ODORA, YERBA DEL VENADO, SLENDER PORELEAF
Porophyllum gracile
Sunflower Family (Asteraceae)

Description: Smooth, bluish green, ill-scented plants 10–30" tall, with many stems, each ending in small, narrow, pale purplish or whitish, rayless head ½" high. Heads with 20–30 disk flowers and only 5 bracts, each bract dotted with a few glands. Leaves linear, ½–2" long, dotted with a few glands. Seedlike fruit very slender, ⅜" long, topped by numerous dull white or tan bristles ¼" long.

Flowering Season: March–October.

Habitat/Range: Dry, rocky slopes, flats, and canyons, common along roadsides, below 4,000', southern California to southern Nevada, southern Arizona and northwestern Mexico.

Comments: This plant has a peculiarly unpleasant odor, rather like pineapple mixed with skunk. Even so, it is apparently relished by cattle and deer, as the name Yerba del Venado suggests ("herb of the deer").

WHITE-PLUME WIRE-LETTUCE
Stephanomeria exigua
Sunflower Family (Asteraccae)

Description: Usually conical, openly branched plants with a prominent central axis, grayish green, wiry, 8–24" tall, with small heads of a few pink, strap-shaped flowers. Strap part of flower ¼–⅜" long, with 5 tiny teeth at end. Bracts around head ¼" long, translucent on margins, the outer bracts much shorter. Seedlike fruit club-shaped, brownish, 5-angled, ⅛–¼" long, topped by feathery, white bristles. Leaves in basal rosette usually withered by flowering time, those on stem very small and linear or lacking. Sap milky.

Flowering Season: April–September.

Habitat/Range: Sandy soil, below 8,000', much of the American Southwest.

Comments: The widespread Brown-Plume Wire-Lettuce *(S. pauciflora)* is broad and bushy, lacking a central axis. It has pale tan plumes on top of fruit.

White-Plume Wire-Lettuce

Orcutt's Woody Aster

ORCUTT'S WOODY ASTER
Xylorhiza orcuttii
Sunflower Family (Asteraceae)

Description: Shrubs up to 5' tall, about as wide, with whitish stems and heads of golden disk flowers surrounded by narrow, vivid lavender or blue-lavender rays. Rays 25–40, 1–1¼" long; disk ½–¾" wide, with 55–140 disk flowers. Slender, seedlike fruits ⅛" long, with many uneven tan bristles at top. Stalks beneath heads 0–4½" long, without hairs or glands. Leaves stiff and leathery, veiny, usually with many spiny teeth along margin, oblong to lanceolate, ¾–2½" long.

Flowering Season: March–April.

Habitat/Range: Clay slopes and gullies, 50–1,000', western edge of Sonoran Desert in southern California.

Comments: Heads more than 1½" in diameter and woodiness of the plants distinguish species of *Xylorhiza* from those in the related genus *Machaeranthera*. All were once included in the very diverse genus *Aster*, but critical studies have shown that smaller, separate genera better reflect relationships. The rare Mecca Aster, *X. cognata*, from extreme northwestern Sonoran Desert region has glandular hairs on stems and flower stalks 0–4½" long.

Mojave Aster

MOJAVE ASTER
Xylorhiza tortifolia
Sunflower Family (Asteraceae)

Description: Coarse, erect plants with spiny-toothed leaves and long-stalked heads with yellow centers surrounded by 25–60 narrow, ½–1½" long, pale- to deep-lavender rays. Bracts around head narrowly lanceolate, softly hairy and glandular, ¼–1" long. Stalks beneath heads 3–9" long. Seedlike fruits slender, ⅛–¼" long, with a tuft of tan bristles at top. Leaves linear to elliptical, softly hairy and glandular, 1–4" long. Stems 8–24" tall, branched mostly in lower half.

Flowering Season: March–May.

Habitat/Range: Rocky slopes, 800–6,500', on edges of Sonoran Desert in southern California, southern Nevada, southwestern Utah, and western Arizona.

Comments: The spectacular, daisylike flower heads seem to fluoresce in the bright desert light. The genus name *Xylorhiza* refers to the stout, woody root.

DESERT WILLOW, MIMBRE
Chilopsis linearis ssp. *arcuata*
Catalpa Family (Bignoniaceae)

Description: Trees or shrubs up to 30' tall, with narrow leaves and pale pink or white bilateral flowers, often with some maroon. Flowers 1–1½" long, almost as wide, with 2-lobed upper lip and 3-lobed lower lip usually marked in center with maroon and yellow. Leaves narrow, curved much like a scythe, 4–12" long, the edges smooth. Pods hanging, slender, 4–12" long, ¼" wide, filled with white-winged seeds.

Flowering Season: April–August.

Habitat/Range: Mostly along washes, below 4,500', southeastern California to Utah, western Texas and northwestern Mexico.

Comments: Leaves are straight in the more eastern subspecies *linearis.* The species, a popular ornamental, may be easily grown from seed, but first trim the wings so the seedling can push through the soil easily.

Desert Willow, Mimbre

WOOLY CRINKLEMAT, OREJA DEL PERRO
Tiquilia canescens var. *canescens*
Borage Family (Boraginaceae)

Description: Plants usually tufted or matted, up to 4" high, 14" across, with gray-hairy foliage and small pink or lavender, rarely white, funnel-shaped flowers. Corolla ¼" long, ¼–⅜" wide, with 5 round lobes. Leaves ovate to lanceolate, ⅜–⅝" long. Fruit spherical, about ⅛" in diameter, smooth or lightly hairy, with 4 equally spaced lines running from tip to base, at maturity breaking along the lines into 4 segments.

Flowering Season: March–September.

Habitat/Range: Open, rocky areas, often on limestone, 1,500–4800', throughout the American Southwest, also northern Mexico.

Comments: The Spanish name means "dog's ear," perhaps in reference to the shape of the hairy leaves. The variety *pulchella,* from southeastern California and western Arizona, has ⅜–½" long flowers.

Wooly Crinklemat, Oreja del Perro

Fanleaf Crinklemat

FANLEAF CRINKLEMAT
Tiquilia plicata
Borage Family (Boraginaceae)

Description: Spreading plants with forked, somewhat glandular, often bronze stems 4–16" long, small pink or lavender flowers, and tiny, pleated leaves. Flowers bell-shaped, 5-lobed, ¼" long. Leaves broadly ovate to nearly round, ³⁄₁₆–½" long, hairy, the 4–7 pairs of veins deeply impressed in upper surface, producing a pleated ("plicate") appearance. Fruit dividing into 4 tiny, shiny, seedlike segments, often 1 or more aborting.

Flowering Season: March–October.

Habitat/Range: Sandy flats, -150–3,000', southeastern California to western Arizona and northwestern Mexico.

Comments: Palmer's Crinklemat *(T. palmeri),* with only 2–3 shallowly impressed veins on the leaves and non-glandular forked stems, occurs below 3,000' on the western edge of the Sonoran Desert and near the Colorado River.

Pink-Flower Hedgehog Cactus

PINK-FLOWER HEDGEHOG CACTUS
Echinocereus fendleri var. *fasciculatus*
Cactus Family (Cactaceae)

Description: Clumps of 5–20 cylindrical stems 5–16" tall, with pale spines and vibrant red-violet flowers. Flower with many petal-like segments 1¼–1½" long, the outer segments much shorter, thicker, reddish or greenish, resembling sepals. Stems 2–3" in diameter, with 8–18 ribs. Spines light brown, reddish brown, or pale gray with darker tips, 1 spine prominent and spreading from stem, 1 or 2 similar but shorter, and 11–13 spines that spread close to stem surface. Fruit narrowly egg-shaped with a flat top, spiny, at first greenish, finally reddish, about 1" long.

Flowering Season: April–May.

Habitat/Range: Sandy, gravelly or rocky areas on hillsides and in washes, 2,500–5,000', southern Arizona, western New Mexico, and northwestern Mexico.

Comments: Pink-Flower Hedgehog Cactus *(E. fendleri)* is common in the American Southwest, its large, brilliant magenta flowers and long spines a clue to its identity. There are a number of varieties. The common variety *fendleri* has only 1 central spine that curves upward, and only usually 1–5 stems. It occurs mostly above 4,000' in northern Arizona and in New Mexico.

GRAHAM'S NIPPLE CACTUS, CABEZA DE VIEJO
Mammillaria grahamii var. *grahamii*
Cactus Family (Cactaceae)

Description: Stems solitary or few in a clump, to 6" tall and 2–3" in diameter, cylindrical or ovate. Spine clusters at tips of nipples, each with 1–2 dark, hooked spines ½–1" long and 18–28 straight, spreading, grayish, tan, or reddish spines ¼–½" long. Flower vivid lavender, pink, or reddish purple, the petal-like segments about 10, ½–1" long, sepal-like segments about as many, smaller. Stamen filaments yellow to red; style branches bright yellow-green. Fruit fleshy, bright red, ½–1" long.

Flowering Season: June–July.

Habitat/Range: Among brush and rocks, 1,000–5,000', southeastern California to southern Utah, across Arizona and New Mexico to western Texas and northwestern Mexico.

Comments: Plants bloom about a week after the onset of summer rains, often blooming again after more rains.

Graham's Nipple Cactus, Cabeza de Viejo

Beavertail Cactus

BEAVERTAIL CACTUS
Opuntia basilaris
Cactus Family (Cactaceae)

Description: Brilliant magenta-pink flowers on low, rounded clumps of ashy gray-green pads. Flowers with many lanceolate petal-like parts up to about 1½" long. Stamens many, the filaments magenta; style white or pink. Pads more or less oval, 2–8" long, usually without large needlelike spines, but with many clusters of hundreds of tiny, reddish brown, barbed bristles. Plants to 20" tall, each branch a chain of 2–5 pads.

Flowering Season: March–June.

Habitat/Range: On dry benches and outwash fans, 400–7,200', southeastern California to southwestern Utah, western Arizona and northwestern Mexico.

Comments: A handsome plant, easy to cultivate in dry, warm areas by placing detached pads in dry soil. Seemingly innocuous, the pad's numerous, tiny spines ("glochids") stick painfully in the skin.

Cactus-Apple, Engelmann's Prickly Pear, Nopal, Abrojo

CACTUS-APPLE, ENGELMANN'S PRICKLY PEAR, NOPAL, ABROJO
Opuntia engelmannii
Cactus Family (Cactaceae)

Description: Bluish green, hemispherical mounds up to 5' tall, 5–15' wide, formed from flattened pads, which in summer bear reddish purple, ovate fruits along upper edges. Pads inversely ovate, mostly 10–16" long, with scattered clusters of 1–4 down-pointing, white or pale gray spines, 1–2" long. Flowers 3" across, with many lanceolate, petal-like parts, blooming in morning, at first yellow but fading to apricot-orange by afternoon.

Flowering Season: April–June.

Habitat/Range: Open, arid ground, 1,000–6,500', southern California to southwestern Utah, east across Arizona and New Mexico to Texas.

Comments: The flattened pads are stems. Individual flowers last only 1 day. Species with edible fruits, as this, are known as *tuna* in Spanish. The genus *Opuntia* was once strictly American, as is true for all but one species of cactus. Since the discovery of the New World, however, species with edible frutis have been introduced in warm, arid regions throughout the world, and are sold in street markets in many countries. Other species have become serious, undesirable rangeland weeds, as in Australia.

Chainfruit Cholla, Brincadora

CHAINFRUIT CHOLLA, BRINCADORA
Opuntia fulgida
Cactus Family (Cactaceae)

Description: Shrub 1–12' tall with hanging, branching chains of greenish fruit, some bearing rose-pink flowers. Flower ¾–1" across, with 5–8 larger, petal-like parts and more smaller, sepal-like parts. Stamens many. Fruits ovate, 1–1¼" long, without spines. Stems 1¼–2" thick, with many elongate-conical swellings, each with 6–12 golden spines ¾–1¼" long spreading in all directions.

Flowering Season: June–August.

Habitat/Range: Open flats, 1,000–4,500', southern Arizona and western Mexico.

Comments: Stems joints are easily detached and, as if they had eyes, seem to jump unerringly from the plant to the skin of the unwary passerby. One fruit is added to the chain's length each year. A fruit may or may not have seed; either way, when one falls to the ground it may root and produce a plant.

Walkingstick Cholla, Cane Cholla

WALKINGSTICK CHOLLA, CANE CHOLLA
Opuntia spinosior
Cactus Family (Cactaceae)

Description: Shrubs 1–10' tall, with cylindrical stems ¾–1¼" thick. Flowers bright redpurple, with many petal-like, lanceolate segments ¾–1" long. Spines 10–20 per cluster, spreading in all directions, ¼–½" long, gray toward base, pinkish toward tip, in the first year covered by a tan sheath that falls away. Spines originate from ¼–½" long swellings. Fruit yellow, ovate, 1–1½" long, very bumpy, often persisting until next flowering season.

Flowering Season: May–June.

Habitat/Range: Dry, open ground, 1,000–5,000', southern Arizona, western New Mexico, northwestern Mexico.

Comments: Tree Cholla (*O. imbricata*), barely entering eastern Sonoran Desert, has stem swellings ¾–1½" long, and spines ½–1¼" long. Opuntias with round stems are often placed in the genus *Cylindropuntia*.

IVY MORNING GLORY
Ipomoea nil
Morning Glory Family (Convolvulaceae)

Description: Twining vines with 3-lobed leaves and funnel-shaped purple or bluepurple flowers. Corolla ¾–1¼" long, the tube nearly white. Sepals ⅝–¾" long, spreadinghairy, tapered to long, narrow, straight, erect tips. Leaves 1–3" long. Stems to 10' long.

Flowering Season: July–September.

Habitat/Range: Cultivated field or waste places, below 4,500', throughout much of the American Southwest, native to tropical America.

Comments: Two other common morningglories are also weedy. Ivy-Leaf Morning Glory *(I. hederacea)* is very similar, but has long, slender sepal tips that curve and arch outward. Common Morning Glory *(I. purpurea)* has lanceolate sepal tips ⅜–⅝" long and corollas 2–2½" long. It is commonly cultivated and, especially in the garden, may have reddish or white flowers.

Ivy Morning Glory

Three-Leaved Morning Glory

THREE-LEAVED MORNING GLORY
Ipomoea ternifolia var. *leptoloma*
Morning Glory Family (Convolvulaceae)

Description: Slender, twining or trailing plants with showy pink or lavender-pink funnel-shaped flowers. Corolla 1–1½" long, as wide or wider, the tube pale cream or white. Leaves divided into 3–5 linear lobes less than ⅛" wide, ¾–3" long, the 2 lobes at base of leaf usually again divided into 3 linear lobes, the lower 2 lobes of the 3 shorter than upper lobe. Fruit an ovate capsule ¼" long, containing a few dark brown seeds. Stems up to 3' long.

Flowering Season: June–October.

Habitat/Range: Grassy areas, 3,000–4,500', southern Arizona and southwestern New Mexico, south deep into Mexico.

Comments: This attractive annual is worthy of cultivation. In years with ample summer rains, it forms spectacular displays on slopes and roadsides; in dry years not a plant will be found.

Arizona Milkvetch

ARIZONA MILKVETCH
Astragalus arizonicus
Bean Family (Fabaceae)

Description: Grayish green plants with spreading stems and upturned, maroon "pea" flowers in spires. Corolla ⅜" long, the banner with a large, white, maroon-veined central spot, the tip of the keel upturned and beaklike. Pod strongly oriented upwards, very slender, ½–1¼" long, more or less triangular in cross section, 2-chambered by a partition running lengthwise along middle. Leaves pinnately compound, ¾–4" long, with 5–17 narrow leaflets ½–¾" long. Stems 6–20" long.

Flowering Season: March–May.

Habitat/Range: Rocky ground, 2,500–5,000', southern Arizona and Sonora.

Comments: The hairs on the surface lie flat, attached by their sides near one end. When pushed with a needle, they can be seen under a lens to twist on their point of attachment.

SALTON MILKVETCH
Astragalus crotalariae
Bean Family (Fabaceae)

Description: Clumped plants with pinnately compound leaves, bright reddish purple "pea" flowers, and swollen tan pods. Flowers ¾–1" long, narrow, the upper petal with a white central blotch. Leaves 2–6" long, with 9–19 broad leaflets ¼–1¼" long, broader in upper half, notched at tip, covered with a few hairs pressed to surface. Pod stiffly papery when mature, with 1 chamber, ¾–1¼" long, ½" wide, on a stout, ⅒" long, stalklike base hidden inside calyx. Stems 6–24" long.

Flowering Season: January–April.

Habitat/Range: Open flats and outwash fans, -150–800', southeastern California to southwestern Arizona and Baja California.

Comments: The swollen pods, almost hairless foliage, and low elevation habitat serve to distinguish this species.

Salton Milkvetch

Fairy Duster, Mesquitilla

FAIRY DUSTER, MESQUITILLA
Calliandra eriophylla
Bean Family (Fabaceae)

Description: Intricately branched shrubs 1–4' tall, with spherical clusters 1–2" wide consisting of pale to deep pink, feathery flowers. Flower heads have hundreds of slender stamens, providing color and showiness. At bases of stamens is a reddish cup with 5 petals and 5 sepals. Fruit a flat pod, swollen by seeds, ¼" wide, 1–3" long, usually reddish, with thick margins. Leaves divided into 1–7 pairs of segments, each with 5–15 pairs of narrow leaflets ⅛–¼" long.

Flowering Season: February–May, and often again August–September after good rains.

Habitat/Range: Gravelly places below 5,000', southeastern California to western Texas, south to central Mexico.

Comments: Fairy Duster is used as an ornamental and is now commonly planted in xeriscaped median of city streets in the American Southwest. It also provides livestock and wildlife browse, and restores nitrogen to the soil through symbiotic actions of bacteria harbored in the root tissue.

Hairy Prairie-Clover

HAIRY PRAIRIE-CLOVER
Dalea mollis
Bean Family (Fabaceae)

Description: Small, softly hairy plants with pinnately compound leaves and reddish lavender to whitish "pea" flowers in short, dense spires. Corolla ³⁄₁₆" long, calyx slightly shorter. Wing petals wide near base, narrowed toward tip, immediately below which is a notch with a dark, dotlike gland. Pods ⅛" long, barely protruding from calyx. Leaves ¾–1½" long, with 9–13 leaflets ⅛–⅜" long, each broader near tip. Stems 2–12" long, reclining at base, the tips turned upward.

Flowering Season: January–April.

Habitat/Range: Sandy or gravelly open places, common along roadsides, below 3,000', southeastern California, western Arizona, and northwestern Mexico.

Comments: Soft Prairie-Clover *(D. mollissima),* from the same region, has ¼" long whitish flowers, not longer than calyx.

ARIZONA LUPINE
Lupinus arizonicus
Bean Family (Fabaceae)

Description: Plants with long, spreading hairs, palmately compound leaves, and spires of magenta "pea" flowers. Corolla ⅜" long, banner with a yellow and white, red-dotted, central spot that becomes deep red-maroon as flower ages. Pod ½–¾" long, ¼" wide, coarsely hairy. Leaflets 6–10, inversely lanceolate, ½–1½" long. Stems 1–several, 4–20" tall.

Flowering Season: January–May.

Habitat/Range: Sandy areas, below 3,500', southeastern California to southern Nevada, western Arizona and northwestern Mexico.

Comments: Annual lupines may line roadsides with bands of color after winters with good rain. Near Gilia Bend along Interstate Highway 8, the westward traveler will notice the change from the blue of Arroyo Lupine *(L. sparsiflorus)* to the magenta of Arizona Lupine.

Arizona Lupine

BAJADA LUPINE
Lupinus concinnus
Bean Family (Fabaceae)

Description: Small, pinkish or purplish, rarely white, "pea" flowers ¼" long in clusters ½–3" long on hairy plants with palmately compound leaves. Banner with a pale cream or yellow center; it and the other petals colored most intensely near the edges. Keel without hairs on margin. Leaflets 5–9, inversely lanceolate, ½–1¼" long, with erect hairs. Pod ½" long, hairy. Stems branched or not, 4–12" tall.

Flowering Season: March–May.

Habitat/Range: Sandy places, below 5,000', throughout the American Southwest, also in northwestern Mexico.

Comments: *Bajadas* are outwash fans, spreading from mountainsides downward; they are often sandy. A less common form of the Bajada Lupine has flowers nearly ½" long. Some plants also may have a few hairs on keel margins.

Bajada Lupine

VELVET-POD MIMOSA, GATUÑO
Mimosa dysocarpa
Bean Family (Fabaceae)

Description: Rose to whitish, cylindrical tufts of tiny flowers at ends of branches on thorny shrubs 2–6' tall. Flower clusters 1½–4" long, about 1½" wide, consisting of many flowers, each with 10 stamens ½" long, the stamens providing the pom-pom appearance of flower cluster. Pod velvety, 1–2" long, often curved, usually constricted between seeds. Leaves twice compound, with 5–12 pairs of segments, each with 6–16 pairs of leaflets ⅛–¼" long.

Flowering Season: May–September.

Habitat/Range: Dry, open areas, 3,300–6,500', southern Arizona to western Texas and northern Mexico.

Comments: So beautiful to behold along the roadsides, so deceptive. To reach to pick a flower-laden branch quickly becomes a painful task of extracting from the hand sharp, curved thorns.

Velvet-Pod Mimosa, Gatuño

Slim-Jim Bean

SLIM-JIM BEAN
Phaseolus filiformis
Bean Family (Fabaceae)

Description: Leaves with 3 leaflets and bilateral, twisted, pink to lavender "pea" flowers on twining, 1–4' long stems. Flowers ⅜–½" long, banner scooped forward like a spoon, wings unequal and bent downward, keel twisted in a brief spiral. Pods curved, 3/16" wide, ½–2" long, slightly wider at tip, finely hairy. Leaflets ovate to diamond-shaped but with rounded corners, ½–1" wide, to ¾–1¼" long, dark green, sparsely stiff-hairy with very short hairs.

Flowering Season: Primarily July–September, but flowering throughout the year.

Habitat/Range: Rocky slopes and canyons, 1,000–4,000', southern Arizona to western Texas and northern Mexico.

Comments: Kin to the garden bean, *P. vulgaris,* several American Southwest species of *Phaseolus* were important food crops to indigenous people.

EMORY'S SMOKEBUSH
Psorothamnus emoryi
Bean Family (Fabaceae)

Description: Round, grayish white, strongly scented, densely branched, 1–7' tall shrubs, with small, red-violet "pea" flowers in compact heads. Corolla ¼" long, wings longest, marked with white along lower edge. Pod ⅛" long, included in calyx, bearing small, dark glands. Leaves ½–3" long, pinnately divided into 5–9 narrow leaflets, terminal leaflet longest. Stems with a feltlike covering and also dotted with tiny orange glands.

Flowering Season: March–May.

Habitat/Range: Dry, open places, usually below 1,000', southeastern California, western Arizona, and northwestern Mexico.

Comments: The lucky observer may find the brown flowers of the rare Stemsucker *(Pilostyles thurberi),* a parasitic plant otherwise completely internal, breaking through the surface of the stems of Emory's Smokebush.

Emory's Smokebush

Filaree, Redstem Stork's-Bill, Alfilerillo

FILAREE,
REDSTEM STORK'S-BILL,
ALFILERILLO
Erodium cicutarium
Geranium Family (Geraniaceae)

Description: Plants with small, rose-lavender flowers and finely divided leaves. Petals 5, each ¼" long, with purplish streaks or spots at base. Sepals bristly at tips. Styles rapidly elongating after fertilization, becoming a beak ¾–2" long, central in the 5-lobed fruit. Leaves ovate in outline, highly divided into segments about ⅒" wide. Stems 1–20" long, in tufts or sprawling.

Flowering Season: February–April, and to July at higher elevations and to the north.

Habitat/Range: Disturbed places, 0–7,000', much of United States.

Comments: This immigrant from Europe is everywhere there is spring moisture, sometimes so dense that it crowds native plants. The 5 ovary segments are attached to elastic styles; the tip is pointed. These segments cling to animals fur and can be distributed widely. The individual styles curl and uncurl in response to changes in humidity (breathe on one as if cleaning glasses and watch it slowly curl). The slow movement of the style, more open in the humidity of morning, more tightly curled on a dry afternoon, helps to nudge the see across the ground, where if may lodge in a safe site for germination.

Desert Stork's-Bill, Heron's Bill

DESERT STORK'S-BILL, HERON'S BILL
Erodium texanum
Geranium Family (Geraniaceae)

Description: Broadly funnel-shaped, red-purple flowers are held on slender stalks barely above triangular, pinnately lobed and scalloped leaves. Petals 5, ⅜–½" long. Fruit divides into 5 sharp, pointed, seedlike segments ¼" long, the style on each developing as a long, elastic, needlelike extension 1–2½" long, which coils when dried. Leaf blades ½–1½" long, about as long as wide, as long as stalk. Stems often reddish, 4–20" long, spreading or lying on ground.

Flowering Season: February–April.

Habitat/Range: Dry, open places, 1,000–4,500', southern California to western Texas and northern Mexico.

Comments: Desert Stork's-Bill is dependent on winter rains for good germination and growth. It is less common in the western part of the Sonoran Desert than in the east.

DAINTY DESERT HIDESEED
Eucrypta micrantha
Waterleaf Family (Hydrophyllaceae)

Description: Weak-stemmed, glandular plants with pinnately lobed leaves and small, usually purplish, bowl-shaped flowers. Corolla ⅛" long, with 5 blue-purple, lavender, or white lobes, the broad tube greenish yellow within. Leaves ¾–2" long, less than ¾" wide, 7–9 lobed, the stalk widened at base and clasping stem. Fruit a spherical capsule hidden within calyx. Seeds curved, black or dark brown.

Flowering Season: February–May.

Habitat/Range: Rocky hillsides, canyon sides, crevices, often among brush, 200–8,000', much of American Southwest.

Comments: Dainty Desert Hideseed is common after winters with sufficient rain but is inconspicuous.

Dainty Desert Hideseed

Purplemat, Morada

PURPLEMAT, MORADA
Nama demissum
Waterleaf Family (Hydrophyllaceae)

Description: Prostrate, forked stems bear most leaves and red-purple, bell-shaped flowers near tips. Corolla 5-lobed, ⅜–½" long. Leaves in clusters, narrowly spatulate, ½–1¼" long. Stems 1–6" long, hairy.

Flowering Season: February–May.

Habitat/Range: Dry, sandy or gravelly ground, common in washes, below 5,000', southeastern California to southwestern Utah, southern Arizona, and northwestern Mexico.

Comments: This common species may color large patches of gully floors and sandy flats with brilliant red-purple. When in full bloom a single plant may be 1' across and so densely flowered that it obscures the ground. As with most desert annuals, growth is very rapid and seeds quickly mature as the soil dries.

Sandbells, Morada

SANDBELLS, MORADA
Nama hispidum
Waterleaf Family (Hydrophyllaceae)

Description: Bell-like flowers with 5-lobed, pink-lavender corollas on plants with linear leaves. Corolla ⅜–½" long. Leaves well-distributed along stem rather than clustered at ends of branches, ½–2½" long, stiffly hairy, sometimes glandular, the edges rolled under. Stems branched, 4–20" long, more or less spreading, bearing hairs that are angled upward.

Flowering Season: February–June, sometimes also in October.

Habitat/Range: Sand or gravel, below 5,000', much of the American Southwest.

Comments: This annual is worthy of cultivation in sandy gardens, responding well to supplementary water, the plants blooming profusely for long periods. Occasionally plants are all white-flowered.

NOTCH-LEAF SCORPION-WEED

Phacelia crenulata var. *ambigua*

Waterleaf Family (Hydrophyllaceae)

Description: Glandular-hairy plants with divided and scalloped leaves and small, purple or blue-purple flowers in branched, coiled clusters. Corolla bell-shaped, 5-lobed, ¼–⅜" long. Stamens 5, ⅜–½" long, conspicuously protruding. Leaves at base with blades 4–16" long, as long as stalk, upper leaves much smaller. Stems 3–24" tall, unbranched or, more commonly, branched from base.

Flowering Season: February–June.

Habitat/Range: Gravelly washes and slopes, below 5,000', southeastern California to southern Nevada, southern Arizona and northwestern Mexico.

Comments: This very common scorpion-weed may form spectacular purple displays on hillsides and roadsides. A small-flowered variety, *minutiflora,* common in the same area, has ⅛" long, purplish blue flowers.

Notch-Leaf Scorpion Weed

Pinstalk Scorpionweed

PINSTALK SCORPIONWEED

Phacelia pedicellata

Waterleaf Family (Hydrophyllaceae)

Description: Glandular, shortly stiff-hairy plants with lavender to blue-violet flowers in coiled clusters. Each flower in cluster on a slender, densely long-hairy, non-glandular, pinlike stalk that becomes longer as fruit matures, to ¼". Corolla bell-shaped, ¼" long, with a tubular base and 5 round, spreading lobes. Leaves 1–5" long, the blade about equal in length to the stalk, blade ovate to round in outline, the lower leaves divided into 3–7 round lobes. Stems with a few branches, or none, 5–20" tall.

Flowering Season: March–May.

Habitat/Range: Sandy or gravelly washes or canyon sides, below 4,500', southeastern California to southern Nevada, western Arizona, and Baja California.

Comments: This is a bad-smelling, very glandular plant that stains hands when handled extensively.

Pima Ratany, Range Ratany, Purple Heather

PIMA RATANY, RANGE RATANY, PURPLE HEATHER
Krameria erecta
Ratany Family (Krameriaceae)

Description: Widely branched, twiggy plants 8–24" high, with inconspicuous leaves and dark purple, bilateral flowers. Sepals 5, petal-like, lanceolate, almost ½" long, cupped forward. Petals 5, small, 3 upper ones purple and joined together at their yellow-green bases; 2 lateral petals maroon, modified as glands. Leaves linear, ⅛–½" long, with hairs that lie against surface. Fruit egg-shaped, ⅜" long, covered with spines that have minute barbs in at least upper third, or spines are not barbed.

Flowering Season: April–October.

Habitat/Range: Open, dry areas, below 5,000', southeastern California to western Texas and northwestern Mexico.

Comments: *Krameria* is the only genus in this small family of 15 species, and the family is restricted to the warmer parts of the Americas. Plants are partially parasitic, through root connections, to plants around them. Small native bees collect saturated fats from the glandular petals to feed their larvae. White Ratany *(K. grayi)* is very similar to Pima Ratany, but has 3 small upper petals free from one another at the base, and has fruits with barbs only at very tips of spines.

Purple Pop-Ups

PURPLE POP-UPS
Pholisma arenarium
Lennoa Family (Lennoaceae)

Description: Above the ground these are columnar or egg-shaped plants 2–8' tall, ¾–3" wide. Corolla about ³⁄₁₆" across, broadly funnel-shaped, with a thin, white, frilly rim. Stamens mostly 6–8. Stems subterranean, whitish, fleshy, slender, 6–12" long, with tan, lanceolate, scalelike leaves ½–¾" long.

Flowering Season: April–July, sometimes also in October.

Habitat/Range: Sand, below 6,200', southern California, western Arizona, northwestern Mexico.

Comments: These uncommon plants are parasites on roots of shrubs, from which they receive nutrition. When the ground is warm, plants swell and elongate quickly, popping up through the ground, pushing minor obstacles aside to expose their flowers. Small bees visit and pollinate flowers, from which seed is produced. Otherwise, existence of *Pholisma* is entirely below ground. Little is known of its biology. In other species with a similar lifestyle, seeds do not germinate until near a root, somehow sensing its presence. Sand Food *(P. sonorae),* its concave head barely protruding above the sand, occurs near the Mexican border. It was eaten by indigenous people.

Blue Dicks, Wild-Hyacinth, Coveria

BLUE DICKS, WILD-HYACINTH, COVERIA
Dichelostemma capitatum
Lily Family (Liliaceae)

Description: Clusters of 2–15 pale lavender to blue-violet flowers nod at top of long, slender, leafless stalk 1–3' tall. Flowers with 6 petal-like segments ¼–½" long spreading from top of narrowly bell-shaped, ⅛–½" long tube. Opening to tube nearly closed by a crown of 3 lanceolate, protruding scales ¼" long. Leaves 2–3, at base of stalk, linear, 4–16" long.

Flowering Season: February–May.

Habitat/Range: Sandy flats and rocky slopes, below 5,000', most of Sonoran Desert in United States, widespread in western United States, southward into Sonora.

Comments: Bulbs are deeply buried, remaining dormant for long periods until stimulated by soaking rains. Then hillsides and flats may be colored by thousands of plants that sway on their long stalks in breezes. Native Americans once dug and ate the bulbs.

DESERT FIVE-SPOT
Eremalche rotundifolia
Mallow Family (Malvaceae)

Description: Lightly bristly plants with round leaf blades on long stalks and globe-shaped, lavender-pink flowers. Petals almost round, ½–1" long, each with a bright reddish spot at base. Stamens many. Leaf blades shallowly and irregularly scalloped on edges, notched at base, ½–2½" wide; leaf stalks ½–4" long. Stems usually reddish, often branched from base, 3–24" tall.

Flowering Season: March–May.

Habitat/Range: Dry, open, usually gravelly places, -150–4,000', southeastern California, southern Nevada, western Arizona.

Comments: The flowers on Desert Five-Spot are exquisite, almost spherical, the 5 brilliant spots within hidden and inconspicuous until one looks directly down into the center of the flower. A pollinating insect must feel it has entered a kaleidoscope.

Desert Five-Spot

PALEFACE, ROCK HIBISCUS
Hibiscus denudatus
Mallow Family (Malvaceae)

Description: Semi-shrubby, spindly plants 1–3' tall with bright lavender-pink or white bowl-shaped flowers. Petals 5, broadly fan-shaped, ¾–1¼" long, dark reddish streaked at base. Stamens many, joined by their filaments. Beneath the 5-lobed calyx there may be a ring of 4–7 small, linear bracts, this sometimes absent. Leaves nearly round to oblong, finely hairy with starlike hairs, the edges coarsely scalloped.

Flowering Season: January–October.

Habitat/Range: Rocky slopes and washes, below 5,000', from southeastern California to southern Nevada and across Arizona and New Mexico to western Texas, south in northern Mexico.

Comments: A desert hillside with many of these plants, their large pink flowers bobbing in the wind, is a delightful sight. Plants in the western Sonoran Desert may have white flowers.

Paleface, Rock Hibiscus

Pink Velvet Mallow

PINK VELVET MALLOW
Horsfordia alata
Mallow Family (Malvaceae)

Description: An open, shrubby plant with few branches, tawny-hairy young stems, velvety leaves, and pink, bowl-shaped flowers. Petals 5, broad, rounded, ½–¾" long. Stamens many, united into a tube in center of flower, the tips free. Fruits with 8–12 wedge-shaped segments, the upper part of the segment expanding into 2 rounded, thin wings. Leaves thick, heart-shaped, 1¼–2" long, densely covered with branched hairs, slightly moist or sticky to the touch. Stems 3–14' tall.

Flowering Season: March–October.

Habitat/Range: Sandy washes, 500–1,500', southwestern Arizona, southeastern California, and northwestern Mexico.

Comments: Pink Velvet Mallow is an ungainly plant with long stems, few branches, and few leaves. The genus, with only 4 species, is restricted to the American Southwest.

Desert Sand Verbena

DESERT SAND VERBENA
Abronia villosa
Four O'Clock Family (Nyctaginaceae)

Description: Plants sprawling, semi-succulent, glandular-hairy, moist and sticky to the touch, with pink-lavender flowers in round clusters 1¼–2½" across. Flowers trumpet-shaped, the flared end ruffled, ¼–⅝" across. Leaves opposite, triangular to round, ½–2" long. Fruits with 3–5 wings, the upper lobes of wings often higher than the central beak. Stems ½–6' long.

Flowering Season: February–May.

Habitat/Range: Sandy soil 0–1600', southeastern California, southwestern Arizona, and northwestern Mexico.

Comments: After ample winter rains Desert Sand Verbena may carpet sandy desert with vibrant pink. Narrow-Leaf Sand Verbena, *A. angustifolia,* from the eastern part of the Sonoran Desert and eastward, is more upright, has shorter hairs, and the beak on the fruit is usually higher than lobes on wings. Characteristic of the family Nyctaginaceae, Desert Sand Verbena has no true petals. A careful examination of a single flower will show that only the 1 series, not both sepals and petals, is present. The united sepals are brightly colored.

Trailing Four O'Clock, Trailing Windmills, Hierba de la Hormiga

TRAILING FOUR O'CLOCK, TRAILING WINDMILLS, HIERBA DE LA HORMIGA
Allionia incarnata var. *Villosa*
Four O'Clock Family (Nyctaginaceae)

Description: Trailing, hairy plants with opposite leaves and 3 bright rose-pink flowers clustered to resemble 1 radial flower. Each flower fan-shaped, ⅛–½" long, scalloped on outer edge, narrowed to a tiny tube near center of cluster. At base of each flower is a broad, ovate bract that envelops fruit. Leaves ovate, smooth or shallowly wavy, ¾–2½" long, those in a pair unequal in size. Fruit with shape of a narrow turtle shell, the sides curved under and with 0–5 broad teeth.

Flowering Season: April–October.

Habitat/Range: Open areas, 0–6,500', southeastern California across the American Southwest to southern Colorado and western Texas, south into Mexico; also South America.

Comments: There are two varieties on the Sonoran Desert, which often grow in the same area. The var. *villosa* has large flowered, the cluster ½-1" across, whereas the var. *incarnata* smaller flower clusters. Flowers in a single cluster mature synchronously, last one morning, then shrivel. Both varieties have large glands on the concave side of fruit that have a sticky secretion that does not dry, perhaps aiding in dispersal.

Scarlet Spiderling

SCARLET SPIDERLING
Boerhavia coccinea
Four O'Clock Family (Nyctaginaceae)

Description: Rank, sprawling, gummy-hairy plants with opposite leaves and tiny heads of vivid violet-red to rose-pink flowers. Individual flowers ⅛" across, with a scalloped rim, 5–15 in a cluster ⅜–½" across. Leaves broadly lanceolate to almost round, ¾–2½" long, unequal in the pair. Fruits club-shaped, ⅛" long, with 5 ribs, covered with gummy hairs. Stems repeatedly branched, 1–6' long.

Flowering Season: April–November.

Habitat/Range: Open places, especially roadsides and in agricultural areas, 0–7,000', from southeastern California across the southern tier of states, south throughout the tropics.

Comments: This common plant is often seen as an unsightly weed, yet the flowers, which open at dawn and close before noon, are beautiful when examined closely.

COLORADO FOUR O'CLOCK, SHOWY FOUR O'CLOCK
Mirabilis multiflora
Four O'Clock Family (Nyctaginaceae)

Description: Usually many-stemmed, leafy plants with bright pink-magenta, trumpet-shaped flowers 1½–2½" long that open in the evening. Several flowers are held within a bell-shaped, 5-toothed 1–1½" long cup. Stamens and style projecting. Fruit dark gray or black, egg-shaped, ¼–⅜" long. Leaves opposite, round to broadly ovate, fleshy, 1–5" long, glandular-hairy, at least when young. Stems to 2½' long.

Flowering Season: April–September.

Habitat/Range: Rocky or sandy places, 100–7,500', from southeastern California to Colorado, western Texas, and northern Mexico.

Comments: In the late afternoon and early morning, the flowers attract hummingbirds; in the evening and night, hawkmoths visit them. Plants are now used as ornamentals in xeriscapes. The large root has been used medicinally.

Colorado Four O'Clock, Showy Four O'Clock

Desert Broomrape, Flor de Tierra

DESERT BROOMRAPE, FLOR DE TIERRA
Orobanche cooperi ssp. *latiloba*
Broomrape Family (Orobanchaceae)

Description: Conelike, dark purple, fleshy plants, usually about 2" wide, 4–16" tall. Flowers bilateral. Calyx ½" long, about equally divided between the teeth (not more deeply so between lower pair of teeth). Corolla 1–1¼" long, the lobes ¼–⅜" long. Hairs on corolla glandular. Stems below ground pale tan, with sparse, scalelike, ¼–½" long leaves.

Flowering Season: January–May.

Habitat/Range: Sandy areas, below 1,600', southeastern California to southwestern Utah, western Arizona, and northwestern Mexico.

Comments: The subspecies *cooperi* has corolla lobes only ⅛–¼" long, the calyx less than ⅜" long. Both varieties are parasitic on roots of shrubs, mostly on those of the Burro-Weed *(Ambrosia dumosa)* and Burro-Brush *(Hymenoclea salsola)*. The name "Broomrape" derives from Broom *(Cytisus,* Fabaceae) and relatives, which are hosts of European species of *Orobanche,* and from Latin *rapere,* "to seize or to snatch." All *Orobanche* are parasites, obtaining their nutrients from the roots of their host. One, *O. ramosa,* Branched Broomrape, from the Mediterranean region, has recently been introduced in California and Texas and is considered a serious threat to broadleaf agricultural crops.

Scarlet-Fruit Passion Flower, Corona de Cristo

SCARLET-FRUIT PASSION FLOWER, CORONA DE CRISTO

Passiflora foetida
Passion-Flower Family (Passifloraceae)

Description: A softly hairy vine with many intertangled, tendril-bearing stems to 8' long or longer. Flowers 1–1½" across. Sepals and petals whitish, ¼" wide, the sepals greenish and hairy on back. Center of flower with a violet corona, its many segments threadlike, about ⅜" long, but innermost a mere fringe ¹⁄₂₅" long. Stamens 5, stigmas 3, all arched outward. Bracts beneath flower divided into narrow, hairy segments. Leaves 3-lobed, 1–1½" long, slightly wider. Fruit round, 1–1¼" in diameter, longer than wide, lightly hairy, red at maturity.

Flowering Season: August–September.

Habitat/Range: Rocky desert hillsides, cliffs, and arroyos, 3,000–5,000', southern Arizona and northwestern Mexico.

Comments: The spectacular flowers open before dawn and close early in the morning. Spanish Catholic missionaries in South America used the flowers to refer to Christ's passion: 3 stigmas symbolize nails of Crucifixion; 5 stamens, his wounds; corona, the crown of thorns; 5 sepals and 5 petals, the apostles, minus Peter and Judas; lobed leaves and tendrils the hands and whips of Christ's tormentors.

DEVIL'S CLAW, DOUBLE CLAW, UNICORN PLANT, AGUARO, CUERNERO
Proboscidea parviflora
Sesame Family (Pedaliaceae)

Description: Stout, moist, and sticky-hairy plants with large, white to reddish purple, bilateral flowers. Corolla 1" wide, 1–1½" long, often with purple blotches on 2 upper lobes, and a broad yellow band along bottom center of tube. Leaf blades round or broadly ovate, up to 10" long and wide, on stout stalks, the edges lobed and scalloped. Fruit with a tapered body about 2–4" long, 1" wide, tip an up-curved horn twice as long as body. Stems erect to sprawling, 1–3' long.

Flowering Season: April–October.

Habitat/Range: Open areas, common along roadsides, 1,000–5,000', from southern California to western Texas, south into Mexico.

Comments: The Tohono O'odham grow Devil's Claw for the black fiber from the fruit, used to weave striking patterns in baskets.

Devil's Claw, Double Claw, Unicorn Plant, Aguaro, Cuernero

RED THREE-AWN, PURPLE THREE-AWN
Aristida purpurea var. *longiseta*
Grass Family (Poaceae)

Description: Purplish, feathery tufts with many stems 6–24" tall bear numerous needle-like spikelets. Each spikelet has a slender, sharply pointed base ½–¾" long and at top 3 slender, flexible, bristlelike awns 1½–4" long. Leaves mostly at base of plant, narrowly linear, 2–6" long.

Flowering Season: April–October.

Habitat/Range: Dry, rocky ground below 5,000', much of western United States and northern Mexico.

Comments: Red Three-Awn often lines roadsides. When the wind blows, the flower heads sway, a dense patch of this grass shimmering pearly pink to iridescent purple in the sun. The sharp spikelets may injure mouths of grazing animals and stick in the feet of pets. The minute grass flower is contained within the spikelet; the awns and sharp point later help disperse the seed.

Red Three-Awn, Purple Three-Awn

Fountain Grass

FOUNTAIN GRASS
Pennisetum setaceum
Grass Family (Poaceae)

Description: Stems stout, 2–7' tall, in massive clumps, with pale pink to rose, feathery, cylindrical flower clusters 3–12" long. Flowers tiny, enclosed in a shiny, hard, seedlike, slightly flattened, egg-shaped spikelet ¼" long, nestled among the numerous bristles of flower cluster. Bristles ¾–1¼" long. Leaves linear, ⅛" wide, 8–24" long, with a long base that forms a sheath around stem.

Flowering Season: June–October.

Habitat/Range: Roadsides, canyon bottoms, 2,500–5,000', widely introduced in western United States, in the Sonoran Desert region, it is most common in southern Arizona.

Comments: A native of Africa, this popular ornamental escaped into the wild soon after its introduction about a half century ago. *Pennisetum* means "feather bristle," in reference to the flower cluster.

BROAD-LEAVED GILIA
Aliciella latifolia
Phlox Family (Polemoniaceae)

Description: Ill-smelling, glandular-hairy plants 4–18" tall, with most leaves near base, and with a widely branched flower cluster of small, pink, trumpet-shaped flowers. Corolla ¼–½" long, the 5 lobes pink on top side, almost white on bottom side. Leaves thick and fleshy, more or less hollylike in appearance, ovate, ¾–4" long, with a few slender, tapered teeth on edges; upper leaves smaller.

Flowering Season: March–May.

Habitat/Range: Sandy soil, especially in washes, below 2,000', southeastern California to southwestern Utah and western Arizona.

Comments: Broad-Leaved Gilia is unusual in its broad, hollylike leaves; most closely related species have pinnately divided leaves. When winter rains are sufficient, Broad-Leaved Gilia is common in its habitat.

Broad-Leaved Gilia

ARIZONA YELLOW-THROAT GILIA
Gilia flavocincta ssp. *flavocincta*
Phlox Family (Polemoniaceae)

Description: Erect, light green plants, with several stems, most leaves near base, and with pink-lavender, funnel-shaped flowers in branched clusters. Corolla ½–1" long, 5-lobed, the tube longer than calyx, lobes pink-lavender, area near opening of tube often dull violet with yellow or white below, the narrow base of tube usually streaked with violet. Leaves at base 1½–3" long, with cobwebby hairs, pinnately lobed, length of lobes greater than width of the central rib of leaf. Upper leaves shorter, less divided.

Flowering Season: February–May.

Habitat/Range: Sandy places in desert mountains, 2,300–5,200', Arizona.

Comments: When in extensive patches, this wildflower may fill the air with a delicate honey scent. Southern Yellow-Throat Gilia (var. *australis*) has corolla tube only as long as calyx.

Arizona Yellow-Throat Gilia

Rock Gilia

ROCK GILIA
Gilia scopulorum
Phlox Family (Polemoniaceae)

Description: Usually branched plants 4–12" tall, the flower-bearing branches glandular, ending in small, trumpet-shaped flowers with 5 pink, lavender, or white lobes. Flower ½" long, the tube white, yellow, or pale violet, more than twice the length of the lightly hairy calyx. Leaves mostly near base 1–3½" long, with small, coarse hairs, prominently toothed, often pinnately divided, the lobes also divided. Fruit spherical, 3/16" long.

Flowering Season: March–April.

Habitat/Range: Gravelly washes and slopes, mostly below 2,500', southeastern California to southern Utah, southwestern Arizona, and northwestern Mexico.

Comments: This species represents the small-flowered gilias, so common in the spring. They vary in nature of hairs, presence of hairs on calyx, length of flower tube, and shape of fruit.

Bristly Calico

BRISTLY CALICO
Langloisia setosissima ssp. *setosissima*
Phlox Family (Polemoniaceae)

Description: Tufted plants ¾–2½" high, with pink-lavender, trumpet-shaped flowers barely extending above bristly leaves. Corolla 5-lobed, ½–¾" long, the ovate lobes about a third as long as tube. Leaf blades ½–¾" long, inversely lanceolate, tapered to stalk, the tip with 3 spine-tipped teeth, usually also a pair of spine-tipped teeth below the leaf tip.

Flowering Season: February–June.

Habitat/Range: Dry, sandy soil, below 3,500', southeastern California to southern Nevada, western Arizona, and northwestern Mexico.

Comments: *Langloisia* is very similar to Desert Calico (*Loeseliastrum*). The former has radial flowers and 2 or 3 bristles in each cluster near base of leaf, whereas *Loeseliastrum* has bilateral flowers and solitary bristles.

DESERT CALICO
Loeseliastrum mathewsii
Phlox Family (Polemoniaceae)

Description: Small, bristly, tufted plants with pinkish lavender, bilateral flowers nestled among leaves. Corolla ½" wide, with 5 narrow lobes at top of a slender tube as long as lobes. Maroon dots form an elaborate pattern on 3 upper lobes; pattern less pronounced on lower 2 lobes. Lower leaves broadly linear, ½–1½" long, pinnately lobed, the lobes tipped with a single pale bristle; upper leaves broader and often shorter. Stems branched, 1–6" long.

Flowering Season: April–June.

Habitat/Range: Sandy and gravelly places, below 5,000', on western and northern edges of Sonoran Desert in California, Nevada, and perhaps Arizona.

Comments: The shape and pattern of the corolla and the extended anthers and style suggest that insect visitors are important in cross-pollination.

Desert Calico

GLAND-LEAF MILKWORT
Polygala macradenia
Milkwort Family (Polygalaceae)

Description: Many crowded stems less than 8" long bear tiny purple, white, and yellow bilateral flowers. Flowers with 2 purple wings ¼" long, spreading to sides. In center of flower 2 narrow white and yellow petals ³⁄₁₆" long project forward over a yellowish keel. Leaves crowded, gland-dotted, narrow, less than ¼" long, covered with dense, short hairs.

Flowering Season: April–July, sometimes again in September.

Habitat/Range: Open, rocky slopes, often on limestone, 1,500–4,500', southern Arizona to western Texas and northern Mexico.

Comments: The odd little flowers are spectacularly beautiful when viewed with a lens; some related species from elsewhere are called gaywings. A tea was made from some species to induce the flow of milk in nursing mothers, giving the name milkwort.

Gland-Leaf Milkwort

Red Maids

RED MAIDS
Calandrinia ciliata
Purslane Family (Portulacaceae)

Description: Succulent plants with spreading stems and brilliant rose-violet or, less commonly, white flowers in leafy clusters. Petals usually 5, broadest in upper half, ³⁄₁₆–½" long. Sepals 2, overlapping one another, persisting until fruit matures. Leaves linear or slightly wider near tip, flat, ½–4" long. Stems 4–16" long.

Flowering Season: February–April.

Habitat/Range: Open areas in sandy or loamy soil, often in cultivated areas, below 6,000', British Columbia to northwestern Mexico, east to New Mexico; also South America.

Comments: Following good winter rains, this is a common early spring annual wildflower in upper elevations of the Sonoran Desert, especially in Arizona. There white-flowered plants may be common, composing almost half of a population.

Purple Owl's-Clover, Escobita

PURPLE OWL'S-CLOVER, ESCOBITA
Castilleja exserta
Figwort Family (Scrophulariaceae)

Description: Glandular-hairy plants 4–18" tall with divided leaves and a dense cluster of pink-purple bracts and flowers at top of stem. Corolla bilateral, pink-purple, the upper lip beaklike and hooked downward at tip, the lower lip swollen and forming 3 pouches, each with a bright yellow tip. Leaves ½–2" long, divided into 5–9 threadlike lobes. Leaves intergrade into pink-purple, lobed bracts of inflorescence.

Flowering Season: March–May.

Habitat/Range: Open areas, 1,500–4,500', California to southern Arizona and north-western Mexico.

Comments: Coloring of the lower corolla lobes may vary. Some races may have white tips, others purple. Occasionally, plants may have white bracts. Until recently classified as *Orthocarpus purpurascens*, careful study has revealed this is actually a *Castilleja*, where, for technical nomenclature reasons it must be called by a completely different name.

VIOLET TWINING SNAPDRAGON, ROVING SAILOR
Maurandella antirrhiniflora
Figwort Family (Scrophulariaceae)

Description: Smooth, twining plants with leaves shaped like arrowheads and bilateral purple or reddish flowers. Corolla ½–¾" long, upper lip 2-lobed, lower lip 3-lobed, with a white hump at base of lower lip next to opening of tube. Fruit a roundish capsule ¼" long nestled in 5 long, narrow sepal-lobes twice the length of the capsule. Leaves ½–1" long. Stems 1–3' long.

Flowering Season: April–October.

Habitat/Range: Stony areas, usually among shrubs, 1,500–6,000', southeastern California to southern Texas, south into Mexico.

Comments: The delicate vines and small snapdragon-like flowers make this plant well worth cultivating, grown from seed and trained on trellises. There are 2 color forms, pale to deep violet, and rose-red.

Violet Twining Snapdragon, Roving Sailor

Yellow-Throat Monkeyflower

YELLOW-THROAT MONKEYFLOWER
Mimulus bigelovii
Figwort Family (Scrophulariaceae)

Description: Densely glandular-hairy plants with bilateral magenta flowers. Corolla ¼–½" long, the flared end ½" across, with 2 upper lobes and 3 lower lobes. Lower interior of tube with finely hairy, yellow ridges. Leaves lanceolate, often wider near tip, ¼–1¼" long. Stems branched or not, 1–10" tall.

Flowering Season: March–June.

Habitat/Range: Desert slopes and washes in the Sonoran Desert, elsewhere in sandy, open places, 400–11,000', much of western United States, where it often blooms into the summer.

Comments: In most years this is a small plant with disproportionately large flowers. In years with ample rain, it may form extensive displays in washes. The genus name comes from Latin for "mime" or "comic," in reference to the impish "face" of the flower of many species.

Parry's Beardtongue

PARRY'S BEARDTONGUE
Penstemon parryi
Figwort Family (Scrophulariaceae)

Description: Smooth, bluish green plants with spires of pink-magenta, bilateral, nodding flowers. Flowers ½–¾" long, the tube minutely glandular-hairy, abruptly flared at end to 2 upper lobes and 3 lower lobes. Fertile stamens 4, the 2 pollen sacs of each anther spread away from one another; 5th stamen sterile, with an expanded tip covered by golden hairs (bearded tongue). Leaves opposite, elliptical to spatulate, often broader near tip, 1½–6" long, ½–1" wide. Stems 1 to many, 1–4' tall.

Flowering Season: February–April.

Habitat/Range: Slopes and canyons, 1,500–5,000', southern Arizona and Sonora, Mexico.

Comments: This wildflower is now used in arid landscaping. It is closely related to Superb Beardtongue *(P. superbus)* of southeastern Arizona, with red flowers ¾–1" long, also used as an ornamental.

ROSY DESERT-BEARDTONGUE
Penstemon pseudospectabilis
Figwort Family (Scrophulariaceae)

Description: Bluish gray plants 2–4" tall, the stem seeming to perforate the united upper leaves. Flowers in long, open clusters at top of stem. Corolla bilateral, vivid rose, ¾–1" long, the 5 lobes short, round. Tube gradually expanded from narrow base to opening ¼–⅜" wide, yellowish and streaked with maroon within. Stamens 5, one sterile and hairless or nearly so at tip. Leaves at base lanceolate to ovate, 2–3" long; leaves on stem ovate, joined by bases, up to 5" from tip to tip. All leaves with fine, sharp teeth.

Flowering Season: February–May.

Habitat/Range: Arid slopes, washes, 300–7,000', southeastern California to southwestern Utah and western New Mexico.

Comments: From central Arizona westward is variety *pseudospectabilis,* glandular-hairy in flower cluster. Eastward is variety *connatifolius,* which is hairless.

Rosy Desert-Beardtongue

GOODDING'S VERVAIN
Verbena gooddingii
Vervain Family (Verbenaceae)

Description: Pink or lavender flowers in dense, 1½–2½" wide, rounded clusters atop stems with opposite leaves. Corolla slightly bilateral, ⅜–½" long, only slightly longer than calyx, the flared end ¼–⅜" wide, with 5 lobes, the lobe facing outward in the floral cluster notched at tip. Hairs on calyx spreading. Mature fruit divides into 4 slender, black or dark brown, seedlike segments ⅛" long. Leaves irregularly and deeply pinnately divided, ½–1½" long, ovate in outline, the stalk more or less flat. Stems 4–18" long.

Flowering Season: Most vigorously March–September, but flowering throughout the year.

Habitat/Range: Dry, open areas, below 5,000', in much of the American Southwest.

Comments: In flower this species often forms showy, hemispherical clumps. Similar species have corollas much longer than the calyx.

Goodding's Vervain

California Fagonia

CALIFORNIA FAGONIA
Fagonia laevis
Caltrop Family (Zygophyllaceae)

Description: Dark green, nearly leafless plants with repeatedly forked stems and propellerlike purple flowers. Petals 5, ¼" long, narrowed at base to a slender stalk. Leaves with 2 small, lanceolate leaflets at base and a larger terminal one ⅛–⅜" long, each spine-tipped. At each side of forked joint on stem is a single, slightly curved, spinelike stipule ⅛" long. Stems 4–24" long, grooved.

Flowering Season: January–April, and sometimes in October.

Habitat/Range: Sandy or rocky areas, 0–2,500', southeastern California, southwestern Utah, western Arizona, and northwestern Mexico.

Comments: *Fagonia* is an arid land genus of about 18 species found also in Chile, the Mediterranean area, and southwest Africa. The other Sonoran Desert species, Sticky Fagonia *(F. pachyacantha)* has straight stipules and ovate leaflets.

BLUE FLOWERS

Desert Bell, Desert Bluebells

Blue flowers often grade into other hues, so you should also check the pink and purple flower section.

Arizona Blue-Eyes

ARIZONA BLUE-EYES
Evolvulus arizonicus
Morning Glory Family (Convolvulaceae)

Description: Flat, round, sky blue flowers on threadlike stalks ½–1¼" long. Corolla ½" wide, with a small white ring around the short tube at center. Leaves broadly to narrowly lanceolate, ½–1" long, lightly hairy. Stems several, erect or leaning, up to 16" long.

Flowering Season: April–October.

Habitat/Range: Open, sunny areas, 3,000–5,000', southern Arizona to southwestern New Mexico and northwestern Mexico; also Argentina.

Comments: The blue flower of this species is unusual among desert plants. It also tests the patience of the photographer, for the flowers held on threadlike stalks on slender stems bounce with the slightest breeze, even that of air rising from warming ground in the morning. Ojo de Víbora ("viper's eyes," *E. alsinoides*) has blue flowers only ¼" wide.

CANYON MORNING GLORY
Ipomoea barbatisepala
Morning Glory Family (Convolvulaceae)

Description: Slender, twining vines, hairless except for sepals, with palmately lobed leaves and bluish to pinkish purple, funnel-shaped flowers. Corolla ¼–1" long, the tube whitish or pale yellow. Sepals thickly beset with stiff, spreading hairs, narrowly lanceolate, ⅜–⅝" long, with long, linear tips. Leaves with 5 or 7 narrow lobes ½–2½" long, ¼–⅜" wide, long-tapered to the tip, widest near the middle, narrowed at base. Stems 1–5' long.

Flowering Season: August–September.

Habitat/Range: Rocky slopes, twining among shrubs, 3,000–5,000', southern Arizona to western Texas, south into Mexico.

Comments: This annual is common in desert canyons at the upper edges of the Sonoran Desert. Flowers quickly wither as the sun strikes them in the morning.

Canyon Morning Glory

Arroyo Lupine

ARROYO LUPINE
Lupinus sparsiflorus
Bean Family (Fabaceae)

Description: Spires of purple-blue "pea" flowers stand above palmately compound leaves. Petals usually slightly less than ½" long, the banner with a white central patch that becomes maroon as flower ages, the center of white patch with a red-spotted yellow blotch. Stalks of keel petals with a few hairs. Pod ½–¾" long, ¼" wide, coarsely hairy. Leaves with 7–11 narrowly lanceolate leaflets ½–1¼" long. Stems and foliage with spreading hairs and also with hairs that lie flat against surface. Stems 6–18" tall.

Flowering Season: January–May.

Habitat/Range: Open, gravelly soil, below 4,500', southeastern California to southwestern Utah, southern Arizona, and northwestern Mexico.

Comments: The size of this common annual is variable, depending on timing and sufficiency of rains.

Parry's False Prairie-Clover

PARRY'S FALSE PRAIRIE-CLOVER
Marina parryi
Bean Family (Fabaceae)

Description: Slender spires of violet-blue "pea" flowers borne on gland-dotted, wiry plants with pinnately compound leaves. Corolla ¼" long, each petal blue and white, the keel longer than banner or wings. Pod ¹⁄₁₀" long, mostly hidden in calyx. Leaves ¾–2" long, with 11–25 roundish leaflets, each ¹⁄₁₆–¼" long. Stems 8–30" long, often in a dense, bushy tangle.

Flowering Season: March–June, often also September–October.

Habitat/Range: Dry, gravelly areas, below 4,000', southeastern California to southern Arizona and northwestern Mexico.

Comments: Only 1 species of this mostly Mexican genus occurs on the United States portion of the Sonoran Desert. It was named for Marina or Malinche, the cacique's daughter who interpreted for Hernán Cortez as he conquered Mexico.

SCHOTT'S SMOKEBUSH, INDIGO BUSH
Psorothamnus schottii
Bean Family (Fabaceae)

Description: Grayish shrubs to about 7' tall, with linear leaves and bright indigo "pea" flowers. Flowers ⅜" long. Leaves ½–1¼" long, ¹⁄₁₀" wide, dotted with darker glands, remaining on plant during dry season. Pod nearly ½" long, dotted with glands.

Flowering Season: March–May.

Habitat/Range: Dry washes and outwash fans, 0–1,000', southeastern California, extreme southwestern Arizona, and Baja California.

Comments: This intricately branched shrub is common in Anza-Borrego Desert State Park. The Smoketree *(P. spinosus)* also has simple leaves; other *Psorothamnus,* all with violet or indigo flowers, have pinnately divided leaves.

Schott's Smokebush

Smoketree, Palo Cenizo

SMOKETREE, PALO CENIZO
Psorothamnus spinosus
Bean Family (Fabaceae)

Description: Intricately branched, twiggy, gray shrubs or trees, 4–30' tall, with small, indigo "pea" flowers. Flower ¼–⅜" long borne in dense clusters of 5–15 flowers, axis of cluster extending as a spine. Pod ¼" long, dotted with orange glands. Leaf inversely lanceolate, gland-dotted, quickly dropping from plant. Stems terminating in sharp spines.

Flowering Season: April–June.

Habitat/Range: Sandy or gravelly washes, roadsides, below 1,500', southeastern California, western Arizona, northwestern Mexico.

Comments: Plants are handsome when in full flower, the intense deep blue-violet flowers often so dense so as to nearly completely cover the shrub. Seed coats must be scratched for water to enter the seed, initiating germination. Usually this occurs by tumbling and grinding in gravel of flooding washes. Such a mechanism helps insure presence of adequate water for seedling establishment.

Desert Bell, Desert Bluebells

DESERT BELL, DESERT BLUEBELLS
Phacelia campanularia
Waterleaf Family (Hydrophyllaceae)

Description: Bell-shaped or broadly funnel-shaped, sapphire blue flowers spread from coiled flower clusters. Corolla ⅝–1½" long, 5-lobed above the broad, tubular base. Stamens 5, projecting from corolla. Leaves ovate or oblong, ¾–3" long, coarsely toothed, upper leaves smaller than lower. Stems branched, 6–24" tall.

Flowering Season: February–April.

Habitat/Range: Dry, gravelly or sandy places, below 5,000', southeastern California and southern Arizona.

Comments: Along the western edge of the Sonoran Desert is variety *campanularia,* with bell-shaped corollas ⅝–1¼" long. Along the northern edge in California is variety *vasiformis,* with broadly funnel-shaped corollas 1–1½" long. The latter is a popular component of wildflower seed mix and is now established in southern Arizona.

BLUE-EYED SCORPION-WEED
Phacelia distans
Waterleaf Family (Hydrophyllaceae)

Description: Pale blue or pale lavender-blue flowers in "fiddleneck" coils, on plants with pinnately divided leaves. Flowers on individual stalks ⅒–⅛" long. Corolla bell-shaped, ⅜–½" across, with a short tube, readily dropping. Stamens 5, protruding. Leaves ¾–6" long, broadly lanceolate in outline, the segments strongly scalloped or toothed. Stems branched, 6–36" long, sparsely stiff-hairy, often tangled in shrubs.

Flowering Season: February–June.

Habitat/Range: Slopes and washes, 800–4,000', California to southern Nevada, southern Arizona, and northwestern Mexico.

Comments: Tansy-Leaf Scorpion-Weed *(P. tanacetifolia)* is similar, occurring mostly north of Sonoran Desert. Its flowers individually are almost stalkless, the corolla semi-persistent.

Blue-Eyed Scorpion-Weed

Arizona Fiesta Flower

ARIZONA FIESTA FLOWER
Pholistoma auritum var. *arizonicum*
Waterleaf Family (Hydrophyllaceae)

Description: Small, bell-like, blue-lavender flowers node in loose clusters at ends of fragile stems. Corolla ¼–½" long, with 5 round lobes and a broad, short tube. Calyx 10-lobed, the lobes narrow, alternately bent backward and forward. Leaves oblong or lanceolate, 5–13 lobed, the lobes often bearing a few teeth. Leaf stalk with a broad flange along each side, the base surrounding and clasping stem. Stems 1–2' long, bearing stout, curved hairs.

Flowering Season: February–April.

Habitat/Range: Among rocks, on banks, usually where partly shaded, below 3,000', California to southern Arizona.

Comments: The curved hairs easily snag, the fragile, usually tangled stems readily breaking. Thus, actual length of stems is not recorded in technical literature.

Bladder Sage

BLADDER SAGE
Salazaria mexicana
Mint Family (Lamiaceae)

Description: Grayish, rounded shrubs 2–6' tall, with many sharp-tipped branches spreading at right angles to parent branch. Corolla ⅝–1" long, with a white or pale violet, hairy, hoodlike upper lip, and 3-lobed, down-bent, deep blue-violet lower lip. Calyx ovate, reddish purple, enlarging as a bladder ½–¾" long at maturity. Leaves opposite, ovate or broadly lanceolate, ⅛–¾" long.

Flowering Season: March–June, often again in October.

Habitat/Range: Sandy or gravelly slopes and washes, below 5,000', southeastern California and southwestern Utah to southern Arizona; also western Texas and northern Mexico.

Comments: Mints usually have 4-sided stems; in Bladder Sage stems are round. Inside the bladdery calyx are 4 seedlike segments of the fruit, dispersed as wind tumbles the detached calyx.

CHIA, CALIFORNIA SAGE
Salvia columbariae
Mint Family (Lamiaceae)

Description: Erect plants 4–20" tall, with dense clusters of flowers forming dark purplish, prickly globes widely scattered in upper part of stem. Calyx tipped with dark purple, ⅜" long, upper lip with 2–3 stiff prickles. Corolla ⅛–¼" across, 2-lipped, upper lip shallowly 2-lobed or not, lower lip 3-lobed, its central lobe much the longest, with whitish patches at base. Leaves mostly at base, 1–4" long, oblong in outline, pinnately divided, the surface crinkled due to impression of veins. Stems 4-sided.

Flowering Season: March–May.

Habitat/Range: Gravelly washes, roadsides, below 3,000', southeastern California to southwestern Utah and southern Arizona.

Comments: Plants have a medicinal, minty odor. Seeds were ground and sweetened, often with mesquite pods, by indigenous people to make nutritious pinole. Seeds were also steeped to make a mucilaginous drink.

Chia, California Sage

Arizona Blue-Curls

ARIZONA BLUE-CURLS
Trichostema arizonicum
Mint Family (Lamiaceae)

Description: Loose clusters of 1–7 flowers spread from axils of upper leaves. Corolla lobes all lavender-blue, or 4 white and the lower, central lobe violet-blue. Lower, central lobe ¼–½" long, its edge ruffled. Stamens 4, curving in a graceful arc between 2 upper petals, ½–1" long. Leaves opposite, oblong to ovate, ½–1½" long. Stems to 2' tall.

Flowering Season: July–October.

Habitat/Range: Rocky slopes at upper edge of Sonoran Desert, 3,500–6,000', southeastern Arizona, southwestern New Mexico and northern Mexico.

Comments: Arizona Blue-Curls is striking, easily spotted along road banks as the traveler ascends arid mountain ranges. The genus name translates as "hair stamen," in reference to the long and graceful stamens that dab pollen on backs of visiting insects.

Meadow Flax

MINIATURE WOOLSTAR
Eriastrum diffusum
Phlox Family (Polemoniaceae)

Description: Small plants, usually widely branched, wiry, and rather easily breaking at branch points, with small trumpet-shaped, pale blue flowers, in headlike clusters. Corolla 5-lobed, ⅜" long, the tube yellow or blue. Stamens 5, unequal in height, slightly protruding from tube. Leaves ½–1" long, linear or divided into linear lobes, intergrading with lobed bracts of heads. Stems 1–8" tall. Fluffy wool often present on bracts of heads and in axils of leaves.

Flowering Season: March–June.

Habitat/Range: Dry, sandy places, below 6,000', much of American Southwest, northwestern Mexico.

Comments: This common annual varies in hairiness. Other less common desert species may be recognized as *Eriastrum* by their blue, trumpet-shaped flowers and stamens all of same length.

MEADOW FLAX
Linum pratense
Flax Family (Linaceae)

Description: Hairless, slender plants with pale blue flowers and buds nodding on threadlike stalks. Petals 5, narrowly fan-shaped, ¼–⅜" long. Styles 5, ¹⁄₁₆–⅛" long, stigmas spherical. Leaves narrowly lanceolate, ½–¾" long. Stems few, branched near base, 2–16" tall.

Flowering Season: February–March.

Habitat/Range: Open areas, often among brush, 1,200–3,500', Arizona eastward to Great Plains.

Comments: Identification of flax species requires attention to stigmas. Common Flax, or Linaza *(L. usatisissimum),* an occasional weed, has sky blue flowers, petals ⅜–½" long, and styles ⅛–³⁄₁₆" long, with slender stigmas. Lewis's Flax *(L. lewisii),* also with sky blue flowers, but from above the Sonoran Desert, has similar petals but styles ³⁄₁₆–⅜" long, with spherical stigmas.

Miniature Woolstar

DESERT WOOLSTAR
Eriastrum eremicum
Phlox Family (Polemoniaceae)

Description: Wiry, branched plants 2–12"
tall, with pinnately divided leaves and slightly
bilateral blue flowers in clusters with woolly
bracts. Corolla ⅝" long, with 3 upper lobes
and 2 lower lobes, the upper lobes each with a
yellow spot at base. Stamens protruding from
tube, slightly bent downward toward lower
lobes. Leaves ¼–2" long, with 5–9 linear
lobes.

Flowering Season: March–June.

Habitat/Range: Open, sandy places, below
5,000', southeastern California, southern
Nevada, southwestern Utah, much of Arizona.

Comments: Occasionally this species is so
abundant it covers broad expanses of the
desert with a sky blue blanket.

Desert Woolstar

Paleflower Skyrocket

PALEFLOWER SKYROCKET
Ipomopsis longiflora ssp. *australis*
Phlox Family (Polemoniaceae)

Description: Pale blue to nearly white, trum-
petlike flowers 1½–2" long at ends of slender
branches. Corolla with 5 lobes up to ½" long
abruptly flared from a long, slender tube.
Leaves distantly spaced on plant; lower leaves
¾–2" long, with 1–3 pairs of linear lobes,
upper leaves smaller and often without lobes.
Fruit a small capsule about as long as calyx.
Stems 4–24" tall, widely and openly branched.

Flowering Season: March–October.

Habitat/Range: Open, sandy, gravelly, or
rocky areas, 1,000–8,000', northwestern to
southern Arizona, southwestern New Mexico,
and northwestern Mexico.

Comments: This plant is common in the arid
grasslands at the upper edge of the Sonoran
Desert. The more northern and eastern subspecies *longiflora* has capsule much longer
than the calyx.

Parish's Larkspur

PARISH'S LARKSPUR
Delphinium parishii
Buttercup Family (Ranunculaceae)

Description: Slender plants with most leaves on basal third of stem, the vivid blue flowers in long, open, loose terminal clusters. Flowers bilateral, ¾–1" across, the 5 sepals petal-like, upper sepal with a backward projecting nectar spur ⅜–½" long. Petals 4, in center of flower, upper 2 often whitish, lower 2 blue, with a notch ⅛" deep. Leaves on long stalks, the blades 5-sided, up to 3" wide, deeply divided into several lobes, each of which is deeply lobed on margin. Stems not branched, or with few branches, 1–3' tall.

Flowering Season: February–April (to June at higher elevations).

Habitat/Range: Among brush in deserts and in juniper woodland, 600–12,000', southeastern California to southwestern Utah, southern Arizona and northwestern Mexico.

Comments: Parish's Larkspur in California may have white flowers. "Larkspur" refers to the spur, shaped like the rear claw of a lark. "Lark's Heel" and "Lark's Claw" were once widely used common names. *"Delphinium,"* from Greek, is also in reference to the spur, in this case fancifully resembling the nose of a little dolphin. Numerous horticultural forms have been developed from several species in the large genus of the northern hemisphere, some annuals, others perennials. In the West native species are detested by ranchers, for they are among the most toxic range plants, often causing death among livestock.

TURPENTINE BROOM
Thamnosma montana
Rue Family (Rutaceae)

Description: Greenish gray, twiggy plants 1–3' tall, with branches seeming to go in all directions, and with barrel-shaped, indigo flowers about ½" long. Petals 5, elliptic, rather leathery. Stems, leaves, and fruits covered with tiny, dark, blisterlike glands that impart the odor of green lemons and turpentine. Leaves linear, ¼–½" long, dropping as they mature. Fruit composed of 2 greenish, united spheres, each ¼" diameter.

Flowering Season: February–April.

Habitat/Range: Dry slopes, below 4,500', from southeastern California to southwestern Utah, southern Arizona and northwestern Mexico.

Comments: The absence of leaves reduces surface area and thus the loss of water. Photosynthesis occurs in the greenish stems. The odoriferous oils discourage plant-eating animals.

Turpentine Broom

Texas Toadflax

TEXAS TOADFLAX
Nuttallanthus texanus
Figwort Family (Scrophulariaceae)

Description: Very slender, smooth plants with bilateral, pale violet-blue flowers in narrow clusters. Corolla ½" long (excluding spur), upper lip angled upward, 2-lobed, lower lip curved downward from a pale, pillowlike swelling at opening, 3-lobed. Spur originating at base of flower, very slender, ¼–½" long, curved downward. Leaves narrowly linear, ½–1½" long, strongly ascending. Stems stiffly erect, to 30" high, often with short, prostrate branches at base.

Flowering Season: February–May.

Habitat/Range: Open areas, 1,500–5,000', much of western United States.

Comments: Plants often occur in patches along roadsides and trails in brushy areas. The slender spur provides nectar for visiting, long-tongued insects.

Chinese Lantern, Purple Ground Cherry

CHINESE LANTERN, PURPLE GROUND CHERRY
Quincula lobata
Nightshade Family (Solanaceae)

Description: Flat, blue-purple flowers nestle on dark green foliage. Corolla about ¾" in diameter, somewhat crinkled, with a 5-point, starlike pattern formed by creases. Stamens 5. Style twisted and bent to one side. Leaves broadly lanceolate to almost linear, 1½–4" long. Fruit a greenish berry surrounded by an inflated, lanternlike calyx about ¾" long, with 5 blunt angles. Stems 4–20" long.

Flowering Season: March–October.

Habitat/Range: Open areas, often on road-sides, 1,000–5,000', southeastern California to Kansas and western Texas, south into Mexico.

Comments: This is often considered to be included in *Physalis,* thus the common name Ground Cherry. Though similar, the blue-purple flower, twisted style, and crystalline hairs serve to distinguish it from that genus.

Silver-Leaf Nightshade, White Horse-Nettle

SILVER-LEAF NIGHTSHADE, WHITE HORSE-NETTLE
Solanum elaeagnifolium
Nightshade Family (Solanaceae)

Description: Purple, lilac, or, rarely, white, star-shaped flowers with conspicuous yellow stamens nod among gray-green foliage. Corolla ¾–1" across, with 5 pointed lobes. Stamens 5, erect. Fruit a hard, round berry about ½" in diameter, mottled green when young, evenly yellow at maturity. Leaves oblong to lanceolate, 1½–6" long, margins usually wavy. Stems 1–3' tall, in patches, with sparse to dense, needlelike prickles.

Flowering Season: May–October.

Habitat/Range: Open areas, especially fields and roadsides, 1,000–6,000', southern California to the southern Great Plains and northern Mexico.

Comments: A pernicious weed, this species forms patches, spreading from deep underground stems (rhizomes), making it difficult to eradicate. Purple Nightshade *(S. xantii)* has broader petal-lobes, green leaves, and no prickles. It barely enters the Sonoran Desert region at higher elevations.

GREEN FLOWERS

Silver Cholla, Golden Cholla

This section includes green flowers, some plants with difficult to classify flowers that have green on them, and plants with green fruits so conspicuous that the flowers are often not noticed. Green flowers often grade into yellow or white, so be sure to check those sections if the plant you're looking for is not here.

Woolly Honeysweet, Espanta Vaqueros

WOOLLY HONEYSWEET, ESPANTA VAQUEROS
Tidestromia lanuginosa
Amaranth Family (Amaranthaceae)

Description: Low-spreading plants with pale gray or ashy-white foliage. Flowers borne in small clusters where leaf joins stem, each flower tiny, inconspicuous, with 5 translucent, greenish yellow sepals. Leaves, ¼–1½" long and nearly as wide, held parallel to ground and densely covered with whitish, intricately branched hairs. Stems dull reddish, 4–20" long, but only 4–6" high.

Flowering Season: June–October.

Habitat/Range: Open flats and hillsides below 5,500', much of the American Southwest and northern Mexico.

Comments: Plants are conspicuous after summer rains, often forming extensive patches of whitish mats. Photosynthesis is most efficient during the hottest part of the day, in temperatures when other plants may slow or cease most cellular activity.

INDIAN-ROOT, SNAKEROOT, SOUTHWESTERN PIPEVINE
Aristolochia watsonii
Birthwort Family (Aristolochiaceae)

Description: Scrambling stems ½–3' long have bent, pipelike flowers hidden among foliage. Flowers 1–1½" long, tubular, curved, greenish, and speckled with brownish purple, with a long, lightly hairy opening. Brownish green leaves are ¾–2½" long and resemble slender arrowheads.

Flowering Season: April–October.

Habitat/Range: Among rocks and on open flats, 2,000–4,500', southern Arizona to western Texas and northern Mexico.

Comments: The bizarre flower of this inconspicuous plant has a musky odor and resembles a rodent's ear. Small blood-sucking flies are fooled into entering the flower, where they are trapped for a day. When they escape and enter another Snakeroot flower, they may pollinate it. The plant was used medicinally for snakebite by Native Americans and early European settlers.

Indian-Root, Snakeroot, Southwestern Pipevine

Mojave Milkweed

MOJAVE MILKWEED
Asclepias nyctaginifolia
Milkweed Family (Asclepiadaceae)

Description: Stout, leafy plants up to 1' tall, with numerous greenish white flowers in loose, round clusters. Flowers have 5 petals, each ½" long, bent backwards; the center of flower has 5 erect, ⅜" long pointed hoods, each concealing a horn curved toward center of flower. The sides of hoods are nearly pressed together. Leaves ovate or lanceolate, 1½–3" long, lightly hairy, with the edges more or less wavy.

Flowering Season: May–September.

Habitat/Range: On plains and flats, often in sandy washes or along roadsides, 1,500–5,000', southeastern California to southwestern New Mexico.

Comments: Although called Mojave Milkweed, the species is found all across southern Arizona. Indigenous people used many plants with milky sap, such as this one, to treat ulcerating sores. The structure of the flowers of *Asclepias* involves a very complex means of pollination. Pollen, in packets attached to a sticky pad which adheres to insects, must be forcibly pulled from the stamens. Insects not strong enough to do so may be stuck and die upon the flower. If the pollen is successfully extracted it then must be precisely inserted into slits in the stigma.

Rush Milkweed, Ajamete

RUSH MILKWEED, AJAMETE
Asclepias subulata
Milkweed Family (Asclepiadaceae)

Description: Clumps of leafless, or nearly leafless, grayish green stems 2½–5' tall with loose, rounded clusters of pale greenish yellow flowers. Flowers have 5 narrow, ⅜" long petals sharply bent back from the center of flower, which has 5 erect hoods as long as the petals and about twice the length of the stamens. Each hood, slightly bent outward, conceals a horn curved toward center of flower. Leaves threadlike, ¾–2" long, usually withering and falling before flowers appear.

Flowering Season: April–December.

Habitat/Range: Dry slopes and flats, below 3,000', southeastern California, southern Arizona, northwestern Mexico.

Comments: The toxic, milky sap contains rubber. Native people used extracts from the plant as a laxative. Today the species is occasionally used in arid landscape design.

SMOOTH TWINEVINE
Funastrum hirtellum
Milkweed Family (Asclepiadaceae)

Description: Vines with many intertangled stems that climb over other vegetation, with dense, short, erect hairs, and many flowers in rounded clusters 2" across. Flowers have 5 ovate, greenish white, ³⁄₁₆" long petals. Centers of flowers have 5 white, inflated sacs less than ⅛" high. Leaves linear to narrowly lanceolate, 1–2" long, covered with minute hairs that stand nearly erect. Stems 3–6' long, bleeding with milky sap when broken.

Flowering Season: March–May.

Habitat/Range: Gravelly or sandy washes and roadsides, 500–4,000', southeastern California and southern Nevada to southern Arizona.

Comments: Climbing Milkweed, *F. cynanchoides*, has hairless foliage, or the hairs lie flat against the surface. Species of *Funastrum* have an unpleasant odor, like that of hot rubber.

Smooth Twinevine

COULTER'S LYRE-POD
Lyrocarpa coulteri
Mustard Family (Brassicaceae)

Description: Branched plants 1–3' tall, covered with dense, grayish, starlike hairs, bearing at ends of branches greenish brown or greenish purple flowers with 4 narrow, twisted petals. Petals ½–1" long, ⅛" wide or less, gently tapering to a slender tip. Leaves ½–6" long, linear to ovate, usually less than ½" wide. Fruit flat, ½–¾" long, about as wide, broadly notched at tip, and divided into 2 equal halves.

Flowering Season: December–April, sometimes in August.

Habitat/Range: Usually among brush in partial shade, below 3,000', southern Arizona, southern California, and northwestern Mexico.

Comments: Plants are difficult to see among other vegetation. The fruit is shaped somewhat like a lyre (a musical instrument), thus the common name. The bizarre flowers are fragrant.

Coulter's Lyre-Pod

LACEPOD, FRINGEPOD
Thysanocarpus curvipes
Mustard Family (Brassicaceae)

Description: Slender plants with stems 5–30" tall, branched or not, with leaves mostly near the base, minute white flowers near the top, and flat, green pods dangling on stalks that curve down from the stems below the flowers. Flowers have 4 ⅛" long petals. Fruit round, ¼–⅜" in diameter, and very flat, the translucent margin scalloped and often perforated with numerous tiny holes. Leaves very narrow, wider in upper half, ½–2½" long.

Flowering Season: January–May.

Habitat/Range: Usually in moist, sandy soil below 4,000', much of western United States, entering northwestern Mexico.

Comments: In the Southwest this slender plant is often diminutive and easily overlooked. The pods are exquisite, very flat, green in the center, and ringed by perforations of unknown function in the thin, decorative edge.

Lacepod, Fringepod

Teddy-Bear Cholla

TEDDY-BEAR CHOLLA
Opuntia bigelovii
Cactus Family (Cactaceae)

Description: Small, treelike cacti 3–8' tall, with short, stubby (3–6" long, 1½–2½" wide), easily detached branches covered with numerous spines. There are 6–10 ½–1" long spines per cluster, spreading in all directions, covered by straw-colored sheaths that eventually fall from spines. The pale greenish or yellowish flowers are sometimes streaked with purple, and the many petal-like segments are ¼–½" long. Fruit ovate, yellowish, and ½–¾" long, with a lumpy surface.

Flowering Season: February–May.

Habitat/Range: Hot, dry slopes, 100–3,000', southeastern California to southern Arizona and northwestern Mexico.

Comments: A teddy bear in appearance only, this ferocious cactus readily buries its exquisitely sharp-barbed spines in the flesh of passers by, the stem-joint readily detaching from the plant and adhering to the unwary. It is most easily removed by inserting a comb beneath the stem-joint and quickly flicking the cactus away from the skin. If firmly embedded, the spines must be cut one by one and pulled with fingers or pliers. In summary, be cautious around this plant.

SILVER CHOLLA, GOLDEN CHOLLA
Opuntia echinocarpa
Cactus Family (Cactaceae)

Description: Densely and intricately branched 3–5' tall shrubs with silvery or golden spines and greenish yellow flowers. Petal-like parts of the flower lanceolate, up to 1" long, the outer parts often streaked or blushed with dull red-purple. Stem joints usually ¾–1" in diameter, less than 4" long, with prominent tubercles only twice as long as wide. Spines 3–12 per cluster, ¾–1½" long, spreading in all directions, the sheaths remaining as covers on spines. Fruit is ½–1" long, ovate, flat at top, densely spiny in upper half, and tan and dry at maturity.

Flowering Season: April–May.

Habitat/Range: Sandy or gravelly flats and slopes, mostly below 3,000', southeastern California to southwestern Utah, western Arizona and northwestern Mexico.

Comments: Plants are common and conspicuous on western parts of the Sonoran Desert.

Silver Cholla, Golden Cholla

Desert Holly

DESERT HOLLY
Atriplex hymenelytra
Goosefoot Family (Chenopodiaceae)

Description: Rounded, compact, grayish, 1–3' tall shrub with toothed, wavy leaves. Flowers small, not showy, male and female flowers on different plants. Female flowers develop into dense clusters of green fruits, each fruit ¼–⅜" long, with 2 round bracts pressed together. Leaves oval or round, ½–1½" long, covered with tiny gray scales, with a few large teeth on each side.

Flowering Season: January–April.

Habitat/Range: Dry slopes and washes, below 5,000', southeastern California to southwestern Utah, western Arizona, and northwestern Mexico.

Comments: The form of the leaf provides the common name, Holly, but there is no close relationship to the holly tree of eastern woods, even though the plants have been collected, dried, and dyed for Christmas ornaments. In most areas the species is now legally protected.

Desert-Mountain Manihot

DESERT-MOUNTAIN MANIHOT
Manihot angustiloba
Spurge Family (Euphorbiaceae)

Description: Smooth, semi-shrubby plants have yellowish green flowers, palmately lobed leaves, and stems 1–7' tall, often reddish. Male flowers have no petals but have 5 narrow, ⅜–½" long sepals that resemble petals; on the female flowers, the sepals drop from the open flower. The 10 stamens are alternately long and short. The leaves are dark green on the upper surface, slightly paler and prominently veined on the lower surface. Each leaf has 5–7 lobes that are 1½–6" long, ⅛–½" wide. Lobes have teeth near base and the teeth themselves are sometimes divided into narrow lobes.

Flowering Season: June–September.

Habitat/Range: Arid flats and slopes, 3,000–5,000', southern Arizona to southern Mexico.

Comments: Species of *Manihot* provide a kind of rubber, tapioca, and cassava. Without appropriate processing, many are toxic. The oil of the seeds is a cathartic and emetic, similar to castor oil.

HALFMOON MILKVETCH
Astragalus allochrous var. *playanus*
Bean Family (Fabaceae)

Description: Usually tufted plants with pinnately compound leaves and bladdery, papery, green pods, which form a plump half-moon in profile. Pods are ½–1¼" long, ½–¾" wide, 1-chambered within, with a short, triangular beak at tip. The "pea" flowers, 4–10 in a slender cluster, are usually whitish, sometimes red-purple, and ¼" long. The ¾–5" long leaves have 11–19 leaflets, each ¼–¾" long. Hairs on plant sparse, lying against the surface. Stems erect to prostrate, 4–20" long.

Flowering Season: March–May.

Habitat/Range: Sandy flats, 1,500–7,000', much of the American Southwest.

Comments: This perennial may act as an annual, flowering within 2 months of germination. The flowers are inconspicuous, but the pods attract attention. The species is toxic to livestock, producing the disease called "loco."

Halfmoon Milkvetch

Mexican Passion Flower

MEXICAN PASSION FLOWER
Passiflora mexicana
Passion-Flower Family (Passifloraceae)

Description: Smooth, hairless, blue-green vines, with stems up to 25' long. The bizarre flowers have 5 greenish, ½" long sepals, usually bent somewhat back. The greenish petals are much smaller. In the center of flower is a crown of numerous, almost hairlike, pink to red-violet segments ½" long, inside of which is a second crown of tiny, erect segments around a yellow center. Stamens green, arching outward from a central column, like the ribs of an umbrella. In the center of the flower are 3 curved styles. Leaves notched to the middle, 1½–5" wide.

Flowering Season: July–September.

Habitat/Range: Among shrubs and trees, often along watercourses, 2,500–5,000', southern Arizona and northern Mexico.

Comments: Although the common names derives from the scientific name, the contrasting, even clashing, colors of the flower are like those of houses in a delightfully painted Mexican village. Plants may festoon trees, and when in flower they fill the air with delicate scent of mothballs.

Woolly Plantain, Woolly Indianwheat

WOOLLY PLANTAIN, WOOLLY INDIANWHEAT
Plantago patagonica
Plantain Family (Plantaginaceae)

Description: Small, woolly plants 2–8" tall, with narrow basal leaves and inconspicuous flowers in dense, green spikes ½–3" long that top leafless stalks. Spikes have linear, green bracts, the lower bracts projecting outward. Sepals ⅛" long, green. Petals 4, spreading, ⅒" long, whitish, translucent. Leaves linear or slightly wider toward tip, ¾–4" long.

Flowering Season: February–May.

Habitat/Range: Sandy areas, 1,500–7,000', much of western North America.

Comments: *P. patagonica* is native to the Sonoran Desert, while a similar plant, Blond Plantain *(P. ovata)*, is common at lower elevations in deserts. Spikes are ¼–1¼" long, with ovate bracts shorter than its sepals. It was possibly introduced from the Mediterranean region. Seeds of a cultivated Eurasian species, *P. afra*, provide psyllium, a bulk laxative and a dietary source of soluble fiber.

Brittle Spineflower

BRITTLE SPINEFLOWER
Chorizanthe brevicornu
Buckwheat Family (Polygonaceae)

Description: Green, skeleton-like, inversely cone-shaped plants densely branched in a forked manner. Flowers barely noticeable, with 5 white sepals, mostly hidden in a ⅛" long cylindrical green tube topped by 6 hooked, stiff bristles. Linear or inversely lanceolate leaves near or at base, ½–1½" long. Stems 2–12" tall.

Flowering Season: March–May.

Habitat/Range: Rocky slopes, flats and washes, below 2,500, much of the arid West to southwestern Arizona and northwestern Mexico.

Comments: This common plant is conspicuous on often otherwise barren, harsh, dry desert pavement. Plants readily break apart at the nodes, sticking tenaciously to clothing and pet fur.

Devil's Spineflower, Spiny-Herb

DEVIL'S SPINEFLOWER, SPINY-HERB
Chorizanthe rigida
Buckwheat Family (Polygonaceae)

Description: Low, erect, often branched plants 1–6" tall, with many long, spiny bracts along stem. The inconspicuous, minute, yellowish flowers are held in funnel-shaped tubes that have 3 spine-tipped teeth up to ½" long. The spiny, flower-bearing tubes are clustered among dense, rigid bracts tipped by stiff needlelike spines up to 1" long. Ovate, ¼–1" long leaves on long stalks wither quickly.

Flowering Season: March–May.

Habitat/Range: Open, dry ground among desert shrubs, below 6,600', southern California to southwestern Utah, western Arizona, and northern Mexico.

Comments: Like sentinels from seasons past, the dark skeletons of dead plants may stand for 1 or 2 years on the baked desert ground, still holding viable seeds. When rains come, young plants grow in the same area, often close to the bases of the dried plants from previous seasons.

IVY-LEAF GROUND CHERRY
Physalis hederaefolia
Nightshade Family (Solanaccac)

Description: Plants few-stemmed and erect, or many-stemmed, branched, and spreading, with hanging, pale yellow or yellow-green flowers and an inflated, bladderlike calyx around a green berry. Most hairs on plant unbranched, some glandular. Stalk beneath flower usually less than ¼" long. Corolla about ½" wide, with 5 bluntly pointed lobes that sometimes bend back, often with darker, yellowish green blotches inside near base of lobes. Berry about ½" in diameter; mature calyx ¾–1¼" long, with 10 ribs. Stems up to ⅛" long.

Flowering Season: April–August.

Habitat/Range: Open places, 2,000–7,000', throughout much of western United States to northern Mexico.

Comments: Caution: although this species is edible, as is the Tomatillo *(P. ixocarpa),* similar *Physalis* fruits are toxic prior to maturity.

Ivy-Leaf Ground Cherry

YELLOW FLOWERS

Greene's Bird's-Foot Trefoil

This section includes flowers ranging from bright golden yellow and yellow-orange to pale, creamy yellow. Since yellow flowers grade into red, green, and white flowers, readers looking for yellow flowers should check the red and orange, green, and white sections of this book as well.

Hairy Fournwort

HAIRY FOURNWORT
Tetramerium nervosum
Acanthus Family (Acanthaceae)

Description: Low plants with cream, bilateral flowers in slender, green-bracted, 4-sided spikes. Floral bracts ¼–½" long, broadly lanceolate, hairy. Petals cream, ½–¾" long, joined at base into a short tube, flared into a spatulate upper lobe that has a maroon spot and veins in center, and 3 lower lobes, the 2 at sides spreading like wings, the central 1 folded like the prow of a kayak. Leaves opposite, lanceolate, ½–3" long, on slender stalks up to ¾" long. Stems up to 1' tall.

Flowering Season: April–October.

Habitat/Range: Rocky slopes and banks, common along washes, 3,000–5,000', southeastern Arizona and southwestern New Mexico to northern South America.

Comments: Flowers open as the day warms, and petals drop in the evening. The Acanthus family is primarily tropical, with relatively few species north of the Mexican border.

DESERT CENTURY PLANT, AMUL, MEZCAL
Agave deserti
Agave Family (Agavaceae)

Description: A stout, candelabra-like flower cluster 8–15' tall, bearing pale yellow flowers, rises from a rosette of stiff, sharp leaves. Flower 1½–2½" long, with 6 petal-like parts ½–¾" long, the stamens protruding from center of flower. Leaves lanceolate, 10-16" long, pale gray-green, very thick, the edge with sparse prickles ¼" long, the tip armed with a formidable dark spine ½–1¼" long.

Flowering Season: May–July, occasionally November–April.

Habitat/Range: Rocky slopes and washes, below 5,000', southern California to western Arizona and northwestern Mexico.

Comments: This century plant requires about 20 years to mature and flower. The rosette then dies, replaced by new rosettes at its periphery. Rings of rosettes up to 20 feet across and estimated to be more than 1,000 years old may form.

Desert Century Plant, Amul, Mezcal

Cockroach Plant, Hierba de la Cucaracha

COCKROACH PLANT, HIERBA DE LA CUCARACHA
Haplophyton crooksii
Dogbane Family (Apocynaceae)

Description: Plants intricately branched, 1–2' tall, dark green, the slender stems bearing 2–3-flowered clusters of brilliant yellow funnel-shaped flowers. Flowers about 1" in diameter, the 5 rounded petal-lobes overlapping much like blades of a pinwheel, joined at the base in narrow tube. Fruit forming a "V" consisting of 2 very slender, cylindrical, but pointed sections 3–4" long. Leaves lanceolate, ½–1½" long.

Flowering Season: July–October.

Habitat/Range: Rocky slopes, often among brush, 2,000–4,500', southern Arizona to western Texas and northern Mexico.

Comments: This plant is toxic, as is a distant relative in the Dogbane Family, the ornamental Oleander *(Nerium oleander)*. An extract of dried leaves mixed with molasses is said to make an effective insecticide.

White-Stem Milkweed, Yamate

WHITE-STEM MILKWEED, YAMATE

Asclepias albicans
Milkweed Family (Asclepiadaceae)

Description: Clumps of few to many, pale gray, leafless stems 3–14' tall have rounded clusters of many dull yellow flowers near the top. Petals 5, greenish white, with some brown or pink, ¼" long, bent backwards. Center of flower with 5 dull yellowish, rounded hoods shorter than the anthers, each hood almost completely concealing a horn curved toward center of flower. Leaves ½–¾" long, thread-like, quickly withering and falling from plant.

Flowering Season: March–May.

Habitat/Range: Dry, rocky places, 0-2,500', southeastern California, southwestern Arizona, and northwestern Mexico.

Comments: The presence of only cylindrical stems reduces the amount of surface exposed to the sun and dry air, while the pale, waxy coating reflects light and heat, all features that help to conserve water.

SILVERLEAF BAHIA

Bahia absinthifolia
Sunflower Family (Asteraceae)

Description: Plants 4–16" tall, with ashy-gray foliage above which are held golden yellow flower heads 1–1½" across. Heads with 10–13 rays ¼–½" long, ⅛" wide or less, a disk about ½" wide, and 12–16 bracts ¼–⅓" long in 2 series. At top of seedlike fruit are 6–9 translucent, pointed scales, each broadest in upper half. Leaves ½ –2" long, lanceolate, with a few teeth near base, divided into 3 lanceolate lobes or, less commonly, palmately divided. Hairs on leaves dense, lying flat against surface, giving the ashy-gray color.

Flowering Season: April–October.

Habitat/Range: Mesas and slopes, 2,500–5,500', southeastern Arizona to southern Texas, south to central Mexico.

Comments: The species is common on calcareous soils near Tucson, Arizona, where it is a frequent roadside plant.

Silverleaf Bahia

Desert Marigold, Hierba Amarilla

DESERT MARIGOLD, HIERBA AMARILLA
Baileya multiradiata
Sunflower Family (Asteraceae)

Description: Grayish, woolly plants 8–12" tall, in large plants hemispheric in form, with brilliant yellow flower heads about 1½" across held well above the foliage. Heads borne singly at ends of stems, each with 30–40 3-toothed rays about ½" long, a central disk about ½" wide, and 2–3 overlapping series of bracts ¼" long. No scales or bristles atop the seedlike fruit. Leaves mostly in the lower half of plant, 1½–3" long, pinnately lobed.

Flowering Season: Throughout the year, most vigorously July–October.

Habitat/Range: Sandy plains, roadsides, 2,000–5,000', southeastern California to southern Utah and western Texas, south into northern Mexico.

Comments: A common wildflower, when blooming vigorously forming bright yellow hemispheres that are spectacular in arid landscapes. Plants may often form dense stands and may line roadsides. When planted in the yard and given supplemental water, a plant may bloom during all the warm months. The species is said to be highly toxic to livestock, but plants are distasteful and usually avoided except under the most severe range conditions.

Laxflower

LAXFLOWER
Baileya pauciradiata
Sunflower Family (Asteraceae)

Description: Grayish, lightly woolly plants 4–30", branched mostly at base, with small, pale yellow flower heads in clusters of 2–3. Rays 4–8, ⅛–⅜" long, more or less translucent, at first spreading and spoon-shaped, soon bent back against head. Disk flowers 8–20. Bracts around head 8–10, narrowly lanceolate, ¼" long, woolly. Seedlike fruit ⅛" long, brown, club-shaped, without bristles or scales at top. Leaves mostly on stem, linear or narrowly lanceolate, sometimes divided into narrow lobes, 1½–5" long.

Flowering Season: December–June, sometimes October.

Habitat/Range: Sandy deserts, below 3,500', southeastern California, southwestern Arizona, northwestern Mexico.

Comments: Laxflower may be single-stemmed and small in dry years, large and bushy after sufficient rain.

SWEETBUSH, CHUPAROSA, JUNCO
Bebbia juncea
Sunflower Family (Asteracee)

Description: A bush up to 3' high with many slender, rushlike branches ending in golden yellow flower heads. Flower heads about ½" tall and ½" wide, with no ray flowers, 20–30 disk flowers, and about 20 bracts in 3 series around head. Seedlike fruit with 15–20 feathery bristles at top. Leaves few, linear, ½–2" long, withering early and falling from the plant.

Flowering Season: April–October, but often with a few flowers most of the year.

Habitat/Range: Dry, gravelly and rocky areas, 100–4,000', southeastern California to southern Nevada and western Texas, south to northwestern Mexico.

Comments: Chuckawallas relish the yellow flower heads, providing a common name of Chuckawalla's Delight. Insects visit the plants for the nectar, giving the Spanish name Chuparosa (from "suck"). Junco, for "rush," refers to the plant's habit.

Sweetbush, Chuparosa, Junco

ARIZONA TICKSEED
Coreopsis californica var. *newberryi*
Sunflower Family (Asteraceae)

Description: Hairless plants with dark green, threadlike leaves all at base and yellow flower heads borne singly on leafless stalks 2–12" tall. Ray flowers 5–12, ½–1" long. Disk ¼–⅜" diameter, with 10–30 flowers. Bracts around head in 2 series: outer series with 2–7 bracts ¼" long, with reddish or yellowish glandular hairs at base, inner series of 5–8 bracts slightly longer, pale and translucent on edges. Seedlike fruit ¼" long, flattened, with winglike edges, brownish, spotted with red in center. Leaves ¾–4" long, sometimes divided into 1–2 threadlike lobes.

Flowering Season: February–May.

Habitat/Range: Gravelly washes, 1,500–3,500', south-central Arizona.

Comments: The genus name comes from Greek, meaning "like a bed bug," in reference to the fruit.

Arizona Tickseed

African Daisy, Cape Marigold

AFRICAN DAISY, CAPE MARIGOLD
Dimorphotheca sinuata
Sunflower Family (Asteraceae)

Description: Showy plants 4–12" tall, with bright yellow or orange rays on heads borne singly at top of long stalk. Rays 1" long, often dark violet at base or tip; disk flowers colored as rays, often purple tipped. Seedlike fruits that develop from ray flowers nearly ¼" long, 3-angled, the surface knobby; those that develop from disk flowers ¼" long or slightly longer, flattened, with wings along edges, the surface smooth. Leaves 1–4" long, often toothed, glandular-hairy, oblong or inversely lanceolate, or upper leaves linear.

Flowering Season: February–April.

Habitat/Range: Roadsides and fields, mostly below 3,000', southern California to southern Arizona.

Comments: This southern African native is a popular annual in gardens. It is added to "wildflower" seed mix spread along highways, reseeding itself in many areas.

Brittlebush, Incienso, Goldenhills

BRITTLEBUSH, INCIENSO, GOLDENHILLS
Encelia farinosa
Sunflower Family (Asteraceae)

Description: Round, shrubby plants 1–5' tall, with brilliant yellow flower heads held well above the silvery-gray foliage. Heads in loose clusters on hairless stems, about 2" across. Rays broadly lanceolate, about ½" long. Seed-like fruits without bristles or scales at top.

Flowering Season: November–May.

Habitat/Range: Dry, rocky slopes, 0–3,000', southeastern California to southern Nevada, southern Arizona, and northwestern Mexico.

Comments: These drought-resistant plants form spectacular globes of yellow when in full bloom and now are popular in xeriscapes in the arid American Southwest. It was burned as incense in churches in northwestern Mexico. Plants exude compounds that when washed from the leaves and deposited in the soil, inhibit germination of other plants, potential competitors for precious resources.

BUTTON BRITTLEBUSH
Encelia frutescens var. *frutescens*
Sunflower Family (Asteraceae)

Description: A round, well-branched shrub 2–5' high with dull yellow, rayless flower heads, usually 1 per stalk held well above the foliage. Heads ½–1" wide, the bracts overlapping in 2–3 series, with stiff, short hairs. Seedlike fruit may have 2 slender scales at top. Leaves broadly lanceolate or ovate, harshly hairy with stiff hairs that have swollen bases. Edges of leaves without teeth or with a pair of poorly defined teeth near base. Stems commonly whitish.

Flowering Season: January–September.

Habitat/Range: Rocky slopes and flats, common along roadsides, below 4,000', southeastern California to southern Nevada, southern Arizona, and northwestern Mexico.

Comments: This very common shrub, though not as showy as its relative, Brittlebush, may color the landscape in a rich, muted yellow.

Button Brittlebush

Turpentine Brush

TURPENTINE BRUSH
Ericameria laricifolia
Sunflower Family (Asteraceae)

Description: A dense, rounded shrub 1–3' tall, with linear leaves and an aromatic, resinous odor. Flower heads yellow, narrow, slightly less than ½" high, in leafy clusters, each with 0–11 narrow rays about ¼" long and 5–16 disk flowers that extend well beyond top of bracts. Bracts of head in several series, overlapping, pointed. Seedlike fruits densely hairy, with very slender, pale tan bristles at top. Leaves ½–¾" long, with glandular dots.

Flowering Season: August–November.

Habitat/Range: Rocky areas, 3,000–6,500', southeastern California to western Texas and northwestern Mexico.

Comments: This is one of the most handsome shrubs when in full flower, now cultivated and used in arid landscape design. It is one of the last plants of the season to bloom.

Interior Goldenbush

INTERIOR GOLDENBUSH
Ericameria linearifolia
Sunflower Family (Asteraceae)

Description: Shrubby plants 1½–7' tall, with linear leaves and golden yellow flower heads with 13–18 narrow rays ⅜–½" long. Base of heads hemispherical, ⅜–½" high, the bracts lanceolate, in 2–3 series, beset with granular glands. Seedlike fruit silky-hairy, ³⁄₁₆" long, the top with a tuft of fine, white bristles ¼" long. Leaves ½–1½" long, dark green, with dotlike glands.

Flowering Season: March–June.

Habitat/Range: Rocky or sandy hillsides and flats, below 6,000', southern California to southwestern Utah, western Arizona, and northwestern Mexico.

Comments: Leaves have a resinous odor when crushed, imparted by the glands, making plants unpalatable to browsing animals. When in full bloom shrubs may be a globe of yellow.

PRINGLE'S WOOLLY-DAISY
Eriophyllum pringlei
Sunflower Family (Asteraceae)

Description: Very low plants with tiny, rayless heads of numerous dull yellow disk flowers nestle among very woolly leaves. Heads hemispherical, ⅛–¼" across, containing 10–25 flowers. Around head are 6–8 boat-shaped, very woolly bracts. Seedlike fruit ¹⁄₁₀" long, silvery-hairy, with 8–12 fringed, translucent, tan scales at top. Leaves wedge-shaped, usually 3-lobed at tip, ¼–½" long. Stems 1–3" long, branched, tufted-spreading.

Flowering Season: March–June.

Habitat/Range: Sandy, open soil, 1,000–7,000', western borders of deserts in southern California, also in southern Nevada and southern Arizona.

Comments: This tiny, often inconspicuous wildflower is common in parts of southern Arizona, often forming grayish yellow patches across suitable habitat.

Pringle's Woolly-Daisy

YELLOW WOOLLY-DAISY
Eriophyllum wallacei
Sunflower Family (Asteraceae)

Description: Dwarf plants with bright yellow heads about ½" across nestled among white, woolly leaves. Rays 5–10, broad and blunt, ⅛" long. Bracts around head usually same number as rays, pointed, ¼" long. Seedlike fruit about ⅒" long, very slender and club-shaped, with a minute crown of scales at top. Leaves broader near tip, ¼–½" long, sometimes 3-toothed at tip. Stems usually reclining on ground, ½–6" long, often forming tufts.

Flowering Season: March–June.

Habitat/Range: Open, sandy or loamy soil, 200–5,000', southeastern California to southwestern Utah, northwestern Arizona, and northwestern Mexico.

Comments: These diminutive plants are common in washes after winter and spring rains. Along the western edge of the desert, rays may be rose-blushed or whitish.

Yellow Woolly-Daisy

Arizona Blanket-Flower

ARIZONA BLANKET-FLOWER
Gaillardia arizonica
Sunflower Family (Asteraceae)

Description: Yellow heads with prominent 3-lobed rays top naked, 4–10" tall stalks that arise from a basal cluster of pinnately divided leaves. Rays fan-shaped, ½" long. Disk ½" wide. Bracts around head lanceolate, in 2–3 overlapping series, hairy, ⅜" long, the tips bending back as fruits mature. Seedlike fruit like a narrow, brownish, hairy, upside-down pyramid ⅛" long, topped by 8-10 scales ⅒" long. Leaves 2–3" long, hairy, lobes scalloped.

Flowering Season: February–July.

Habitat/Range: Arid, open areas, 1,000–4,000', southern Nevada and Utah to southern Arizona .

Comments: There are two varieties: *arizonica* has scales atop the seedlike fruit blunt at tip, without well-defined midribs; *pringlei* has scales, each with a midrib extending into a sharp point.

Desert Sunflower, Desert Gold

DESERT SUNFLOWER, DESERT GOLD

Geraea canescens
Sunflower Family (Asteraceae)

Description: Coarsely hairy plants 1–2½' tall, with golden flower heads 2–3" across held well above grayish green leaves. Rays 10–21, ½–¾" long, shallowly toothed at ends. Bracts around head in 2–3 series, lanceolate, ¼–½" long, hairy. Each disk flower in center of head enfolded by a scale. Seedlike fruit ¼" long, flat and wedge-shaped, edges white and long-hairy; at top of each edge is an erect spine. Leaves mostly near base of plant, lanceolate to oval, 1–4" long, those near base with broad, flat stalks, those near top without stalks.

Flowering Season: October–June.

Habitat/Range: Sand, below 3,000', southeastern California to southwestern Utah, western Arizona, and northwestern Arizona.

Comments: The genus name derives from a Greek word for "old," in reference to the dense gray hairs on the ring of bracts on the flower head. Desert Sunflower, a handsome plant in dense stands, or when there is sufficient water, is used occasionally for an ornamental. It occasionally hybridizes with Brittlebush *(Encelia farinosa)*.

STICKY SNAKEWEED, SMALL-HEAD SNAKEWEED
Gutierrezia microcephala
Sunflower Family (Asteraceae)

Description: Low, many-branched shrublet 1–2½' tall, with thousands of tiny yellow flower heads, each with 1–2 disk flowers and 1–2 ray flowers ⅛" long. Heads cylindrical or slightly swollen, ⅛" high, in clusters of 2-5. Bracts whitish yellow, slightly swollen in middle. Seedlike fruits ⅒" long, lightly hairy, with a few minute scales at top. Leaves linear, ¾–2" long.

Flowering Season: Summer–fall.

Habitat/Range: Open desert, plains, and woodland, 1,000–7,000', southern California to western Texas and Colorado.

Comments: Plants are entirely yellow when the thousands of flowers are in bloom. The related Broom Snakeweed, Matchweed, or Kindlingweed *(G. sarothrae)*, even more widespread in western North America, has tiny bell-shaped heads with 2–8 ray flowers and about as many disk flowers.

Sticky Snakeweed, Small-Head Snakeweed

COMMON SUNFLOWER, MIRASOL, GIRASOL
Helianthus annuus
Sunflower Family (Asteraceae)

Description: Tall plants, sparsely harsh-hairy, usually branched, bearing large heads with a dark brown center and yellow rays. Flower heads with disk 1–3" across, with 12–35 lanceolate rays 1–2" long. Bracts around head in several series, smooth to rough hairy, ovate, ½–1" long, tapered to a long, slender tip. Seedlike fruit enfolded by stiff scale on disk, more or less flattened, light gray, ⅛–½" long, with 2 broad scales at edges at top. Stems 3–10' tall, often branched.

Flowering Season: March–October.

Habitat/Range: Disturbed areas, 100–7,000', much of North America.

Comments: This plant is called Mirasol, "it looks at the sun," because the heads face the sun from morning to evening, returning to face east in the morning. Many variations of this species have been cultivated for seed, oil, and ornamental plants.

Common Sunflower, Mirasol, Girasol

Blueweed

BLUEWEED
Helianthus ciliaris
Sunflower Family (Asteraceae)

Description: Smooth, greenish blue plants, usually in patches, bearing heads about 1½" across, with yellow rays. Disk dark brown, ½–1" across. Rays 12–18, ½–¾" long. Bracts around head in several series, ovate, hairy on edges, ¼" long. Seedlike fruit enfolded by scales on disk, black or dark gray, slightly flattened, ⅛" long, with 2 broad, pointed scales at top at edges. Midstem leaves opposite, linear to broadly lanceolate or oblong, either not lobed or pinnately lobed, 1½–3" long. Stems 20–30" tall.

Flowering Season: June–November.

Habitat/Range: Clay, often where saline, especially in low spots or along canals, 1,000–6,500', southern California to western Texas, south into Mexico.

Comments: This plant has deep, creeping rootstocks, and can be an aggressive weed in agricultural areas.

PLAINS SUNFLOWER
Helianthus petiolaris
Sunflower Family (Asteraceae)

Description: Grayish, hairy plants bearing heads 2–3" across with 10–30 yellow rays. Disk brown, ½–1" across. Rays ¾–1" long, 3-toothed. Bract around head lanceolate or ovate, rough with short hairs, ⅜–½" long. Seedlike fruit enfolded by scales on disk, grayish, pale striped, silky-hairy, 3/16" long, with 2 scales at top at edges. Scales in center of disk long-hairy. Leaves lanceolate, triangular, or ovate, 1½–6" long, hairy, the edges smooth or toothed. Stems often several, usually branched, 2–7' tall.

Flowering Season: March–October.

Habitat/Range: Sandy places, 500–7,500', much of western United States and Mexico.

Comments: When vigorous, plants form a large, rounded mass of yellow flower heads, attractive in gardens. Finches relish the seedlike fruits.

Plains Sunflower

Longleaf False Golden-Eye

LONGLEAF FALSE GOLDEN-EYE
Heliomeris longifolia var. *annua*
Sunflower Family (Asteraceae)

Description: Slender, erect, wiry plants with linear leaves and small golden yellow heads. Rays about 12, broad, commonly curled back, ¼–½" long. Disk ¼–⅜" across. Bracts around head in 2 series, lanceolate, tapered to a fine point, with hairs that lie flat against surface. Seedlike fruit ⅒" long, blackish, hairless, without scales or hairs at top. Leaves 1¼–2½" long, ⅛" wide, with a prominent midvein, edges rolled under. Stems 8–28" tall.

Flowering Season: May–October.

Habitat/Range: Open hills and plains, 2,500–7,000', southern Arizona to western Texas and northwestern Mexico.

Comments: This species is sometimes so common it colors the landscape over broad areas. In quantity plants are toxic to cattle; it is apparently good forage for sheep.

Camphorweed

CAMPHORWEED
Heterotheca subaxillaris
Sunflower Family (Asteraceae)

Description: Erect, hairy, glandular plants up to 7' tall, with yellow flower heads in an array of spreading branches at top of leafy, few-branched stem. Rays 15–45, ¼–½" long; disk ⅜–½" wide, with 25–45 disk flowers. Many bracts on head, lanceolate, overlapping, hairy, glandular, forming a cup ¼" high. Seedlike fruits flattened, broader near top, those of disk flowers topped with brownish bristles, those of ray flowers without bristles. Leaves ovate to elliptical, 1½–4" long, toothed on edges or not, those on stem without stalks.

Flowering Season: March–November.

Habitat/Range: Abundant along roadsides and ditches, 1,000–5,000', much of the American Southwest.

Comments: The open cluster of bright flowers above the dark, leafy stems resembles a burst of fireworks, a distinctive form that helps recognition.

YELLOW THIMBLEHEAD
Hymenothrix wislizeni
Sunflower Family (Asteraceae)

Description: Branched plants 2–5' tall, with small yellow flower heads in clusters at ends of branches. Heads ⅛" high and wide, with about 8 shallowly 3-toothed rays ⅛" long. Disk flowers with a conspicuously expanded throat above the slender tube. Seedlike fruits black, 4- or 5-angled, pointed at base, flat at top, topped with 10–15 lanceolate, translucent, long-pointed, ³⁄₁₆" long scales. Scales have a dark midvein extending into the slender point. Leaves mostly near base, 2–5" long, divided into 3 divisions, each division again 3-divided into linear or oblong segments.

Flowering Season: June–December.

Habitat/Range: Sandy soil, 2,500–5,000', southern Arizona, New Mexico, northwestern Mexico.

Comments: Plants are common along roadsides where they receive extra water from pavement runoff.

Yellow Thimblehead

Bitterweed, Poison Rubberweed

BITTERWEED, POISON RUBBERWEED
Hymenoxys odorata
Sunflower Family (Asteraceae)

Description: Pinwheel heads of yellow flowers on branched plants 4–24" tall. Rays 6–13, ¼–½" long, each narrowly fan-shaped, 3-toothed at tip; many disk flowers form a yellow button in center. Bracts on head ¼" long, outer ones joined and thickened at base. Seed-like fruit ¹⁄₁₀" long, indistinctly 4-angled, covered with silvery hairs that lie flat against surface, with 5–8 narrowly pointed scales ¹⁄₁₀" long at tip. Leaves up to 2" long, pinnately divided into 3–15 linear segments.

Flowering Season: January–June.

Habitat/Range: Clay soil, 0–6,000', throughout southwestern United States, northern Mexico.

Comments: Bitterweed is restricted to low areas on the Sonoran Desert, often coloring small basins golden yellow. Elsewhere, prior to about 1925 bitterweed was abundant only in such small basins and in low areas of rangeland. Intensive grazing and reduction in perennial grasses and other plants is believed to have contributed to the spread of this weed into rangeland. It is toxic to sheep. Only about 1 percent of their body weight, consumed in a short time or over several months, is lethal. It is distasteful, and therefore seems to be avoided by horses and cattle.

Jimmy-Weed, Rayless Goldenrod

JIMMY-WEED, RAYLESS GOLDENROD
Isocoma pluriflora
Sunflower Family (Asteraceae)

Description: Semi-woody plants 1–4' tall, with narrow leaves and rounded or flattened clusters of small, yellow flower heads. Flower heads without rays: disk flowers 7–15, about ¼" long, abruptly expanded above the narrow tube. Ring of bracts around head ³⁄₁₆" high, the bracts ovate, straw-colored at base, greenish at tip. Seedlike fruit about ¹⁄₁₀" long, silky-hairy, with numerous tiny, straw-colored bristles at top. Leaves linear, ⅛–½" wide, usually without teeth, or those near the base sometimes with teeth.

Flowering Season: June–October.

Habitat/Range: Sandy or clay soils, often where saline, below 5,000', from southwestern Arizona to Utah, Colorado, Texas, and northern Mexico.

Comments: This plant is toxic to livestock, causing "trembles," but is distasteful and is rarely eaten.

CALIFORNIA GOLDFIELDS
Lasthenia gracilis
Sunflower Family (Asteraceae)

Description: Slender plants with opposite leaves and golden flower heads ¾" across. Rays 6–13, ¼–⅜ long, narrowly oval. Disk flowers many. Base of head hemispherical, with 4–13 broadly lanceolate, hairy bracts. Seedlike fruit linear or club-shaped, hairy, ⅛" long, 4-angled, gray or black, with 2–6 slender, lanceolate scales at top, or scales lacking. Leaves linear or lanceolate, often broader toward tip. Stems branched or not, 6–16" tall.

Flowering Season: March–May.

Habitat/Range: Open areas, below 4,500', Oregon through California to southern Arizona, Baja California.

Comments: Extensive areas may be carpeted in gold by this plant. When crowded, stems of individual plants are often unbranched; when plants are alone in the open, stems may be widely branched and have many heads.

California Goldfields

LACY TANSEY-ASTER, CUTLEAF IRONPLANT
Machaeranthera pinnatifida
Sunflower Family (Asteraceae)

Description: Golden yellow flower heads with narrow rays top plants with pinnately toothed, bristle-tipped leaves. Rays 15–30 or more, ⅜" long; disk flowers many, also yellow, on a disk ⅜–½" wide. Bracts around head narrow, overlapping in several series, tapered to a fine, often bristle-tipped point. Leaves oblong in outline, ½–2½" long. Stems few to many, 8–24" tall, the stems and foliage usually lightly woolly, sometimes also glandular.

Flowering Season: March–October.

Habitat/Range: Dry, open areas, 2,000–5,000', much of the American Southwest and Great Plains.

Comments: This common perennial is variable, with several subspecies and many varieties. It has a plethora of scientific names because local variants have been named and have been placed in several genera as specialists sought a satisfactory classification during the past 2 centuries.

Lacy Tansey-Aster, Cutleaf Ironplant

Fendler's Desert-Dandelion

FENDLER'S DESERT-DANDELION
Malacothrix fendleri
Sunflower Family (Asteraceae)

Description: Yellow flower heads about 1" across, with only strap-shaped flowers, are held on branched stalks above a rosette of leaves. Bracts around head narrowly lanceolate, with pale, translucent edges, the inner bracts equal, about ⅓" long, the 2-3 outer bracts very short. Leaves lanceolate in outline, usually deeply lobed, 1–4" long. Seedlike fruit cylindrical, ⅒" long, with 15 ribs, bearing at top numerous soft bristles that all fall off as a unit, leaving behind usually 1 stouter bristle. Stems 4–10" tall.

Flowering Season: March–June.

Habitat/Range: Sandy and rocky areas, 2,000–5,000', southern Arizona to western Texas.

Comments: The similar Scalebud, *Anisocoma acaulis,* has broad, overlapping, rounded bracts with broad, translucent edges. It barely enters the northern edge of the Sonoran Desert.

Desert Dandelion

DESERT DANDELION
Malacothrix glabrata
Sunflower Family (Asteraceae)

Description: Bright yellow flower heads are held above dark green, deeply divided leaves. Heads with only strap-shaped flowers, the outer ones ½–¾" long, those toward center much shorter, each with 5 tiny teeth on the blunt tip. Young heads have a central "button" of maroon buds. Bracts around head lanceolate, sharply pointed, outer about half the length of inner. Seedlike fruit slender, ⅛" long, prominently ribbed, with a few irregular bristles at top. Leaves mostly at base, 3–6" long, divided into a few linear lobes. Stems 2–16" tall, usually few-branched.

Flowering Season: March–June.

Habitat/Range: Coarse, sandy soil, below 6,000', Oregon, Idaho, Utah, and south to Mexico.

Comments: After wet winters, Desert Dandelion may carpet the desert floor with extensive patches of brilliant yellow.

CHINCHWEED, MANSANILLA DEL COYOTE
Pectis papposa
Sunflower Family (Asteraceae)

Description: Low, mounded plants with opposite, linear leaves, small yellow flower heads in clusters, and an odor reminiscent of lemon-scented furniture polish. Heads with 8 oval rays ⅛–¼" long. Bracts around head usually 8, narrow, pointed, ³⁄₁₆" long. Seedlike fruit narrowly cylindrical, lightly hairy, ⅛" long, topped by a low crown of tiny scales. Leaves ½–2½" long, the edges bearing embedded, circular oil glands and with 2–5 pairs of bristly hairs near base. Stems 4–10" long, repeatedly forked.

Flowering Season: June–December.

Habitat/Range: Sandy soil, 0–5,000', much of Arizona, New Mexico, southeastern California, and northwestern Mexico.

Comments: Chinchweed usually appears after summer rains, sometimes becoming so frequent that expanses of sandy desert are covered in yellow.

Chinchweed, Mansanilla del Coyote

Pigmy-Cedar, Romero

PIGMY-CEDAR, ROMERO
Peucephyllum schottii
Sunflower Family (Asteraceae)

Description: Dark green, densely leafy shrubs 2–10' tall, with linear leaves and pale yellow flowers in rayless heads. Disk flowers 12–21, ¼–⅜" long, the anthers conspicuously protruding. Bracts around head in 1 series, narrowly lanceolate, ⅜–½" long, gland-dotted near slender tip. Seedlike fruit ⅛" long, club-shaped, blackish, bristly hairy, with a tuft of fine bristles and sometimes also narrow scales at top. Leaves ½–¾" long, dotted with glands.

Flowering Season: December–May.

Habitat/Range: Rocky slopes and banks, below 5,000', southeastern California to southern Nevada, western Arizona, and northwestern Mexico.

Comments: There is only 1 species of *Peucephyllum*, the name meaning "fir leaf," in reference to the needlelike leaves. The glands give a resinous odor.

Turtleback, Desert Velvet

TURTLEBACK, DESERT VELVET

Psathyrotes ramosissima
Sunflower Family (Asteraceae)

Description: Grayish, dome-shaped plants 2–5" high, 2–12" broad, with small, yellow, rayless flower heads tucked among the leaves. Flower heads ¼–½" tall, with 5 outer bracts and 12–15 slightly longer inner bracts. Leaf blades on long stalks, roundish, ¼–¾" long, deeply scalloped, whitish, densely velvety, the veins deeply impressed on the upper surface. Seedlike fruits densely hairy, ⅛" long, with many fine, brownish bristles at top. Stems brittle, repeatedly branched, to 6" long.

Flowering Season: Mostly March–June, but may flower any time of year.

Habitat/Range: Dry, open places, mostly below 3,000', southeastern California to southern Nevada, southwestern Utah, western Arizona, and northwestern Mexico.

Comments: The genus names derives from Greek for "brittleness," in reference to the brittle stems. The leaves are closely adjacent to one another, forming a dome reminiscent of a turtle's shell.

WHITE-STEM PAPER-FLOWER
Psilostrophe cooperi
Sunflower Family (Asteraceae)

Description: Densely branched, white, woolly plants have yellow flower heads with 3–6 broad rays. Rays almost round, ⅜–¾" long, with 3 small teeth at end. Bracts form a cylinder ⅛" across, ¼" long, the 5–8 outer bracts lanceolate, hairy, the 4–5 shorter inner bracts translucent. Seedlike fruits brown, slender, somewhat angled, ⅛" long, topped by 4–6 transparent scales ¹⁄₁₀" long. Leaves linear, ½–3" long. Stems 8–24" long.

Flowering Season: Mostly April–June, and October–December, but other times of year as well.

Habitat/Range: Sandy or gravelly soil, 500–5,000', southeastern California to southwestern Utah, southern Arizona, and northwestern Mexico.

Comments: When in full flower the plants form handsome, brilliant yellow globes. As flowers age, rays become dry and papery, finally fading to dull white. Dried flowers may be used in floral arrangements.

White-Stem Paperflower

SMOOTH THREADLEAF RAGWORT
Senecio flaccidus var. *monoensis*
Sunflower Family (Asteraceae)

Description: Somewhat shrubby, dark green plants 1–4' tall, with narrowly linear, usually divided leaves, and yellow flower heads. Rays narrow, ½–¾" long, usually 8 or 13, surrounding a disk ⅜" wide. Pointed bracts around head ¼–⅜" long, about 13 or 21 in number, the inner ones lined up side by side, the outer ones irregularly placed, nearly half the length of inner. Seedlike fruit narrow, hairy, ³⁄₁₆" long, topped by numerous fine white bristles ¼" long. Leaves 1–4" long, usually with at least a few linear lobes.

Flowering Season: Mostly March–May, but flowering throughout the year.

Habitat/Range: Dry slopes and washes, 1,000–6,600', much of the American Southwest and northern Mexico.

Comments: Hairy Threadleaf Ragwort *(S. flaccidus* var. *douglasii),* with grayish, hairy foliage, is common around the upper edge of the Sonoran Desert and beyond.

SmoothThreadleaf Ragwort

Dandelion, Blowball, Chicória

DANDELION, BLOWBALL, CHICÓRIA
Taraxacum officinale
Sunflower Family (Asteraceae)

Description: Heads of bright yellow, strap-shaped flowers are borne singly on hollow, 2–10" tall stalks originating at center of a rosette of jaggedly toothed leaves. Heads ¾–1¼" wide. Seedlike fruit ⅛" long, slender and tapered at both ends, at the top with a very slender extension that grows longer as fruit matures, putting the feathery, parachute-like end into the wind. Leaves inversely lanceolate in outline, 2–12" long. Stalk and leaves bleed milky sap when broken.

Flowering Season: Mostly October–April, but flowering in cool places much of the year.

Habitat/Range: A weed in watered areas in the Sonoran Desert region, below 10,000', throughout much of the world.

Comments: Early settlers probably introduced this plant. Leaves make good salad greens, and flower heads make delicate wine.

FIVE-NEEDLE PRICKLYLEAF, PARRALENA
Thymophylla pentachaeta var. *belenidium*
Sunflower Family (Asteracee)

Description: Round plants 4–8" high, with small golden flower heads about ½" wide held above the foliage on slender, 1–4" long stalks. Ray flowers usually 13, about ⅛" long. Bracts around head hairless in 2 sets, the outer with 3–5 very short and triangular bracts, the inner with 12–17 bracts about ¼" long, united along their edges more than half their length, dotted with a few dark glands near tips. Seedlike fruit topped with scales, some having stiff, pinlike tips. Leaves stiff, divided into 3–5 linear, prickle-tipped lobes.

Flowering Season: March–October.

Habitat/Range: Dry slopes and flats, 2,500–6,000', southeastern California to western Texas, northern Mexico; also South America.

Comments: Other varieties vary in number of lobes on leaves, hairiness, or characteristics of scales atop the fruit.

Five-Needle Pricklyleaf, Parralena

YELLOWDOME, YELLOWHEAD
Trichoptilium incisum
Sunflower Family (Asteraceae)

Description: Tufted, woolly-hairy plants with conspicuously toothed leaves and yellow, rayless flower heads borne singly on slender stalks. Heads nearly ½" high, surrounded by lanceolate bracts ¼" long. Stalks beneath heads 1–5" tall. Seedlike fruit ⅛" long, broadest at upper end, hairless or densely hairy, topped by 5 feathery scales ¼" long, each divided into many bristles. Stems 2–10" long.

Flowering Season: February–May, sometimes also October–November.

Habitat/Range: Dry slopes and flats, below 3,300', southeastern California to southern Nevada, western Arizona, and Baja California.

Comments: The genus name derives from Greek words meaning "feathery bristle," in reference to the feathery scales on the top of the seedlike fruit. The bright yellow heads contrast attractively against the soft gray foliage.

Yellowdome, Yellowhead

American Threefold, Trixis, Plumilla

AMERICAN THREEFOLD, TRIXIS, PLUMILLA
Trixis californica
Sunflower Family (Asteraceae)

Description: Semi-shrubby plants 1–3' high, with 9–25 small, bilateral yellow flowers in heads aggregated in branched, leafy clusters. Heads ½–¾" long. Individual flower with 3-lobed lower lip, this usually spreading, and a 2-lobed upper lip that is usually curled back. Seedlike fruit cylindrical, 5-nerved, ½" long, densely hairy, topped by a tuft of soft, straw-colored bristles. Leaves lanceolate, ¾–2" long.

Flowering Season: Most vigorously February–April, but throughout the year.

Habitat/Range: Rocky slopes, below 5,000', southern California to western Texas and northwestern Mexico.

Comments: The genus name and the English common name refer to the 3-lobed lower lip of the flower. The Spanish name means "little feather," in reference to the fruiting head.

Silverpuffs

SILVERPUFFS
Uropappus lindleyi
Sunflower Family (Asteraceae)

Description: Heads of seedlike fruits with silvery, daggerlike scales form conspicuous spheres about 1½" wide. Flower heads yellow, about ½" across, consisting of only strapshaped flowers. Bracts around head narrowly lanceolate, ½–1" long, the outer bracts progressively shorter. Seedlike fruit blackish, very slender, ¼–½" long, tapered to tip, bearing 5 lanceolate scales at top, ¼–½" long, each with a brownish midvein ending in a bristle tip ¼" long. Leaves in a basal rosette, 2–12" long, linear, often with small, sparse, linear lobes. Stems 2–28" tall, sap milky.

Flowering Season: March–June.

Habitat/Range: Open areas, below 6,000', much of western United States and in northwestern Mexico.

Comments: In the sunlight the silvery heads glisten and are conspicuous from a distance.

COWPEN DAISY, GOLDEN CROWNBEARD
Verbesina encelioides
Sunflower Family (Asteraceae)

Description: Bright yellow flower heads about 1½" across are held on long stalks above leaves. Rays ovate, ½" long, deeply 3-toothed at the ends; disk flowers many, forming a large button in center of head. Seedlike fruit broader at upper end, flattened, with fine, winglike extensions on narrow edges, with 2 short spines at top of fruit that easily drop off. Leaves mostly opposite, narrowly triangular, up to about 6" long, edges toothed. Stems 6–60" tall.

Flowering Season: April–November.

Habitat/Range: Disturbed areas, where often receiving extra water, 0–6,000', throughout the American Southwest and in northern Mexico.

Comments: Infusions made from this plant were used by early settlers and Native Americans to treat skin diseases, insect bites, and, as a tea, stomach disorders, diarrhea, or rheumatism.

Cowpen Daisy, Golden Crownbeard

Yellow Trumpetbush

YELLOW TRUMPETBUSH
Tecoma stans
Catalpa Family (Bignoniaceae)

Description: A many-stemmed shrub to 10' tall, with pinnately compound leaves and large, bright yellow, bilateral flowers. Flower about 2" long, the open end with 2 lobes flared upward and 3 downward. Leaves opposite, with 3–9 lanceolate, toothed, 2–5" long leaflets. Fruits hanging, 3–8" long, about ½" wide, filled with flat seeds with papery white wings.

Flowering Season: May–October.

Habitat/Range: Rocky slopes, 2,500–5,500', southern Arizona to Texas, south into tropical America.

Comments: This is now a popular ornamental that with a little water provides spectacular blooms all summer long. Horticultural variants with coral-tinged flowers are now available. Plants may freeze to the ground each year; in the frost-free areas they become small trees or robust shrubs.

Mexican Yellowshow

MEXICAN YELLOWSHOW
Amoreuxia palmatifida
Lipstick-Tree Family (Bixaceae)

Description: Large, yellow-orange, bowl-shaped flowers twisted to 1 side are held just above palmately lobed leaves. Stamens many, in 1 long set and 1 short set. Two petals opposite the set of long stamens each have 2 maroon spots at base; side petals with 1 spot; petal next to long stamens with no spots. Leaves 1½–8" wide, with 7–9 coarsely toothed lobes ¾–1½" wide. Plants 10–20" tall.

Flowering Season: July–August.

Habitat/Range: Rocky slopes and flats, 3,500–5,500', southeastern Arizona and adjacent New Mexico; also in Sonora.

Comments: This striking wildflower occurs at the upper edge of the Sonoran Desert, to be discovered as the enthusiast climbs into desert mountain ranges near the Mexican border. Fruits and roasted roots were used as food by Native Americans.

RANCHER'S FIREWEED, DEVIL'S LETTUCE
Amsinckia menziesii var. *intermedia*
Borage Family (Boraginaceae)

Description: Small, yellow-orange flowers bloom at the top of a fiddleneck flower cluster on bristly-hairy plants. Corolla trumpet-shaped, 5-lobed, ¼–⅖" long, ⅛–¼" wide; calyx with 5 narrowly lanceolate lobes joined near base, about half the length of the corolla. Leaves linear to narrowly lanceolate, ¾–6" long, those at base much larger. Fruit divides into 4 tiny, seedlike, minutely warty nutlets. Stems 8–40" tall, repeatedly forking.

Flowering Season: March–May.

Habitat/Range: Weedy or grassy places, mostly below 5,000', western United States and northwestern Mexico.

Comments: The stiff, sharp hairs make these plants unpleasant to touch. The flower cluster progressively uncoils, keeping newly opened flowers on top and easily available to pollinators.

Rancher's Fireweed, Devil's Lettuce

BLACK MUSTARD
Brassica nigra
Mustard Family (Brassicaceae)

Description: Sparsely to densely stiff-hairy plants 1–10' tall, bearing yellow flowers with 4 petals in terminal clusters on the branches. Petals ½" long, with a narrow stalklike base and a broad blade. Fruit a narrow, pod ½–¾" long, angled upward, and almost pressed against the stem. Leaves up to 1' long at base, shorter on stem, pinnately lobed, the lobes sharply toothed, the terminal lobe the largest.

Flowering Season: February–June.

Habitat/Range: Roadsides, waste areas near agricultural land, and in old fields, below 1,000–5,000' in the Sonoran Desert region, much of North America.

Comments: Seeds of this native of Europe, cultivated in many areas, are the source of most commercial mustard. The leaves of some variants are used for mustard greens.

Black Mustard

WESTERN WALLFLOWER
Erysimum capitatum
Mustard Family (Brassicaceae)

Description: Erect plants 1–4' tall, 1 to few stems ending in dense clusters of vivid yellow flowers with 4 petals. Petals ¾–1" long, with a very slender stalk included within sepals and a broad, bent back, terminal half. Stamens 6, 2 of them shorter than others. Fruit a very slender, more or less 4-sided pod 1½–6" long, angled strongly upward on stem. Leaves spreading in basal rosette and angled strongly upward on stem, lanceolate or oblong, coarsely toothed or not, 1–10" long.

Flowering Season: March–April in Sonoran Desert region, often later elsewhere.

Habitat/Range: Open areas, often washes and roadsides, 2,500–9,500', much of western United States.

Comments: Outside Sonoran Desert area, where flowers may be whitish, yellow, orange, or rust colored, the species descends to sea level or occurs as high as 13,000'.

Western Wallflower

Gordon's Bladderpod

GORDON'S BLADDERPOD
Lesquerella gordonii
Mustard Family (Brassicaceae)

Description: Slender, grayish plants with several 4–16" long stems, bright yellow 4-petaled flowers, and round, pea-sized pods. Petals broad, ⅜" long. Stamens 6, 4 long, 2 short. Pod spherical, hairless on exterior and on interior, ³⁄₁₆–⅜" diameter. Leaves oblong or lanceolate, often broader in upper half, coarsely toothed, ½–3" long, upper leaves less prominently lobed, smaller.

Flowering Season: February–May.

Habitat/Range: Sandy open places, below 5,000', southern Arizona to the southern Great Plains and northern Mexico.

Comments: This early wildflower may color extensive flats with yellow. The similar Moapa Bladderpod *(L. tenella),* from western Arizona and southeastern California, has pods sparsely hairy on exterior, densely so on interior.

GOLDEN PRINCE'S PLUME
Stanleya pinnata
Mustard Family (Brassicaceae)

Description: Plants 1½–6' tall, with dense spires of bright yellow flowers held above pinnately divided leaves. Petals 4, ½–¾" long, the blade and stalk about same length, the stalk with brownish hairs on inner surface. Stamens 6, about as long as petals. Ovary on a stalk ½–1" long. Fruit a slender pod 1½–3" long, with a silvery, lengthwise partition. Leaves grayish green, 2–8" long, divided into narrow segments.

Flowering Season: April–September.

Habitat/Range: Dry areas among brush, 1,000–5,000', much of the western United States.

Comments: Plants grow only on selenium-bearing soil, and thus are toxic to livestock. Under normal conditions animals avoid the plant. The species occurs on the northern margins of the Sonoran Desert, and sporadically at upper elevations within it.

Golden Prince's Plume

Santa Rita Pricklypear

SANTA RITA PRICKLYPEAR
Opuntia santa-rita
Cactus Family (Cactaceae)

Description: Purplish gray, densely branched cactus, usually spineless, up to 7' tall, 10' wide. Flowers with many lanceolate, yellow, petal-like parts, often reddish at base, the longest 1–1½". Pads round, 6–8" diameter, with many tufts of brownish, needlelike bristles ⅛–¼" long, occasionally with a few reddish brown spines on upper edge. Fruit ovate, reddish, 1–1½" long.

Flowering Season: March–April.

Habitat/Range: Open areas, 2,000–4,000', southern Arizona to western Texas, northwestern Mexico.

Comments: The brown bristles (glochids) are painfully irritating. The purple stems and yellow flowers are attractive in combination, making the plant popular as an ornamental. Purple Pricklypear *(O. macrocentra)* is similar, but has long, black spines along upper edges of pads.

Yellow Bee-Plant

YELLOW BEE-PLANT
Cleome lutea
Caper Family (Capparaceae)

Description: Widely branched, 1–7' tall plants, with palmately compound leaves and yellow flowers with 4 petals. Petals ½" long, oblong or ovate. Stamens usually 6, longer than petals. Fruit a pod 1½–2½" long, ¼" wide, hanging from a slender stalk that has a joint in the middle. Lower leaves usually with 5 lanceolate leaflets ½–2½" long; upper leaves usually with 3 leaflets.

Flowering Season: May–September.

Habitat/Range: Sandy soil, usually along streams or in low, water-collecting areas, 1,000–4,000' (higher outside Sonoran Desert area), much of western United States.

Comments: Plants have a foul odor. The southern Arizona plant has been called variety *jonesii,* distinguished by generally larger petals and fruits than more northern plants have.

BLADDERPOD BUSH, EJOTILLO
Isomeris arborea
Caper Family (Capparaceae)

Description: Shrubs 2–7' tall, with pinnately divided leaves, yellow flowers in elongate clusters at ends of branches, and hanging, bladdery, green pods beneath flowers. Petals 4, gently curved outward, ⅜–½" long. Stamens 6, ¾–1" long. Ovary on a stalk in center of flower, developing into an inflated, 1–2" long, hanging pod that ultimately becomes tan and leathery. Leaves grayish green, usually with 3 oval leaflets ½–2" long.

Flowering Season: Most of the year, most vigorously January–March.

Habitat/Range: Desert washes, 500–4,000', southern California and Baja California.

Comments: There is only 1 species of *Isomeris.* It also extends west of the mountains that delimit the western edge of the desert into the coastal scrub vegetation, descending there to sea level.

Bladderpod Bush, Ejotillo

JACKASS CLOVER
Wislizenia refracta ssp. *refracta*
Caper Family (Capparaceae)

Description: Profusely branched plants ½–8' tall, with compound leaves and tiny, yellow flowers. Petals 4, ⅒–¼" long. Fruit with 2 round segments ⅛" in diameter, on a stalk bent downward at elbowlike joint, ¼–⅜" long between fruit and joint. Style hairlike between the 2 fruit halves, 3⁄16" long. Leaves with 3 leaflets, each wider in upper part, ½–1½" long.

Flowering Season: April–November.

Habitat/Range: Washes, flats, roadsides, usually where alkaline, 1,000–6,500', southern California to western Texas and northwestern Mexico.

Comments: These ill-smelling plants are toxic to domestic animals, but are seldom eaten. The flowers produce a fine honey. The var. *palmeri*, at 0–1,000', has the upper leaves with only 1 leaflet, most likely an adaptation to conserve water.

Jackass Clover

Gila Live-Forever

GILA LIVE-FOREVER
Dudleya collomae
Stonecrop Family (Crassulaceae)

Description: Succulent plants have narrow, tapering leaves and narrow, yellow flowers in pink-stemmed, open, forked clusters. Petals 5, ½–⅝" long, erect, narrow, joined at base, the pointed tips curved outward. Leaves 10–20 in each rosette, 1½–6" long, widest at or near base, gently tapered to a long, pointed tip. Stems 6–24" tall, bearing small, triangular, spreading leaves.

Flowering Season: March–May, also October.

Habitat/Range: Rocky slopes, 2,000–6,000', central Arizona.

Comments: Worthy of cultivation, this handsome plant should not be taken from the field. Rather, it should be purchased from responsible dealers. Chalky Live-Forever *(D. pulverulenta* ssp. *arizonica),* from western Arizona and southern California, has red or yellow petals ½" long, a chalky powder on leaves, and an abrupt taper to leaf tips.

Melon-Loco

MELON-LOCO
Apodanthera undulata
Squash Family (Cucurbitaceae)

Description: Coarse, dark green plants with trailing stems up to 10' long, roundish, jagged-edged leaves, and yellow flowers with long, slender tubes. Flowers with 5 lobes about 1½" long, either male and in loose clusters, or female and solitary, both on the same plant, the female flowers larger and on younger parts of stem. Leaves kidney-shaped, 2–6" wide, irregularly pleated. Fruit spherical or oval, 2½–4" long, dark green, with about 10 longitudinal ridges.

Flowering Season: June–September.

Habitat/Range: Dry, often sandy or gravelly soils, 1,500–5,500', southern Arizona to western Texas and northern Mexico.

Comments: The plants have a disagreeable odor, and the flesh of the fruits is bitter, both deterrents to animals that might eat them. Oil may be pressed from the seeds.

BUFFALO GOURD, CALABAZILLA
Curbita foetidissima
Squash Family (Cucurbitaceae)

Description: Coarse, bluish green, trailing plants up to 20' long, with large, triangular, rough-hairy leaves. Flowers orange-yellow, urn-shaped, 5-lobed, about 4" long, the base ribbed and veiny. Male flowers with contorted stamens; female flowers with 3–5 bilobed stigmas. Leaves 4–12" long, on stout stalks slightly shorter. Fruits spherical, smooth, 2–4" in diameter, at first dark green with pale stripes, ultimately maturing to even yellow.

Flowering Season: May–August.

Habitat/Range: Sandy and gravelly soil, 1,000–7,000', southern California across the American Southwest to the southern plains, south into Mexico.

Comments: Plants have an unpleasant odor; *foetidissima* means "most smelly." The root is massive, sometimes weighing more than 100 pounds. Seeds are good sources of protein and oils.

Buffalo Gourd, Calabazilla

Coyote Melon

COYOTE MELON
Cucurbita palmata
Squash Family (Cucurbitaceae)

Description: Trailing stems 1–4' long with bluish green, rough-hairy, palmately divided leaves. Flowers yellow-orange, 2–3" long, urn-shaped, 5-lobed (varying 4–6). Male flowers with contorted stamens; female flowers with 3–5 2-lobed stigmas. Fruits spherical, light green with whitish bands and splotches, becoming yellow in age. Leaves 2–3½" long and broad, with 5 broadly to narrowly triangular lobes that meet about halfway to the point of attachment to leaf stalk, each lobe with a few irregular teeth.

Flowering Season: April–September.

Habitat/Range: Sandy areas, below 4,000', southeastern California to western Arizona and Baja California.

Comments: "Coyote" is a modifier referring to wild relatives of domestic plants. In O'odham lore, the rascal coyote ruins useful objects by defecating on them. Fingerleaf Gourd *(C. digitata)* has very narrow leaf lobes that are separate almost to the leaf stalk.

Maricopa Milkvetch

MARICOPA MILKVETCH
Astragalus lentiginosus var. *maricopae*
Bean Family (Fabaceae)

Description: Plants coarse, 12–20" tall, almost hairless, with pinnately compound leaves and slender, open spires of pale yellow "pea" flowers. Flowers ⅝" long, the banner longest, wings mid-length, keel shortest. Pod oriented upward on stem, ¾–1¼" long, ³⁄₁₆" wide, pointed at tip, slightly curved, when cut crosswise seen to be 2-chambered by a partition running the length in middle. Leaves 2–6" long, with 17–25 ovate, ¼–¾" long leaflets.

Flowering Season: March–May.

Habitat/Range: Rocky washes and roadsides, 1,100–2,300', south-central Arizona.

Comments: This plant is common in neighborhoods of the greater Phoenix suburban area. Yucca Milkvetch *(A. lentiginosus* var. *yuccanus),* from slightly north and west, also with pale yellow or whitish flowers, has pods ½" in diameter.

WAND HOLDBACK
Caesalpinia virgata
Bean Family (Fabaceae)

Description: Slender, widely branched, wand-like plants 2–7' tall with bilateral yellow flowers in spires, only a few flowers at any one time in bloom. Flowers ½–¾" across. Petals 5, upper petal innermost, slightly darker yellow than other petals, red-streaked at base. Pods sickle-shaped, flat, ¾–1" long, sprinkled with tiny, dark glands. Leaves divided into segments, the 2 segments at side ¼–½" long, the terminal segment ½ –1½" long, each segment divided in 3–10 pairs of ⅛" long leaflets.

Flowering Season: March–May, sometimes again in October.

Habitat/Range: Dry, hot slopes, washes and roadsides, 300–1,500', southeastern California, western Arizona, and northern Mexico.

Comments: Leaves are deciduous during drought, only the canelike stems evident.

Wand Holdback

BLUE PALO VERDE, PALO VERDE AZUL
Cercidium floridum
Bean Family (Fabaceae)

Description: Densely twiggy trees 6–25' tall, with smooth, bluish green bark. Branches tend to droop to ground. Flowers ¾" across, with 5 petals, upper petal orange-spotted. Leaves ¾–1¼" long, forked into 2 segments each with 1–3 pairs of oval leaflets ⅛–⅜" long. Leaves drop shortly after maturing. Spine at base of leaf ⅛–⅜" long.

Flowering Season: March–May.

Habitat/Range: Washes, 0–3,500', southeastern California to southern Arizona and northwestern Mexico.

Comments: Foothills Palo Verde *(C. microphyllum)*, has pale yellow flowers with upper petal white, branches stiff, erect, spine-tipped, and leaf segments with 4–8 pairs of tiny leaflets. Mexican Palo Verde *(Parkinsonia aculeata)* has upper petal orange in age, and persistent, drooping central stalk of leaf 8–12" long.

Blue Palo Verde, Palo Verde Azul

Hog Potato, Pignut, Camote de Ratón

HOG POTATO, PIGNUT, CAMOTE DE RATÓN
Hoffmanseggia glauca
Bean Family (Fabaceae)

Description: Bilateral, yellow flowers in loose clusters above feathery, twice pinnately compound leaves. Petals 5, ½" long, each tapered to a narrow stalk with scattered dark glands, the upper petal oriented innermost. Calyx and flower stalk also covered with dark, stalked glands. Leaves 2–5" long, grayish green, with 5–11 segments, each segment with 5–11 pairs of leaflets ⅛–⅜" long. Stems 1–several, 4–12" tall.

Flowering Season: April–September.

Habitat/Range: Open ground, 100–5,000', from southeastern California to the southern plains, south to central Mexico.

Comments: Tuberous enlargements on the roots provide valuable feed for wildlife and when roasted were eaten by Native Americans. Plants form large colonies and can become an unwelcome weed in agricultural areas.

Greene's Bird's-Foot Trefoil

GREENE'S BIRD'S-FOOT TREFOIL
Lotus greenei
Bean Family (Fabaceae)

Description: Upturned yellow "pea" flowers are held above the foliage on stalks ½–1" long on these spreading or matted, grayish hairy plants. Flowers about ½" long, the banner suffused with brick red on the back. Opening buds brick red. Leaves ½" long, with 3–7 leaflets each ⅛–⅜" long, covered with spreading hairs. Pod nearly straight, linear, ½–¾" long, spreading perpendicular to the stalk.

Flowering Season: March–May, sometimes again in August.

Habitat/Range: Gravelly banks and slopes, 3,000–5,000', southern Arizona and New Mexico, northwestern Mexico.

Comments: This species is common at the upper edges of the southeastern part of the Sonoran Desert. When in full flower it forms spectacular yellow mats, the brick red accent contrasting with the vivid yellow of the petals.

BROOM BIRD'S-FOOT TREFOIL, DESERT ROCKPEA
Lotus rigidus
Bean Family (Fabaceae)

Description: Plants coarse, broomlike, the stems 1–3' tall, with few leaves and with 1-3 yellow "pea" flowers per stalk. Petals ½–¾" long; banner with some rusty red on back. Leaves pinnate, ½–¾" long, with 3–5 narrow leaflets, with a few hairs that lie flat against the surface. Pod 1¼–1½" long, straight, about ⅛" wide, nearly hairless.

Flowering Season: February–May.

Habitat/Range: Dry slopes and washes, 200–5,500', southeastern California to Utah and Arizona, south to Baja California.

Comments: This is the most arid-adapted *Lotus* in Arizona. *Lotus* is the ancient Greek name for this large, almost worldwide genus. "Trefoil" refers to 3 leaflets, a common number in many species. In some species the pods are in clusters, spreading much like the toes of a bird.

Broom Bird's-Foot Trefoil, Desert Rockpea

California Broom

CALIFORNIA BROOM
Lotus scoparius var. *brevialatus*
Bean Family (Fabaceae)

Description: Usually erect, bushy-branched, broomlike plants 1½–7' tall, with small, yellow "pea" flowers in rings on stem. Corolla ⅜" long, the keel longer than other petals. Pod slender, ½" long, curved, spreading or drooping on stem. Leaves ½–1" long, divided into 3–6 broad, ¼–½" long leaflets, leaves on upper part of stem usually with only 3 leaflets.

Flowering Season: March–August.

Habitat/Range: Rocky slopes and washes, below 5,000', western edge of desert in California, western Arizona, and Baja California.

Comments: The short *(brevi)* winged *(alatus)* flowers mark this variety. Other varieties occur north and west. All have nitrogen-fixing bacteria associated with roots, helping to make this critical element available to plants and animals.

Desert Bird's-Foot Trefoil, Desert Lotus

DESERT BIRD'S-FOOT TREFOIL, DESERT LOTUS

Lotus strigosus var. *tomentellus*
Bean Family (Fabaceae)

Description: Matted plants with small, yellow "pea" flowers borne singly, nestled among pinnately compound leaves, on stalks less than ¼". Corolla ¼–⅜" long. Lobes of calyx as long as tube. Fruits slender, ½–1" long. Leaves with 4–9 broad, thick, ⅛–⅜" long leaflets, lightly to densely hairy. Stems branched, 4–12" long or longer.

Flowering Season: March–June.

Habitat/Range: Gravelly areas, mostly below 4,000', throughout Sonoran Desert in United States.

Comments: Other mat-formers are variety *strigosus*, from western edge of desert, with flowers ⅜" long, on stalks at least ½" tall; Foothill Bird's-Foot Trefoil *(L. humistratus)*, softly spreading-hairy, with calyx lobes 1–2 times length of tube; and Coastal Bird's-Foot Trefoil *(L. salsuginosus)*, with thick leaves, usually with 2–4 flowers on stalk.

SPINY SENNA

Senna armata
Bean Family (Fabaceae)

Description: Mostly leafless 2–5' tall, gray-green shrubs, heavily branched, when in flower covered by deep yellow, slightly bilateral flowers. Petals 5, nearly round, each on a slender, short stalk, ⅜–½" long, upper petal slightly ahead of other petals. Pod lanceolate, straight, 1–1½" long. Leaves pinnate, when present, 2–6" long, with 1–4 pairs of oblong leaflets ¼" long; midrib of leaf elongates after leaflets fall, and becomes spine-tipped.

Flowering Season: February–May, sometimes again October–November.

Habitat/Range: Sandy washes, flats, and slopes, 600–3,500', southeastern California to southern Nevada, western Arizona, and Baja California.

Comments: For most of the year, shrubs are an inconspicuous, tangled mass of grayish living and dead twigs. For a week or so, it may be spectacular when in full bloom.

Spiny Senna

Desert Senna, Daisillo, Hojasen

DESERT SENNA, DAISILLO, HOJASEN
Senna covesii
Bean Family (Fabaceae)

Description: Plants with bright yellow flowers about 1¼" across and pinnately compound leaves. Flowers slightly bilateral, the upper petal held innermost to the other 4, each petal broadly oval, about ⅝" long. Leaflets 2–3 pairs, each broadly elliptical, pointed, ½–1¼" long. Pods ¾–1½" long, ¼" wide, with hairs pressed against the surface. Between the lowest pair of leaflets, on the top of the leaf stalk, is a peglike gland. Stems 1–2' tall.

Flowering Season: April–October.

Habitat/Range: Open, dry areas, 1,000–3,000', southeastern California to southwestern New Mexico; northwestern Mexico.

Comments: On this and other sennas, the unusual stamens each have a terminal pore. Bumblebees land on the flower, hang upside down, and "buzz" to shake loose the pollen, which collects on their bodies.

Slim-Pod Senna

SLIM-POD SENNA
Senna hirsuta var. *glaberimma*
Bean Family (Fabaceae)

Description: Tall, green, hairless or almost hairless plants with pinnately compound leaves and bilateral yellow flowers in clusters. Petals 5, broadly oval, ½" long. Two lower stamens much longer than upper stamens. Leaves up to 16" long, with 3–8 pairs of lanceolate, 1½–4" long leaflets, stalk of the leaf bearing a stout, conical gland just above the base. Pods slender, ⅛–¼" wide, up to 10" long, usually arched outward from stem.

Flowering Season: July–September.

Habitat/Range: Along washes and roadsides, 2,500–5,500', southern Arizona and southern New Mexico and northern Mexico.

Comments: As with other species of *Senna,* pollen is shaken from the pores of the anthers by buzz vibrations of visiting bumblebees. Senna, a cathartic, is obtained from dried leaves of Old World species.

SCRAMBLED-EGGS
Corydalis aurea
Fumitory Family (Fumariaceae)

Description: Smooth, soft plants with divided leaves and strongly bilateral yellow flowers in open, elongate clusters at tips of stems. Flower ½–¾" long, with 4 petals. Upper petal projects forward like a visor and bears a saclike spur behind point of attachment. Lower petal extends forward, much like the prow of a boat. Two interior petals, at sides, enclose the stamens in their ladle-like tips. Leaves grayish green, 1–8" long, repeatedly divided into many linear segments ⅛–¼" long. Stems erect or reclining, often in bunches, 4–16" long.

Flowering Season: February–June.

Habitat/Range: Open areas or often in protection of brush, 1,500–9,500', much of North America.

Comments: Plants are toxic to livestock, particularly to sheep.

Scrambled-Eggs

Whispering Bells

WHISPERING BELLS
Emmenanthe penduliflora var. *penduliflora*
Waterleaf Family (Hydrophyllaceae)

Description: Yellow or cream, bell-shaped flowers nod on branched plants with pinnately lobed or toothed leaves. Stems and leaves covered with glandular, odorous hairs. Corolla ¼–½" long, 5-lobed. Stamens not protruding from corolla. Leaves long and narrow, ½–5" long. Stems 2–30" tall.

Flowering Season: March–May.

Habitat/Range: Dry, open places, common on slopes, roadsides, washes, often under bushes, below 4,000', California to southern Utah and southern Arizona.

Comments: As the corolla dries it becomes papery, the slightest breeze shaking corollas to make a whispering sound. As the developing fruit enlarges, it is enclosed by the dried corolla. *Emmenanthe* comes from Greek, meaning "abiding flower," in reference to the persistent corolla.

Desert Rock Nettle, Desert Stingbush

DESERT ROCK NETTLE, DESERT STINGBUSH
Eucnide urens
Loasa Family (Loasaceae)

Description: Densely leafy plants with large, translucent, pale yellow, tulip-shaped flowers held just above the foliage. Flowers with 5 petals 1¼–2" long, broader in upper half, pointed at the tip; stamens many. Leaves ovate, ¾–2½" long, coarsely toothed, covered with conspicuous, stiff hairs. Plants form rounded clumps 1–2' high.

Flowering Season: April–September.

Habitat/Range: Dry, rocky places, 300–4,500', southern Utah and Nevada to southeastern California and western Arizona.

Comments: The scientific name means "strongly nettlelike, burning." The plants are lovely to admire, but the hairs deliver an irritating sting. For a plant that grows in hot, inhospitable places, the stinging hairs are very likely an effective defense against animals that might like to eat it.

SAND BLAZING-STAR, SILVER BLAZING-STAR
Mentzelia involucrata
Loasa Family (Loasaceae)

Description: Flowers with 5 pearly, pale yellow, ½–2½" long petals, pointed at tip, bloom on plants with pinnately lobed, rough-hairy leaves. Beneath flower is a pair of jagged-edged, ½–1¼" long bracts, translucent white in center, green on margins. Leaves narrowly lanceolate in outline, 1½–5" long, covered with barbed hairs that give the feeling of a cat's tongue. Stems white or pale apricot, with a pearly sheen, 4–16" tall.

Flowering Season: January–May.

Habitat/Range: Sandy, gravelly, or rocky places, below 4,000', southeastern California, southwestern Arizona, northwestern Mexico.

Comments: Spiny-Hair Blazing-Star *(M. tricuspis)* from below 2,000' in eastern California and western Arizona is very similar, but beneath flowers has bracts that are mostly green, with white only at base.

Sand Blazing-Star, Silver Blazing-Star

Jones' Blazing-Star

JONES' BLAZING-STAR
Mentzelia jonesii
Loasa Family (Loasaceae)

Description: Stems pale and smooth, often sprawling or tangled in shrubs, the intensely brilliant yellow flowers with 5 petals. Stamens many, the outer longer than inner. Petals ¼–¾" long, broadest in upper half, sometimes with orange spot at base. Bracts beneath flower triangular-ovate, not lobed. Fruit slender, ⅛" wide at flared tip, ½–1½" long, curved in a "C" or an "S".

Flowering Season: February–May.

Habitat/Range: Rocky washes, slopes, and roadsides, 700–5,000', southeastern California to southern Nevada and western Arizona.

Comments: This species is extremely variable in flower size and size of plants. In the open, plants may be small, with a single stem; on a shaded bank, plants may be branched many times.

Adonis Blazing-Star

ADONIS BLAZING-STAR
Mentzelia multiflora
Loasa Family (Loasaceae)

Description: Branched plants to 3' tall, with pearly whitish stems, leaves rough like a cat's tongue, and bright yellow flowers with 10 petals. Petals ½–1" long, in 2 sets, broad petals alternating with shorter, narrower petals. Stamens many, the outer ones with broad filaments. Styles ½" long. Fruit a cylindrical capsule ½–¾" long. Leaves lanceolate in outline, up to 6" long, 1¼" wide, usually lobed along margins, or in very narrow leaves nearly unlobed.

Flowering Season: February–October.

Habitat/Range: Open areas, often sandy, 100–7,500', much of the American Southwest.

Comments: Flowers of this widespread and variable species open in the evening. The smaller, shorter petals are actually expanded, sterile stamens. Surface of leaves have barbed hairs that readily cling to clothing.

DESERT VINE, SLENDER JANUSIA, FERMINA
Janusia gracilis
Malpighia Family (Malpighiaceae)

Description: Slender vines to 10' long with yellow flowers. Flowers with 5 crinkled petals about ¼" long, each with a slender stalk at base and a broad, paddlelike end. Fruits 2- or 3-winged, resembling maple fruits, each wing paper thin, about ½" long, often suffused with dull red. Leaves opposite, narrowly lanceolate, ½–1½" long, with straight, stiff hairs that lie against the surface.

Flowering Season: April–October.

Habitat/Range: Dry, rocky slopes, among brush, 1,000–5,000', southern Arizona to western Texas and northern Mexico.

Comments: *Janusia* is an American genus of about a dozen species found from southern North America to Argentina. Desert Vine may be so completely entangled in shrubs that it is nearly impossible to extricate. Desert tortoises feed upon the plant.

Desert Vine, Slender Janusia, Fermina

YELLOW INDIAN-MALLOW
Abutilon malacum
Mallow Family (Malvaceae)

Description: Branched plants covered by a grayish velvet composed of branched, starlike hairs. Petals 5, narrowly fan-shaped, ⅜–⅝" long. Calyx ¼" long, divided about halfway to base, the free part of the sepals lanceolate. Stamens many, united by their filaments. Leaves 1¼–3½" long, round, ovate, or heart-shaped, the tip blunt or tapered to a fine point. Fruit about ¼" wide, divided into 5 wedge-shaped sections, each with 3 minutely hairy black seeds.

Flowering Season: August–October.

Habitat/Range: Rocky, arid hills, 2,500–5,000', from southern Arizona to western Texas, and south into Mexico.

Comments: In identifying species of *Abutilon,* some of which are very similar, attention must be paid to the nature of hairs covering plant, number of fruit segments, shape of sepals, and coloring of petals.

Yellow Indian-Mallow

CURLY BLADDER MALLOW
Herissantia crispa
Mallow Family (Malvaceae)

Description: Plants with heart-shaped, velvety-hairy leaves and small, pale yellow, starlike flowers. Petals 5, ¼–⅜" long. Stamens many, clustered in center. Flowers on slender stalks with a joint above middle that bends increasingly as fruit matures. Leaves ½–3" long, with irregular teeth on edges, the veins impressed on the upper surface and conspicuously netlike. Fruit maturing as 8–15 bladdery segments arranged in a ring ½–¾" in diameter. Stems soft and trailing or semi-woody and erect, velvety-hairy when young, up to 3' long.

Flowering Season: February–October.

Habitat/Range: Dry slopes among shrubs, below 3,500', southeastern California to western Texas, also Florida, and south into tropical America.

Comments: The jointed flower stalk distinguishes this common species.

Curly Bladder Mallow

Desert Rose-Mallow

DESERT ROSE-MALLOW
Hibiscus coulteri
Mallow Family (Malvaceae)

Description: Spindly shrubs with few large, bowl-shaped, pale yellow flowers on long stalks. Petals 5, broadly fan-shaped, ¾–1½" long, commonly with reddish streaks at the base. Stamens many, joined by their filaments. Beneath 5-lobed calyx is a ring of 10–14 linear, ¼–¾" long bracts. Lower leaves broadly ovate, toothed; upper leaves divided into 3 narrow, toothed lobes, the entire leaf about 1" across. Stems 1–4' tall.

Flowering Season: Most vigorously July–September, but flowering throughout the year.

Habitat/Range: Rocky slopes, 1,500–4,500', southern Arizona to western Texas and northern Mexico.

Comments: The flowers of Desert Rose-Mallow are spectacular when encountered among desert brush, borne on spindly, otherwise inconspicuous shrubs. This is a temperate representative of a genus of nearly 200 species, mostly tropical. Flamboyant hybrids are popular ornamentals, the first introduced to horticulture about 100 years ago. The fleshy red calyx of Roselle *(H. sabdariffa),* originally African but now widespread, is used to make the popular tea jamaica (pronounced *ha–mi–ca*). Other species are used for fiber, timber, and oil.

SPREADING FANPETALS, BUEN DÍA
Sida abutifolia
Mallow Family (Malvaceae)

Description: Trailing or matted plants usually with reddish 6–24" long stems and apricot-yellow to nearly white flowers. Petals about ⅜" long, fan-shaped, notched in the broad tip, 1 of the 2 resulting lobes shorter than the other. Leaves broadly lanceolate to almost round, ¼–1¼" long, scallop-toothed on edges. Calyx and stems with long, straight, spreading hairs. Fruit with 5 wedge-shaped segments ⅛" long.

Flowering Season: April–October.

Habitat/Range: Plains and mesas, usually in gravelly or sandy soil, common on roadsides, 2,500–6,000', across the southern United States to northern South America.

Comments: Flower symmetry reverses in adjacent flowers on the stem, the short lobes on the right in 1 flower, on the left in the next, and so on.

Spreading Fanpetals, Buen Día

Rough Menodora, Twinberry

ROUGH MENODORA, TWINBERRY
Menodora scabra
Olive Family (Oleaceae)

Description: Dark green, many-stemmed plants 2–2½' tall, with small upper leaves and bright yellow flowers. Petals 5, each ¼–⅜" long, more or less ovate, joined into a narrow tube at base about ½" long. Sepals 8–11, narrow, usually at least slightly rough-hairy. Fruit consists of 2 translucent spheres each up to ¼" in diameter, at first green, later tan. Leaves few, the lower narrowly lanceolate, up to 1" long, the upper leaves much smaller.

Flowering Season: March–September.

Habitat/Range: Dry flats and slopes, 1,500–7,500', southeastern California to southern Utah and western Texas, south in northern Mexico.

Comments: Broom Menodora *(M. scoparia)*, sometimes not considered to be distinct from Rough Menodora, is smooth and has 5–8 sepal lobes.

Golden Suncup

GOLDEN SUNCUP
Camissonia brevipes ssp. *brevipes*
Evening Primrose Family (Onagraceae)

Description: Plants 2–30" tall, with leaves mostly in a basal rosette, and with brilliant yellow flowers in loose, nodding clusters. Petals 4, broad, rounded, ¼–¾" long, without red spots at base. Petals attach to end of tube ⅛–⅜" long at top of slender, stalklike ovary. Fruit a slender, straight or gently curved pod 2–4" long, ⅛" wide or less, not wider at top, with a stalk at base. Leaves to about 6" long, pinnately divided or not, when divided the terminal segment much larger than lateral segments.

Flowering Season: February–May.

Habitat/Range: Sandy areas, -200–6,000', southeastern California to southwestern Utah and western Arizona.

Comments: Flowers open at dawn and close as the day warms. With its brilliant yellow, often comparatively large flowers, this is one of the most showy Suncups.

CALIFORNIA SUNCUP
Camissonia californica
Evening Primrose Family (Onagraceae)

Description: Stiffly erect, spindly plants ½–6' tall, with sparsely scattered, bright yellow flowers. Petals 4, broadly ovate, ¼–½" long, often red-spotted near base, attached to a very short tube at top of stalklike ovary. Fruit very slender, bent downward, 1½–4½" long. Leaves of basal rosette lanceolate, pinnately lobed, 2–6" long, dying early, the leaves on stem progressively smaller upward.

Flowering Season: March–May.

Habitat/Range: Dry, usually disturbed places, below 5,000', California to western Arizona and northwestern Mexico.

Comments: This species is common along roadsides, strongly resembling members of the Mustard Family (Brassicaceae). However, the position of the ovary, below other flower parts, places it in the Evening Primrose Family. Flowers close by midday.

California Suncup

Heartleaf Suncup

HEARTLEAF SUNCUP
Camissonia cardiophylla
Evening Primrose Family (Onagraceae)

Description: Softly spreading-hairy plants with roundish, broadly heart-shaped, rather thick leaves, and bright yellow or cream flowers with 4 petals. Sepals and petals attached to a tube ³⁄₁₆–½" long at top of long, slender, hairy ovary. Petals almost round, ⅛–½" long. Fruits cylindrical, ascending, ¾–2½" long. Leaves ½–2½" long, irregularly toothed. Stems branched, mostly 4–20" tall, sometimes taller.

Flowering Season: February–May.

Habitat/Range: Sandy or rocky areas, often on canyon sides, 0–5,000', southeastern California, western Arizona, northwestern Mexico.

Comments: Flowers open at dusk and close before the heat of the next day, the petals turning rusty orange as they wilt. The species name, *cardiophylla*, means "heart leaf."

Yellow Desert Evening Primrose

YELLOW DESERT EVENING PRIMROSE
Oenothera primiveris ssp. *primiveris*
Evening Primrose Family (Onagraceae)

Description: Stemless plants with large, pale yellow flowers in center of a rosette of leaves. Petals 4 per flower, heart-shaped, ½–⅞" long. Leaves inversely lanceolate in outline, deeply pinnately lobed, ½–5" long. Fruit square in cross section, tapering, ¼" thick, ¾–2" long.

Flowering Season: February–May.

Habitat/Range: Desert flats and gentle slopes, 1,600–5,300', from southeastern California to western Texas and northwestern Mexico.

Comments: Unusual among evening primroses, some plants in a single population can self-fertilize whereas others must outcross. The subspecies *bufonis* from California, Nevada, and Utah has 1–1½" long petals; subspecies *caulescens* from low elevations in California and adjacent Arizona also has large petals but has stems 4–16" long.

MEXICAN GOLD POPPY, AMAPOLA DEL CAMPO
Eschscholzia californica ssp. *mexicana*
Poppy Family (Papaveraceae)

Description: Yellow or orange-yellow, cup-shaped flowers held erect above smooth, grayish green leaves. Petals 4, fan-shaped, ½–¼" long, often more deeply colored at base. Stamens many. At base of petals is a pink rim ¹⁄₄₀–¹⁄₁₀" wide. Sepals form a cone over bud, falling from flower as it opens. Leaves with 3 dissected lobes. Stems 4–16" tall

Flowering Season: January–May.

Habitat/Range: Sandy or rocky areas, 1,000–4,600', from southeastern California to Utah, western Texas and northwestern Mexico.

Comments: Mexican Gold Poppy is annual. The very similar California Poppy *(E. californica* ssp. *californica)*, usually a perennial, may be annual in arid situations. It has a pink rim ¹⁄₁₀–¼" wide. It is commonly included in seed mixes and may be found in gardens and along highways.

Mexican Gold Poppy, Amapola del Campo

DESERT GOLDEN-POPPY
Eschscholzia glyptosperma
Poppy Family (Papaveraceae)

Description: Smooth, bluish green plants 2–24" tall, with cup-shaped, golden yellow flowers at ends of stalks and leaves all in a tuft at base. Petals 4, fan-shaped, ½–1" long. No pinkish rim at top of stalk beneath petals. Stamens many. Leaves repeatedly divided in a forked manner into linear lobes, the entire lobed portion ¾–1½" long, borne on a long stalk. Pod very slender, tapering, 1½–2½" long

Flowering Season: February–May.

Habitat/Range: Desert washes, flats, and slopes, especially where sandy or gravelly, 200–2,000', southeastern California to southwestern Utah and western Arizona.

Comments: The buds of Desert Golden-Poppy nod at the ends of their stalks, becoming upright as the flower opens. The calyx is in the form of a dunce cap, and is pushed off the flower upon blooming.

Desert Golden-Poppy

Pygmy Golden-Poppy, Little Gold Poppy

PYGMY GOLDEN-POPPY, LITTLE GOLD POPPY
Eschscholzia minutiflora
Poppy Family (Papaveraceae)

Description: Smooth, pale bluish plants with divided leaves at base and also higher on stem among golden yellow flowers. Petals 4, fan-shaped, ⅛–¼" long, less commonly ½–1" long. Stamens about 12. Leaf blades mostly ½–2" long, repeatedly divided into slender lobes, the lobes becoming broader from base to tip. Fruit slender and tapering, 1½–3" long, held erect.

Flowering Season: February–May.

Habitat/Range: Sandy and gravelly places, mostly below 4,500', southeastern California to southwestern Utah, southern Arizona and northwestern Mexico.

Comments: Pygmy Golden-Poppy differs from other *Eschscholzia* on the Sonoran Desert by having leaves scattered along the stem in addition to a tuft at base. Petal size varies greatly, the name *minutiflora* (tiny flower) not always appropriate.

Desert Unicorn Plant, Yellow Devil's Claw, Uña de Gato

DESERT UNICORN PLANT, YELLOW DEVIL'S CLAW, UÑA DE GATO
Proboscidea althaeifolia
Sesame Family (Pedaliaceae)

Description: Stout, moist, and sticky-hairy plants with large yellow or orange-yellow, bilateral flowers. Flowers 1¾" wide, about as long, with dotted maroon or brownish lines at the mouth of tube. Leaves round or broadly ovate, ¾–3" long and wide, on stout stalks, the edges lobed and scalloped. Fruit with a tapered body about 2–3" long, ¾" wide, with an up-curved horn at tip twice as long as body. Stems spreading, often reddish, up to 2½" long.

Flowering Season: July–September.

Habitat/Range: Sand, 100–4,000', southeastern California to western Texas, southward into Mexico.

Comments: Plants grow from a stout root that stores nutrients, usually flowering after substantial summer rains. As the fruit dries it darkens, and the curved horn splits into 2 slender claws.

GOLDEN DESERT-TRUMPETS
Linanthus aureus ssp. *aureus*
Phlox Family (Polemoniaceae)

Description: Brilliant yellow, trumpet-shaped flowers ¼–½" long are held on threadlike, erect or spreading stems 2–6" long. Corolla with 5 broad, yellow lobes, with the upper part of the tube deeper yellow or maroon. Leaves opposite, mostly at widely spaced branch points on stem. Each leaf divided into 5–7 prickle-tipped linear ⅛–¼" long lobes.

Flowering Season: March–June.

Habitat/Range: Sandy areas, below 6,000', southern California to southern Nevada and western Texas, also northwestern Mexico.

Comments: This annual may be so common as to color broad swatches of ground brilliant yellow. The subspecies *decorus,* found in the same area, but usually not mixed with subspecies *aureus,* has white or cream corollas with the tube maroon in upper part.

Golden Desert-Trumpets

Desert Trumpet, Guinagua

DESERT TRUMPET, GUINAGUA
Eriogonum inflatum
Buckwheat Family (Polygonaceae)

Description: Spindly, grayish green plants 4"–5' tall, with several branches attached at 1 point, much like ribs of an umbrella. Below branches stem is swollen, then gently tapers to slender portion below. Individual flowers gathered in small clusters in tiny 5-toothed cups, the flowers yellow, about ⅛" across, with white hairs on backside of each of 6 pointed, petal-like lobes. Leaves all at base, on long stalks, the blades oval or kidney-shaped, ½–2" long, usually rather convex and wrinkled.

Flowering Season: March–July, sometimes also September–October.

Habitat/Range: Open, gravelly or rocky areas, -50-6,600', from southern California eastward to Colorado and New Mexico, south into northwestern Mexico.

Comments: The swelling results from irritation by a tiny moth larva that lives inside the stem. Uninfected stems do not swell.

Purslane, Verdolaga, Little Hogweed

PURSLANE, VERDOLAGA, LITTLE HOGWEED
Portulaca oleracea
Purslane Family (Portulacaceae)

Description: Plants smooth, shiny, fleshy, with small yellow flowers near stem tips. Flowers with 5 petals up to 3/16" long, notched at tip. Leaves spatulate, broader near roundish tip, 1/2-1 1/2" long. Fruit tiny, cup-shaped, with a circular lid; seeds black, iridescent, 1/25" across, covered with peglike projections. Stems often bronze, spreading, up to about 1' long.

Flowering Season: July–September.

Habitat/Range: Moist soil, 1,500-5,000', temperate and tropical regions worldwide.

Comments: Purslane has been used as a potherb by many peoples throughout history. In the American Southwest it is stewed with tomatoes and onions and various spices. Taxonomy of the group is not settled; some botanists recognize several similar species based upon spacing and prominence of the minute projections on the seeds.

ORANGE FLAMEFLOWER
Talinum aurantiacum
Purslane Family (Portulacaceae)

Description: Succulent plants with narrow leaves and orange to yellow flowers with 5 petals and 20 or more stamens. Petals broadest near tip, 3/8–1/2" long. Sepals 2. Leaves linear or narrowly lanceolate, 1/2–2 1/2" long, 1/10–1/4" wide. Stems 4–16" long.

Flowering Season: July–September.

Habitat/Range: Rocky slopes and plains, 2,500–5,000', southern Arizona to western Texas and northern Mexico.

Comments: Native Americans cooked and ate the large, fleshy roots. Plants from above 3,500' tend to have orange or even reddish tinged flowers, stout stems, and comparatively broad leaves. Such plants thoroughly intergrade with plants from lower elevations that have yellow flowers, slender stems, and very narrow leaves, which have been named *T. angustissimum* but are now considered to be part of 1 variable species.

Orange Flameflower

Golden Columbine

GOLDEN COLUMBINE
Aquilegia chrysantha var. *chrysantha*
Buttercup Family (Ranunculaceae)

Description: Golden yellow flowers with 5 long spurs tip upward above fernlike foliage. Petals 5, like sugar scoops, each with a spur 1½–2½" long; sepals lanceolate, petal-like, spreading between petals, ¾–1½" long. Stamens many, protruding from center of flower. Leaves 3 times divided into roundish or fan-shaped, scalloped leaflets ½–1¾" long. Plants up to 4' tall.

Flowering Season: April–September.

Habitat/Range: At springs and along streams, 3,000–11,000', southeastern Arizona to Colorado, Texas, and northern Mexico.

Comments: Permanent water is rare on the Sonoran Desert, but along streams in canyons one might find spectacular displays of this bright and cheery wildflower. It is a popular ornamental in the semi-shaded, moist garden.

Chaparral Bush-Beardtongue

CHAPARRAL BUSH-BEARDTONGUE
Keckiella antirrhinoides var. *microphylla*
Figwort Family (Scrophulariaceae)

Description: Shrubs 2–8' tall, with mostly opposite leaves and bilateral, pale yellow flowers. Corolla tubular, ⅝–1" long, the upper lip hoodlike, arched forward, ⅜–⅝" long, lower lip reflexed downward, 3-lobed. Stamens 5, the 4 fertile ones hairy at point of attachment to the corolla, but with hairless anthers, the sterile stamen protruding from mouth of corolla, densely yellow-hairy at tip. Leaves more or less lanceolate, ¼–¾" long. Stems densely and finely hairy.

Flowering Season: March–May.

Habitat/Range: Desert hills and mountains, 1,500–5,000', southern California to southern Arizona, northwestern Mexico.

Comments: These shrubs form spectacular yellow displays on hillsides. This was once in the genus *Penstemon,* distinguished by its stamens, which are hairless at the base.

COMMON, SEEP, OR YELLOW MONKEY-FLOWER
Mimulus guttatus
Figwort Family (Scrophulariaceae)

Description: Vivid yellow, bilateral flowers bloom on soft stems with opposite, coarsely toothed leaves. Corolla ⅜–1¼" long, 2 lobes of upper lip slightly bent back, 3 lobes of lower lip spreading. Lower lip with a pillowlike swelling, speckled with red, that closes opening to tube. Calyx bell-shaped, ¼–⅝" long, swollen in fruit. Upper tooth of calyx 2–3 times longer than others, in fruit, the 2 side and 2 lower teeth closing over opening. Leaves ovate to round, ½–4" long. Stems 2–36" long, usually erect, sometimes the base leaning on ground, or sometimes stem creeping and rooting where it touches ground.

Flowering Season: March–September.

Habitat/Range: Wet places, 500–9,500', much of western North America.

Comments: Well-washed leaves may be used for salad greens.

Common, Seep, or Yellow Monkey-Flower

Ghost Flower

GHOST FLOWER
Mohavea confertiflora
Figwort Family (Scrophulariaceae)

Description: Moist, glandular hairy plants with deeply cup-shaped, bilateral, translucent, pale yellow flowers 1–1½" long, maroon-spotted within. Sides of corolla cleft, the corolla with a pronounced lower lip with a large maroon spot on swelling at base, and an upper lip. At base of corolla, on lower side, is a pouchlike swelling. Leaves linear to lanceolate, ½–2½" long. Stems branched or not, 4–16" tall.

Flowering Season: February–April.

Habitat/Range: Sandy washes and gravel slopes, 0–3,500', southeastern California, southern Nevada, western Arizona, northwestern Mexico.

Comments: As is true for so many desert annuals, Ghost Flower varies with rainfall. Small plants may be unbranched, with only 1 or few flowers; large plants may be extensively branched, as wide as tall, and with many flowers.

Yellow Twining Snapdragon

YELLOW TWINING SNAPDRAGON
Neogaerrhinum filipes
Figwort Family (Scrophulariaceae)

Description: Yellow, bilateral flowers dangle from inconspicuous, threadlike, hairless stems that twine through brush. Corolla ½" long, the upper lip with 2 lobes angled upward, the lower lip with 3 lobes bent downward. Near opening, the lower lip is convex, red-dotted. Lowermost leaf blades ovate, ¼–¾" long, on stalks about as long; upper leaves smaller and narrower. Stems 1–3" long.

Flowering Season: February–May.

Habitat/Range: Sandy places in brush, 0–4,500', southeastern California to southwestern Utah, western Arizona, northwestern Mexico.

Comments: This plant is extremely inconspicuous, but once noticed among shrubs in a wash, others are often easily found nearby. It so thoroughly twines through shrubs that it is nearly impossible to extricate it without breaking its stems.

TREE TOBACCO, TABACO AMARILLO, DON JUAN
Nicotiana glauca
Nightshade Family (Solanaceae)

Description: A few-branched shrub 2–25' tall, with smooth, blue-green leaves and hanging, tubular, yellow flowers. Corolla 1¼–1½" long, constricted just below the 5 blunt lobes near open end. Leaves ovate, 2–8" long, with a pale, powdery covering on leaves that easily rubs off ("glaucous," giving the specific epithet). Flower stalk curves upward as capsule inside enlarging calyx matures.

Flowering Season: Most vigorously May–September, but flowering throughout the year.

Habitat/Range: Roadsides, ditches, streams, below 3,000', southern California to central Texas and northern Mexico.

Comments: This South America native is now found in many semi-arid regions of the world. Tree Tobacco has mostly anabasine, a carcinogen, which like the toxin nicotine, acts as a natural insecticide.

Tree Tobacco, Tabaco Amarillo, Don Juan

Yellow Ground-Cherry, Tomatillo del Desierto

YELLOW GROUND-CHERRY, TOMATILLO DEL DESIERTO
Physalis crassifolia
Nightshade Family (Solanaceae)

Description: Intricately branched, leafy plants mostly 8–20" tall, with flat, round, yellow flowers ½–¾" wide. Petals 5 but fully united, indicated as 5 broad angles at edge of corolla. Stamens 5, erect in center of flower. Calyx at first ⅛–¼" long, but as fruit matures calyx enlarges and forms an ovate, 10-ribbed, green bladder ¾–1" long around the smooth, green berry.

Flowering Season: March–May.

Habitat/Range: Sandy and rocky areas, below 4,000', southeastern California to southern Nevada, western and southeastern Arizona, and northwestern Mexico.

Comments: Fendler's Ivy-Leaf Ground-Cherry *(P. hederifolia* var. *fendleri)* is found at 2,500' and higher. It has greenish yellow corollas with a greenish or purplish brown blush at base of each petal lobe.

Buffalo Bur, Mala Mujer

BUFFALO BUR, MALA MUJER
Solanum rostratum
Nightshade Family (Solanaceae)

Description: Prickly plants with star-shaped, yellow flowers and pinnately divided leaves. Flowers 1" across, with 5 pointed lobes. Stamens 5, somewhat swept toward bottom of flower, the lowest much the largest, opening by terminal pores. Leaves 3–7 lobed, up to 2' wide and 5' long, prickly especially on veins on underside, the veins deeply impressed, giving a crinkled appearance. Fruit a round, densely spiny berry ½" in diameter. Stems prickly, 12–30" tall.

Flowering Season: May–August.

Habitat/Range: Open areas, common on roadsides, 1,000–7,000', a native of the Great Plains now found throughout much of the American Southwest and northern Mexico.

Comments: This is an unwelcome weed on intensively grazed rangeland. Bees "buzz" the flower to shake pollen free for collection. Mala Mujer ("bad woman") refers to the spiny, unpleasant nature of the plant.

Goat Head, Puncture Vine, Torito, Toboso

GOAT HEAD, PUNCTURE VINE, TORITO, TOBOSO
Tribulus terrestris
Caltrop Family (Zygophyllaceae)

Description: Trailing plants with opposite, pinnately compound leaves and small, yellow flowers with 5 petals, ⅛–¼" long. Fruit ½" in diameter, excluding spines, with 5 wedge-shaped sections, each section with 2 stout spines ¼" long. Leaves ½–2" long, with 3–6 pairs of leaflets ¼–½" long. Stems to 3' long.

Flowering Season: March–October.

Habitat/Range: Open areas, particularly where disturbed and weedy, below 7,000', throughout Sonoran Desert, much of warmer parts of world.

Comments: This immigrant from the Mediterranean region is a noxious weed in many states. Plants are toxic to livestock, and ingested fruits may cause internal injury. Spines on fruits are painful to bare feet and will puncture bicycle tires. Seeds may last several years in the soil.

RED AND ORANGE FLOWERS

Desert Mariposa

This section includes red and orange flowers, as well as those with a maroon or brownish cast. Some plants with bright red fruits are also included here. Since red flowers grade into pink and purple, and orange flowers grade into yellow, readers looking for red or orange flowers should check the pink and purple and yellow sections of this book as well.

Desert Honeysuckle, Chuparosa

DESERT HONEYSUCKLE, CHUPAROSA
Anisacanthus thurberi
Acanthus Family (Acanthaceae)

Description: Shrubs 3–7' tall, with opposite leaves, or leaves in clusters on older stems. Corolla red-orange or salmon, 1½–2" long, with a slender tube, the upper lip narrow and not lobed, lower lip much broader and 3-lobed; stamens 2. Leaves lanceolate, ¼–3" long.

Flowering Season: Most vigorously March–May, but almost throughout the year when conditions are right.

Habitat/Range: Rocky slopes and along washes, 1,800–5,500', southern Arizona, southwestern New Mexico, and northwestern Mexico.

Comments: The flowers have nectar deep within the tube and are visited by hummingbirds *(chuparosa)*. The colorful flowers contrast with the dark green foliage, giving the plant good potential as an ornamental in a dry-land garden.

Chuparosa, Hummingbird-Bush

CHUPAROSA,
HUMMINGBIRD-BUSH
Justicia californica
Acanthus Family (Acanthaceae)

Description: Grayish green, sparsely leafy or leafless shrubs 2–7' tall, with numerous intertangled, stiffly spreading, opposite branches. Flowers scarlet to red-orange, sometimes dull, rarely yellow, with a slender tube 1¼–1½" long that flares to a hoodlike upper lip and a tonguelike lower lip, each lip ½" long. Leaves broad, rounded at base, pointed at tip, ½–3" long, withering and dropping.

Flowering Season: Most vigorously March–June, but almost throughout the year when conditions are right.

Habitat/Range: Gravelly or rocky slopes and flats, common in washes, 0–4,000', southeastern California, southern Arizona, and northwestern Mexico.

Comments: *Chuparosa,* meaning "it sucks the rose," is one Spanish word for hummingbird. Another name sometimes used locally is Honeysuckle, since nectar may be sucked from the base of the flower. The plants are used in water-conserving xeriscaping in the American Southwest where winters are warm, providing attractive masses of red or yellow when in full bloom. Temperatures much below freezing will damage or kill the plants, restricting their use as an ornamental elsewhere.

Emory Barrel Cactus

EMORY BARREL CACTUS
Ferocactus emoryi
Cactus Family (Cactaceae)

Description: Barrel-shaped or columnar plants with stout, hooked or curved spines and deep red flowers. Stems 2–8' tall, 1–2" in diameter, with 20–30 ribs. Spine clusters each with 8–10 large, grayish red or grayish spines, each somewhat flattened and with fine cross-ribs, the longest 2–2½", the central spine hooked at tip. Flowers near top of plant, about 1½" long, with many petal-like parts. Fruits yellow, barrel-shaped, 1¼–1¾" long.

Flowering Season: June–September.

Habitat/Range: Rocky, gravelly, or sandy areas, 1,500–3,000', southwestern Arizona and northwestern Mexico.

Comments: The absence of fine, bristlelike spines helps to distinguish this from Southwestern Barrel Cactus *(F. wislizenii)*. Plants often grow from cracks and ledges in dark rock in open sun, providing striking contrast.

SOUTHWESTERN BARREL CACTUS
Ferocactus wislizenii
Cactus Family (Cactaceae)

Description: Barrel-shaped or columnar plants with stout, hooked spines and red or yellow flowers. Stems 2–10' tall, 1½–2½' in diameter, with 20–28 ribs. Spine clusters with 12–20 spreading, ashy gray, slender spines that twist and bend, and with 4 large, somewhat flattened, grayish red spines 1½–2" long, with fine cross-ribs, at least some lower spines hooked at tip. Flowers 1–2" long, with many petal-like parts. Fruits yellow, barrel-shaped, up to 1¼–1¾" long.

Flowering Season: July–September.

Habitat/Range: Rocky or gravelly areas, 1,000–5,600', southern Arizona to western Texas and northwestern Mexico.

Comments: California Barrel Cactus *(F. cylindraceus)* is more slender and has more than 4 stout spines per cluster. Clustered Barrel Cactus *(Echinocactus polycephalus)* has woolly stem tips.

Southwestern Barrel Cactus

Buckhorn Cholla

BUCKHORN CHOLLA
Opuntia acanthocarpa
Cactus Family (Cactaceae)

Description: Shrubs 3–12' tall, with cylindrical, spiny stems and with tan fruits that drop the first season after maturation. Flowers 2–3" across, with many petal-like parts of varying shades of bronze-red, purple, or greenish yellow. Fruits ovate, 1–1½" long, spiny, falling late summer or fall. Stems 1–1½" in diameter, with raised tubercles ½–1" long, sometimes longer, at least 3 times as long as wide. Spines ½–1¼" long, 6–25 per cluster, spreading in all directions, at first covered by a straw-colored sheath, the spine within tan or reddish, darker with age.

Flowering Season: April–May.

Habitat/Range: Desert slopes and flats, 500–3,000', southeastern California to southwestern Utah, southern Arizona and northwestern Mexico.

Comments: Staghorn Cholla *(O. versicolor)* is similar but with reddish fruits that tend to stay on the stems more than a year.

Redstar, Star-Glory

REDSTAR, STAR-GLORY
Ipomoea coccinea var. *hederifolia*
Morning Glory Family (Convolvulaceae)

Description: Twining, climbing vines with lobed leaves and scarlet, trumpet-shaped flowers. Corolla ¾–1¼" long, the flared end cup-shaped, ½–¾' wide. Leaves up to 4" long, 3" wide, those near base of plant usually shallowly 3-lobed, pointed at tip, deeply indented at base. Leaves in upper part of stem deeply divided into 3 or 5 narrow lobes, each lobe narrower at base than at middle. Stems 2–10' long.

Flowering Season: May–October.

Habitat/Range: Seasonally moist soil, hillsides and canyons, 2,500–6,000', southern Arizona to western Texas, south into Mexico.

Comments: This is the only morning glory in the Sonoran Desert area with scarlet flowers. The variety *coccinea* has mostly unlobed, heart-shaped leaves. In the American Southwest it occurs mostly at 4,000–6,000'.

SCARLET MILKVETCH
Astragalus coccineus
Bean Family (Fabaceae)

Description: Long, scarlet-red, "pea" flowers bloom in loose clusters above grayish-hairy, pinnately compound leaves. Corolla 1½" long, banner much longer than wings or keel. Pods 1–1½" long, plump, curved, pointed, and covered with velvety-woolly hairs clustered at end of stalk, lying on ground. Leaves 1½–4" long, clumped near base of plant, each with a stout stalk and 7–15 more or less lanceolate or elliptical leaflets ¼–½" long. Stems usually in tufts, including flower stalks up to 1' tall.

Flowering Season: March–May.

Habitat/Range: Gravelly ridges and canyon sides, 2,000–7,000', southeastern California, western Arizona and Baja California, occurring on western edge of Sonoran Desert and in Kofa Mountains.

Comments: The long, scarlet flowers—rare in the genus—probably attract hummingbirds.

Scarlet Milkvetch

WESTERN CORAL-BEAN, CHILCOTE
Erythrina flabelliformis
Bean Family (Fabaceae)

Description: Shrubs with scarlet, 2" long flowers in loose clusters blooming before or as leaves appear. Upper petal folded, nearly concealing the others. Leaves divided into 3 fan-shaped leaflets 1–3" long. Stems to 15' tall, usually much shorter, with tiny, very sharp prickles.

Flowering Season: April–May, sometimes again in September.

Habitat/Range: Dry, rocky slopes at upper margin of desert, 3,000–5,500 feet, southern Arizona, adjacent New Mexico, and northern Mexico.

Comments: The large red seeds, used in necklaces, are toxic. The long, slender flowers, basically "pea" flowers, attract hummingbirds. The long period of leaflessness and sensitivity to cold detract from ornamental potential of this plant. In Mexico Coral-Bean may be a tree up to 25' tall.

Western Coral-Bean, Chilcote

Ocotillo, Coachwhip

OCOTILLO, COACHWHIP
Fouquieria splendens
Ocotillo Family (Fouquieriaceae)

Description: Shrubs 3–30' tall, with spiny, long, canelike stems in an inverted cone, when flowering tipped by brushlike clusters of scarlet flowers. Corolla ⅝" long, with 5 round lobes that curl outward. Stamens protrude beyond corolla. Leaves spatulate or inversely lanceolate, ¾–2" long, when present borne in clusters in axils of gently curved or straight spines ½–1¼" long.

Flowering Season: March–June, sometimes again October–November.

Habitat/Range: Dry slopes and flats, below 5,000', southeastern California to Texas, northern Mexico.

Comments: One of 13 species in a mostly Mexican family of very remote relationship to other plants, the bizarre Ocotillo seems a symbol of the American Southwest. Leaves clothe stems quickly after rains, yellowing and falling as the soil dries.

Scarlet Hedge-Nettle

SCARLET HEDGE-NETTLE
Stachys coccinea
Mint Family (Lamiaceae)

Description: A rather harshly hairy plant with a spicy odor, opposite leaves, and bilateral bright red flowers. Flowers about 6 in each well-spaced ring in upper part of stem. Each flower ¾" long, with a gently curved tube ending in a visorlike upper lip and a down-turned, 3-lobed lower lip. Stamens 4, projecting from under upper lip. Leaves elliptical to more or less triangular, ¾–3" long, the veins impressed on upper surface, the edges with many round-tipped teeth. Stems 4-sided, usually in clumps, 12–28" tall.

Flowering Season: March–October.

Habitat/Range: Moist, rich soil in canyons, often near water, 1,500–8,000', southern Arizona to western Texas and much of Mexico.

Comments: Scarlet Hedge-Nettle responds well to cultivation, blooming throughout the summer, attracting hummingbirds. This is a large genus, with about 300 species, many in Eurasia. Some produce potato-like swellings on subterranean stems that are edible when pickled or boiled. Lamb's Ears *(S. lanata),* from the Mid-East, is a popular ornamental with densely silvery-hairy leaves and purple flowers.

DESERT MARIPOSA
Calochortus kennedyi var. *kennedyi*
Lily Family (Liliaceae)

Desert Mariposa

Description: Intensely deep orange, bell-shaped flowers are held erect on smooth, grayish green stems 4–16" tall. Flowers several in a loose cluster. Petals 3, fan-shaped, 1¼–2" long, each with club-shaped hairs near base and a dark nectary surrounded by a fringed membrane. Leaves very narrow, grayish green, 3–8" long, channeled on upper side, those at base withering by flowering time.

Flowering Season: March–May.

Habitat/Range: Dry slopes and flats, 2,000–6,000', southeastern California to southern Nevada, southern Arizona, and northwestern Mexico.

Comments: Bulbs may remain dormant for years, until deep soaking rains stimulate them. Floral displays may then be spectacular. Flowers of more western populations may be red. *C. kennedyi* var. *munzii*, occasional throughout the range, has yellow flowers.

Apricot Globemallow, Desert Globe Mallow

APRICOT GLOBEMALLOW, DESERT GLOBE MALLOW
Sphaeralcea ambigua
Mallow Family (Malvaceae)

Description: Usually robust plants 2–4' tall, with several to many stems, and with sprays of orange-red flowers, but flower color varying from white through pink and rose to apricot and red-orange. Petals 5, ⅝–1½" long. Fruit hemispherical, ⅛–¼" high, with 9–13 wedge-like segments, the sides of which are coarsely netted, the notch on interior angle deep and conspicuous. Leaves ⅝–2" long, shallowly 3-lobed, scalloped on margins.

Flowering Season: Much of the year, most vigorously March–April.

Habitat/Range: Open places, mostly below 3,500', southeastern California to southwestern Utah, Arizona, and northwestern Mexico.

Comments: Plants may have 100 stems and when in flower are spectacular. East of Phoenix populations are multicolored, forming a festive display along roads in the spring.

Coulter's Globemallow

COULTER'S GLOBEMALLOW
Sphaeralcea coulteri
Mallow Family (Malvaceae)

Description: Red-orange flowers held in narrow clusters on plants with palmately lobed leaves. Petals 5, ⅜–½" long; stamens many. Fruit divides into about 15 dry, wedgelike, kidney-shaped segments ⅒" tall, each in side view with the part above notch much narrower than heavily netted part below notch. Leaf triangular or heart-shaped, 3- or 5-lobed, the margin scalloped. Stems sprawling, leaning at base, or erect, ½–4' long.

Flowering Season: January–May.

Habitat/Range: Open, usually sandy areas, below 2,500', southeastern California, southwestern Arizona, and northwestern Mexico.

Comments: Species of *Sphaeralcea* are difficult to identify, and the crucial features are in aspects of fruit segments. Coulter's Globemallow is the only one that is unquestionably an annual.

CALICHE GLOBEMALLOW
Sphaeralcea laxa
Mallow Family (Malvaceae)

Description: Few- to many-stemmed, often grayish plants, with palmately lobed leaves and long, open wands of orange-red flowers. Petals 5, ½–¾" long, fan-shaped. Stamens many, anthers dark purple. Fruit hemispherical, 3/16–¼" high, dividing into 12–14 wedge-shaped segments; segments as viewed from side have upper part tapering to a point, lower part prominently netted, with membranous, transparent windows in net. Leaves about as long as wide, triangular or heart-shaped, ½–2" long, shallowly to deeply 3-lobed, the lobes scalloped. Stems 1–3' tall.

Flowering Season: March–November.

Habitat/Range: Calcareous soils, 2,000–6,000', southern Arizona to Texas and northern Mexico.

Comments: Caliche, a rain-induced deposit of white calcium carbonate beneath the soil surface, is common in deserts.

Caliche Globemallow

HUMMINGBIRD TRUMPET, ZAUSCHNERIA
Epilobium canum ssp. *latifolium*
Evening Primrose Family (Onagraceae)

Description: Clumped, slightly shrubby plants, with clusters of long, bright-red flowers. The 4 petals are ⅜–⅝" long, cleft at tip, and attached to top of a broad, ¾–1¼" long tube. Sepals shorter than petals, set between them, also attached to top of tube. Stamens 8. Leaves ½–1" long, ovate, green, lightly hairy, and often also glandular, sometimes with teeth on edges. Stems 4–24" long.

Flowering Season: June–December.

Habitat/Range: Damp places, often in canyons, 2,500–7,000', Oregon to southern California, eastward to New Mexico, also northwestern Mexico.

Comments: This plant is popular in arid landscaping where a little extra water is provided. It is also called California Fuchsia because its flowers resemble Fuchsia, a popular ornamental in the same family.

Hummingbird Trumpet, Zauschneria

DESERT RHUBARB, CANAIGRE, CAÑA AGRIA, SAND DOCK
Rumex hymenosepalus
Buckwheat Family (Polygonaceae)

Description: Erect plants with long, dense clusters of small, pinkish bronze, membranous-winged fruits. Flowers small and green, with 6 sepals, the 3 inner enlarging to about ½" long, producing the wings on the heart-shaped fruit. Leaves mostly near base of stem, dark green, thick, lanceolate to oblong, 6–12" long. Stem stout, bronze, 1–4' tall.

Flowering Season: March–April.

Habitat/Range: Sand, 0–6,000', Wyoming to Mexico, southern California to western Texas.

Comments: Canaigre has been used medicinally, to make dye, as a substitute for rhubarb in pies, and, with sugar, as stewed or roasted greens. The clustered, swollen roots were a source of tannin for curing hides. Chewed, they helped alleviate pyorrhea. A tea prepared from them was used to treat sore throats.

Desert Rhubarb, Canaigre, Caña Agria, Sand Dock

Copper Purslane

COPPER PURSLANE
Portulaca suffrutescens
Purslane Family (Portulacaceae)

Description: Erect plants 6–12" tall, with linear leaves and coppery orange flowers ¾–1¼" across. Petals 5, fan-shaped, notched at tip, deep reddish at base. Stamens many, filaments deep red. Leaves cylindrical, fleshy and succulent, ½–1" long. Fruit a capsule, the top popping off like a small lid, exposing many tiny, curled seeds.

Flowering Season: July–September.

Habitat/Range: Sandy and gravelly places, 3,000–5,500', from southern Arizona east to Texas and Arkansas, south into Mexico.

Comments: People indigenous to the American Southwest once used seeds from native species of *Portulaca* to make mush and bread. Of the native purslanes, Copper Purslane has the largest flowers, which open as the morning warms and close about midday. The genus *Portulaca* has about 200 species, found worldwide in temperate and tropical regions, 3 giving rise to garden portulacas through selection for large and "doubled" flowers.

Crownpod Purslane

CROWNPOD PURSLANE
Portulaca umbraticola var. *coronata*
Purslane Family (Portulacaceae)

Description: Plants smooth, shiny, fleshy, with erect or spreading stems 3–8" long, and with small flowers near stem tips. Petals are red near tip and yellow near base or less commonly only yellow, ³⁄₁₆" long, and rounded at tip. Leaves linear or spatulate, ½–1¼" long. Fruit a capsule ¼" wide, surrounded by a thin, translucent, crownlike rim attached just below the lid. Capsule filled with many tiny, black, curled seeds.

Flowering Season: August–September.

Habitat/Range: Sandy or gravelly places, 2,500–6,000', southern Arizona to western Texas, south into Mexico.

Comments: This common species is often overlooked. Plants germinate and mature rapidly after summer rains, and the small but showy flowers open in the morning and close by midday.

Fire-Cracker Bush, Trompetilla

FIRE-CRACKER BUSH, TROMPETILLA
Bouvardia ternifolia
Coffee Family (Rubiaceae)

Description: Small shrubs 1–3' tall with leaves arranged in rings of 3–4 around stem, and with slender, trumpet-shaped, scarlet flowers at tips of branches. Corolla 1–1½" long, with usually 4, sometimes 5, pointed lobes at end of tube, the tube lightly hairy externally, and densely hairy within at base. Leaves 1½–3" long, ovate to lanceolate, tapered to a slender, pointed tip.

Flowering Season: May–October.

Habitat/Range: Canyons, usually in partial shade, 3,000–9,000', southern Arizona to western Texas and northern Mexico.

Comments: This species may be found on cooler, brushy slopes in the mountains near the upper limits of the Sonoran Desert. It is spectacular when in full flower, attracting hummingbirds, which feed on its nectar.

DESERT PAINTBRUSH
Castilleja chromosa
Figwort Family (Scrophulariaceae)

Description: Harshly hairy plants 6–18" tall, with divided leaves and a cluster of bright red flowers and bracts at top of each stem. Calyx tubular, ¾–1" long, bright red at tip, 4-lobed, more deeply cleft above than below, very shallowly cleft on sides. Corolla beaklike, ¾–1¼" long, usually protruding from calyx, green on top, with red-orange flanges on sides. Leaves 1–2½" long, linear near base of plant, divided into a few slender lobes on upper stem, intergrading with red-lobed bracts among flowers.

Flowering Season: March–April, at higher elevations until August.

Habitat/Range: Rocky areas, 2,000–8,000', much of western United States.

Comments: This species occurs along the northern edge of the Sonoran Desert in Arizona. Classification varies; by some specialists this is *C. applegatei* var. *martinii*.

Desert Paintbrush

WOOLLY INDIAN PAINTBRUSH

Castilleja lanata
Figwort Family (Scrophulariaceae)

Description: Woolly, pale gray plants 1–3' tall, with linear leaves, and clusters of bright red bracts and flowers at tops of stems. Calyx tubular, red at tip, ¾–1" long, the 4 lobes about one half length of calyx. Corolla beaklike, barely protruding from calyx, green on top, with red-orange flanges on sides. Leaves 1–3" long, intergrading into bright red, 3-lobed bracts among flowers.

Flowering Season: November–March, and at higher elevations throughout the summer and early fall.

Habitat/Range: Dry, rocky slopes, often among brush, 2,500–7,000', southern Arizona to western Texas, northern Mexico.

Comments: Paintbrushes are not common in the Sonoran Desert region. This species occurs in the mountains in the eastern portion of the desert, and even then it is not very frequent. The ragged flower cluster is the "paintbrush."

Woolly Indian Paintbrush

Crimson Monkeyflower

CRIMSON MONKEYFLOWER

Mimulus cardinalis
Figwort Family (Scrophulariaceae)

Description: Robust plants, usually with softly hairy foliage that is moist to the touch, and with large, bilateral crimson flowers. Flowers on slender stalks 2–3" long. Corolla 1½–2¼" long, much longer than calyx, the upper lip arched forward, the lower lip strongly bent downward. Leaf blades ¾–3" long, oblong or inversely lanceolate, toothed on edges, with 3–5 veins originating at point of attachment of leaf stalk. Stems 10–30" long.

Flowering Season: March–October.

Habitat/Range: Wet places in canyons, 2,000–8,500', southern California to western New Mexico, north to Utah and Oregon; also northwestern Mexico.

Comments: This is a spectacular wildflower to come upon when one is hiking in wet canyons in desert mountains. Hummingbirds visit the brilliant flowers.

Eaton's Firecracker

EATON'S FIRECRACKER
Penstemon eatoni ssp. *exsertus*
Figwort Family (Scrophulariaceae)

Description: Plants with opposite leaves and brilliant red, tubular flowers mostly turned to 1 side in long clusters. Corolla 1–1½" long, with 5 short, rounded lobes (2 upper, 2 lateral, and 1 down-curved lower lobe). Stamens project beyond lobes of corolla—4 are fertile, with hairy anthers, and 1 is sterile and hairless or sparsely hairy at tip. Leaves lanceolate to ovate, green, 2–5" long. Stems 1–4' tall.

Flowering Season: February–June.

Habitat/Range: On banks and flats, often among brush or trees, 2,000–7,000', southern Arizona.

Comments: Other varieties of Eaton's Firecracker, mostly to the north, have stamens that do not project beyond corolla lobes. The species is now a popular ornamental in southern Arizona, adding brilliant color to gardens and roadside parkways.

ARIZONA SCARLET-BUGLER
Penstemon subulatus
Figwort Family (Scrophulariaceae)

Description: Brilliant red, slightly bilateral, tubular flowers spread in loose, long clusters on plants with linear, opposite leaves. Corolla ¾–1" long, the tube ⅛–¼" wide at opening, the 5 short, round lobes spreading. Stamens 5, the sterile 1 hairless at tip or nearly so. Leaves 1–3" long, green or slightly grayish with a waxy bloom. Stems 8–30" tall, usually several in a clump.

Flowering Season: February–May.

Habitat/Range: Rocky hillsides and washes, 1,500–4,500', central and southern Arizona.

Comments: The red, tubular flowers attract hummingbirds, providing nectar for energy on their migration to the north or to higher elevations in mountains, where they will spend the summer. On their return, late-blooming plants of other species will supply nectar.

Arizona Scarlet-Bugler

Arizona Poppy, Orange Caltrop

ARIZONA POPPY, ORANGE CALTROP
Kallstroemia grandiflora
Caltrop Family (Zygophyllaceae)

Description: Sprawling plants with opposite, pinnately compound leaves and orange, bowl-shaped flowers, maroon in center. 5 fan-shaped petals, ½–1½" long. Leaves 1–3" long, with 4–8 pairs of elliptical leaflets ⅓–1" long. Fruit broadly ovate, but with a beak ¼–¾" long. Stems up to 4' long.

Flowering Season: February–September.

Habitat/Range: Open areas, especially where disturbed, 1,000–5,000', southeastern California to western Texas and northwestern Mexico.

Comments: The orange flowers bear a superficial resemblance to the California Poppy *(Eschscholzia californica)*, but there is no relationship. This similarity also is expressed in alternate common names of Desert Poppy, Mexican Poppy, or Summer Poppy. The species is occasionally cultivated as a summer annual.

LOSSARY

Alternate—placed singly along a stem, one after another, usually each successive item on a different side of the stem from previous. As one traces the orientation from one item to the next above, a spiral is drawn around the stem. Usually used in reference to arrangement of leaves on a stem (*see* Opposite and Whorl for comparison).

Annual—a plant that completes its life cycle, from seed germination to production of new seeds, within a year, then dying (*see* Perennial and Biennial for comparison).

Anther—a sac at the tip of the stamen where the pollen is formed.

Axil—the region in the angle formed by the upper side of the leaf or leaf stalk, where it joins the stem.

Banner—the upper petal in many of the flowers of the Bean Family (*see* "Pea" flower), often bent upward or even backward, usually broader than the other petals, and always covering them in the bud; also called "standard."

Basal—at the base or bottom of; generally used in reference to leaves located at the base of the stem, at ground level.

Biennial—a plant completing its life cycle in two years and normally not producing flowers during the first year (*see* Annual and Perennial for comparison).

Bilateral—in reference to the shape of a flower as viewed "face on," a shortened term for "bilaterally symmetrical," and substitution for the technical term "zygomorphic." A bilateral flower is one that can be divided into

mirror images in only one plane through the center of the flower. Mammals, fish, birds, and insects, for example, are bilateral (*see* Radial for comparison).

Blade—the broad, flat part of a structure, usually in reference to leaves or petals, often contrasting with the stalk of the structure.

Bract—reduced or modified leaf, often associated with flowers, either green or not, sometimes scalelike.

Bristle—a stiff hair, usually erect or curving away from its attachment point.

Bulb—underground plant part that is a short, swollen stem covered by fleshy, modified, usually non-green, food-storing, scalelike leaves (example is the onion).

Calyx—a collective term for the outer set of flower parts, composed of sepals, which may be separate or joined to one another; usually green. If there is only one set of parts outside the stamens or pistil, it is by definition the calyx, even though it may resemble a corolla (*see* Corolla and Petal-Like Parts for comparison).

Capsule—a dry fruit that releases seeds through splits or holes; as used in this guide, usually not elongate (*see* Pod for comparison).

Clasping—surrounding or partially wrapping around a stem or branch.

Cluster—any grouping or close arrangement of individual flowers; "flower cluster" is used as a substitute for the commonly used but more technical term "inflorescence."

Compound Leaf—a leaf that is divided to its midrib or stalk into two to many leaflets, each of which resembles a complete leaf. A leaf will have a bud in its axil, whereas leaflets do not (*see* Palmately Compound Leaf, Pinnately Compound Leaf, and Simple Leaf in the introduction for comparison).

Corolla—collective term for the set of flower parts interior to the calyx and exterior to the stamens (if present), composed of petals, which may be free or united; often white or brightly colored, rarely green (*see* Calyx and Petal-Like Parts for comparison).

Deciduous—a term referring to the more or less synchronized shedding of structures, usually leaves. Shrubs and trees that drop all their leaves at the end of the growing season are "deciduous," or leaves may be said to be "deciduous." Many desert plants are evergreen, but will shed their leaves during severe drought, and then are "drought deciduous" (*see* Evergreen for comparison).

Disk Flower—small, tubular, usually trumpet-shaped flowers in the central portion of the flower head of plants in the Sunflower Family (Asteraceae) (*see* illustration p. 32; *see* Ray Flower and Strap-Shaped Flower for comparison).

Elliptical—in reference to the shape of a plane cut obliquely through the axis of a cone, usually in reference to leaf shape (*see* illustration p. 31).

Entire—usually in reference to a leaf margin that is plain, not lobed or toothed (*see* illustration p. 30).

Erect—standing more or less perpendicularly to the surface.

Evergreen—plants that bear green leaves throughout the year. Leaves may be shed asynchronously or synchronously, but in either case, new leaves are in place before old ones are shed (*see* Deciduous for comparison).

Family—a group of related genera, usually easily recognized by sharing similar features (such as floral features, fruit types, stem anatomy, etc.).

Fiddleneck—coiled and resembling the carved, coiled end of the neck of a violin; in this guide used to describe a flower cluster that is coiled, the buds on the inside of the coil, open flowers on the outside, and maturing fruits somewhat distant on the stem below the coil. As the flowers bloom, the cluster slowly uncoils, exposing new buds to bloom.

Filament—the usually slender stalk of a stamen, tipped by the anther.

Flower Head—as used in this guide, a dense and continuous group of flowers, without obvious branches or spaces between them; often mistaken for a single "flower" until structure is understood. The term is used especially in reference to the grouping of flowers in the Sunflower Family (Asteraceae).

Fruit—the mature ovary of a plant, containing ripe seeds; a fruit may be fleshy or hard, large or small, and may consist of other parts of the flower or plant.

Genus—a group of closely related species, sharing many characteristics in common; plural "genera."

Genera—*see* Genus.

Glandular—bearing glands, structures that secrete something. Glands in plants are often borne at tips of hairs, the exuded substance usually moist or sticky and odoriferous, or they may be part of the surface layer and appear as darkened spots. Glandular secretions on the surface of plants usually inhibit or repel potential insects or other animals that might eat the plant.

Herbaceous—a term that means "not woody." Such a plant is usually soft and green.

Hood—a curved or folded structure, often somewhat scoop shaped, associated with the corolla. In this guide "hoods" are those scoop-like structures interior to the petals and exterior to the stamens in milkweeds (Asclepiadaceae); since most milkweeds have reflexed petals, the hoods are typically the most prominent feature of the flowers. Species with bilateral flowers also often have the upper lip "hoodlike," that is, much like a deeply cupped visor.

Inflorescence—the structure on which flowers are borne, in this guide called the "flower cluster;" various specialized terms describe the form of the inflorescence.

Involucre—a distinct series of bracts or leaves that subtend a flower or a flower cluster. Often used in the description of the flower head of the Sunflower Family (Asteraceae), where in this guide "ring of bracts" is substituted.

Keel—referring especially to the two joined petals forming the lower part of the flower in the Bean Family (Fabaceae), which resembles the prow of a boat (*see* illustration p. 32); any structure that is a sharp, narrow ridge.

Lanceolate—narrow and pointed at both ends, usually broader just below the middle, much like the tip of a lance. When describing a structure that is basically lanceolate but broader above the middle, in this guide the term "inversely lanceolate" is used, substituting for the technical term "oblanceolate."

Leaf—the flattened, usually photosynthetic and therefore food-producing organ of the plant, attached to the stem.

Leaf Blade—the broadened, flattened part of the leaf, in contrast to the leaf stalk.

Leaf Stalk—the slender portion of a leaf, distinguished from the blade, continuous with the midrib, and attaching the leaf to the stem; technically the "petiole."

Leaflet—a distinct, leaflike segment of a compound leaf.

Linear—long and very narrow, with parallel or nearly parallel sides—*see* illustration p. 31.

Lobe—a segment of an incompletely divided plant part, typically rounded at tip; often used in reference to the partial segmentation of the leaf blade.

Midrib—the central or main vein of a leaf.

Node—the region of the stem where one or more leaves are attached. Buds are commonly borne at nodes, in axils of leaves.

Nutlet—a term for a small, hard, one-seeded fruit or segment of a fruit.

Oblong—a shape with more or less parallel sides, longer in one direction than the other, as used here, with rounded ends; commonly used with leaf shape—*see* illustration p. 31.

Opposite—paired directly across from one another along a stem or axis (*see* Alternate and Whorl for comparison).

Ovary—the portion of the flower where seeds develop, usually a swollen area below the style (if present) and stigma; develops into the fruit.

Ovate—more or less egg shaped in outline, often bluntly pointed at tip.

Pads—used here in reference to flattened stem-joints of *Opuntia*. The pads are part of the stem, the spine clusters (technically areoles) derived from branch systems, the needles modified from leaves.

Palmate—referring to an arrangement where segments attach to a common point, much like fingers attach to the palm of a hand. Used commonly to describe lobing of a leaf (palmately lobed) or compound leaves (palmately compound). A palmately compound leaf is one that has three or more leaflets attached at the tip of the leaf stalk (leaves of lupines in the Bean Family, Fabaceae)—*see* illustration p. 30).

Parallel—side by side, about the same distance apart for the entire length; often used in reference to veins or edges of leaves.

Pappus—in the Sunflower Family (Asteraceae) the modified calyx, consisting of a crown of scales, bristles, or soft hairs at the top of the seedlike fruit.

"Pea" Flower—as used in this guide, a reference to the flower shape seen in many of the species in the Bean Family (Fabaceae), a flower that has a banner, two wings, and a keel—*see* illustration p. 32)

Perennial—a plant that normally lives for more than one year (*see* Annual and Biennial for comparison).

Petal—a unit of the corolla, usually flattened and brightly colored.

Petal-Like Parts—referring to parts of a flower that resemble petals but technically are not petals, or where the distinction between petals and sepals is not immediately evident; in technical works the term "tepals" may be used. In this guide "petal-like parts" is used in the Cactus Family (Cactaceae), where sepals are thoroughly intergradient with petals, in the Lily Family (Liliaceae), where sepals may be brightly colored like the petals, and in the Four O'Clock Family (Nyctaginaceae), where there are no petals and the calyx is brightly colored and fragile, like a delicate corolla.

Photosynthesis—the process by which plants use energy in light to rearrange and join molecules of carbon dioxide from the air, all to store the sun's energy in molecules of sugar built from the carbon dioxide and water, the plant's "food." Except for rare instances (such as around deep sea vents), all life on Earth depends on this process.

Pinna—the primary division of a compound leaf (plural pinnae), often equivalent to a leaflet (as in *Astragalus* and *Lupinus*). In a twice compound leaf, as in Velvet-Pod Mimosa *(Mimosa dysocarpa)*, this guide uses "segment" in place of pinna, the leaflets being the small leaflike structures resulting from division of the pinna.

Pinnate—referring to an arrangement where parts are aligned along opposite sides of an axis, much like the barbs of a feather are aligned along each side of the common central axis. Used commonly to describe lobing of a leaf (pinnately lobed) or compound leaves (pinnately compound). A pinnately compound leaf is one that has two or more leaflets arranged along opposite sides of a common axis (leaves of many members of the Bean Family, Fabaceae)—*see* illustration p. 30).

Pistil—the female part of the flower, consisting of ovary, style, and stigma; a flower may have one pistil or several pistils.

Pod—as used in this guide, a dry, elongate fruit that splits open upon maturity to release seeds (*see* Capsule for comparison).

Pollen—tiny, often powdery male reproductive cells formed in the anther, ultimately producing the sperm prior to fertilization of the egg within the ovary of the plant.

Pulvinus—a swelling at the base of a leaf stalk (petiole) or at the base of a leaflet that often aids in the movement of leaves or leaflets.

Radial—in reference to the shape of a flower as viewed "face on," a shortened term for "radially symmetrical," and substitution for the technical term "actinomorphic." A radial flower is one that can be divided into mirror images by several planes through the center of the flower. A starfish is radially symmetrical (*see* Bilateral for comparison).

Ray Flower—a flower at the periphery of the head of the Sunflower Family (Asteraceae), the corolla extended far to one side, flattened and shaped like a single petal; a flower head may have no, one, several, or many ray flowers; when several or many are present, they usually extend outward like the rays of a star—*see* illustration p. 32.

Rosette—a dense cluster of leaves very closely spaced around the stem, often at ground level, but in members of the Agave Family (Agavaceae), sometimes at the top of a stout trunk.

Scale—any thin, membranous, usually translucent structure that somewhat resembles scales of fish or reptiles.

Seedlike—resembling a seed; in this guide used to refer to the fruits of various plants, especially members of the Sunflower Family (Asteraceae), where the "seed" (as in the sunflower "seed") is technically a one-seeded fruit, the outer covering consisting of ovary wall joined to the bases of other flower parts, the true seed contained inside.

Sepal—a unit of the calyx, typically flattened and green but occasionally brightly colored (*see* "Petal-Like Parts" for comparison).

Shrub—a multi-stemmed, woody plant of moderate to low height with stems arising at ground or near ground level.

Simple Leaf—a leaf that is not compound. A simple leaf may have a plain (entire) margin, or the margin may be toothed or deeply lobed. As long as clefts between the lobes do not extend to the midrib, the leaf is simple. A deeply lobed oak leaf, for example, is "simple."

Spatulate—referring to a shape broader in upper half, round at the tip—*see* illustration p. 31.

Species—seemingly a simple concept, but one argued extensively by naturalists; usually a grouping of very similar individuals using their environment in a similar manner, capable of mating with one another. Because many plants reproduce asexually (e.g., Dandelion, *Taraxacum*) or tend to self-pollinate and self-fertilize (e.g., some suncups, *Camissonia*), the definition is more difficult to apply in plants than in many animal groups. Species are internationally referred to by a scientific name, a binomial, such as *Taraxacum officinale,* where the first name is the genus name and is a noun, and the second is the specific epithet and modifies the genus name. The binomial structurally is Latin, and usually has meaning. For example, *"Taraxacum"* is an ancient name for this plant, the precise meaning now lost, possibly of Greek or Arabic origin, perhaps meaning "to stir up;" *"officinale"* refers to "of the office," or an apothecary shop. Both names hint at medicinal properties. The term "species" is both singular and plural.

Specific Epithet—*see* Species.

Spike—an elongate, unbranched, often dense cluster of stalkless or nearly stalkless flowers.

Stalk—as used in this guide, a stemlike structure supporting a leaf, flower, or flower cluster (technically "petiole," "pedicel," and "peduncle," respectively).

Stalkless—lacking a stalk; when stalkless a leaf blade or a flower is directly attached to the stem.

Stamen—the male part of the flower, consisting of the slender, stalklike filament and the saclike anther, in which pollen forms.

Standard—*see* Banner.

Stigma—portion of the pistil receptive to pollen; usually at the top of the style and often appearing fuzzy or sticky.

Style—the portion of the pistil between the ovary and the stigma, often slender; each pollen grain will produce a tube that traverses the style, delivering sperm to the eggs within the ovary.

Strap-Shaped Flower—in reference to the type of flowers found in the heads of dandelions *(Taraxacum)* and their relatives in the Sunflower Family (Asteraceae). The flowers throughout the head are strap shaped, the corolla extended conspicuously toward the periphery of the head, the flowers in the center smaller than those near the edge of the head. Usually each corolla has five tiny teeth at tip. These are contrasted with ray flowers, which are similar but which are found only at the periphery of the head.

Subshrub—Semi-woody plants, particularly near base, often small; not as robust and woody as plants called shrubs, but not with soft, green stems throughout, either.

Subspecies—a group of individuals within a species that have a distinct range, habitat, and structure; in plants, usually not conceptually different from variety, but both terms remain in use because of historical reasons.

Subtend—situated below or beneath, often encasing or enclosing something.

Succulent—thickened, fleshy, and juicy.

Tendril—a slender, coiling or twining structure by which a climbing plant grasps its support.

Toothed—bearing teeth, or sharply angled projections, along an edge.

Tubercle—A small, rounded or conical projection.

Umbel—A flower cluster where each of the individual flower stalks attach at a common point at the tip of the main stalk of the flower cluster, much like the ribs of an umbrella attach at the top of the umbrella.

Variety—a group of individuals within a species that have a distinct range, habitat, and structure; in plants, usually not conceptually different from subspecies, but both terms remain in use because of historical reasons.

Veins—bundles of small cylindrical cells, some of which carry water and minerals, others of which carry a sugar solution. Water and sugar solutions may move in opposite directions through different series of cells in the same vein.

Whorl—three or more parts attached at the same point around a stem or axis (*see* Alternate and Opposite for comparison).

Wings—flat, thin, extended portions; in the Bean Family (Fabaceae), specifically referring to the two side petals of the flower, flanking the keel.

ADDITIONAL READING

Anderson, Edward F. *The Cactus Family.* Portland, Ore.: Timber Press, 2001.

Axelrod, D. I. *Age and Origin of Sonoran Desert Vegetation.* California Academy of Sciences, Occasional Papers. San Francisco, Calif.: Calif. Academy of Sciences Press, 1979.

Bender, Gordon L. (ed.). *Reference Handbook on the Deserts of North America.* Westport, Conn.: Greenwood Press, 1982

Correll, Donovan S., and Marshall C. Johnston. *Manual of the Vascular Plants of Texas.* Renner, Tex.: Texas Research Foundation, 1970.

Curtin, L. S. M. *Healing Herbs of the Upper Río Grande.* Los Angeles, Calif.: Southwest Museum, 1965.

Durant, Mary. *Who Named the Daisy? Who Named the Rose?* New York, N.Y.: Dodd, Mead & Co.

Felger, Richard S. *Flora of the Gran Desierto and Río Colorado of Northwestern Mexico.* Tucson, Ariz.: University of Arizona Press, 2000.

Fleming, T. H. "Pollination of Cacti in the Sonoran Desert." *American Scientist* 88:432-439, 2000

Hickman, James C. (ed.). *The Jepson Manual – Higher Plants of California.* Berkeley, Calif.: University of California Press, 1993.

Jaeger, Edmund C. *A Source-book of Biological Names and Terms* (3rd ed.). Springfield, Ill.: Charles C. Thomas, Publisher, 1955.

Kearney, Thomas H., and Robert H. Peebles. *Arizona Flora* (with supplement). Berkeley, Calif.: University of California Press, 1960.

Mabberley, D. J. *The Plant-book.* Cambridge, England: Cambridge University Press, 1989.

Munz, Philip A., and David D. Keck. *A California Flora.* Berkeley, Calif.: University of California Press, 1959.

Paredes Aguilar, R., T. R. Van Devender, and R. S. Felger. *Cactáceas de Sonora, México: su Diversidad, Uso y Conservación.* Tucson, Ariz.: Arizona-Sonoran Desert Museum Press, 2000.

Parson, Mary E. *The Wild Flowers of California.* San Francisco, Calif.: California School Book Depository, 1930.

Phillips, S. J., and P. W. Comus (eds.). *A Natural History of the Sonoran Desert.* Tucson, Ariz.: Arizona-Sonora Desert Museum Press; Berkeley, Calif.: University of California Press, 2000.

Roberts, Norman C. *Baja California Plant Field Guide.* La Jolla, Calif.: Natural History Publishing Co., 1989.

Robichaux, Robert H. (ed.). *Ecology of Sonoran Desert Plants and Plant Communities.* Tucson, Ariz.: University of Arizona Press, 1999.

Wasowski, Sally, and Andy Wasowski. *Native Landscaping from El Paso to L. A.* Chicago, Ill.: Contemporary Books.

Wiggins, Ira L. *Flora of the Sonoran Desert,* part II of Forrest Shreve and Ira L. Wiggins, *Vegetation and Flora of the Sonoran Desert.* Stanford, Calif.: Stanford University Press, 1964.

$\mathcal{I}$NDEX

A

Abert's Wild Buckwheat 65
Abrojo 86
Abronia villosa 104
Abutilon malacum 193
Acanthaceae
    Anisacanthus thurberi 212
    Dicliptera resupinata 74
    Justicia californica 213
    Ruellia nudiflora 74
    Siphonoglossa longiflora 34
    Tetramerium nervosum 148
Acanthus Family. *See* Acanthaceae
Achyronychia cooperi 51
Acourtia
    nana 76
    wrightii 77
Adonis Blazingstar 192
African Daisy 153
Agavaceae
    Agave deserti 149
    Yucca baccata 34
    Yucca elata 35
    Yucca schidigera 35
Agave deserti 149
Agave Family. *See* Agavaceae
Agria, Caña 221
Aguaro 109
Aizoaceae
    Sesuvium verrucosum 75
Ajamete 138
Alfilerillo 95
Algodoncillo 59
Aliciella latifolia 110
Alkali Mallow 59
Allionia incarnata 105
Amapola del Campo 198
Amaranthaceae
    Gomphrena sonorae 36
    Tidestromia lanuginosa 136
Amaranth Family. *See* Amaranthaceae
Amarilla, Hierba 151
Amarillo, Tabaco 207
American Threefold 171

Amoreuxia palmatifida 174
Amsinckia menziesii var. *intermedia* 174
Amsonia tomentosa 36
Amul 149
Anemone, Desert 68
Anemone tuberosa var. *tuberosa* 68
Anemopsis californica 69
Anisacanthus thurberi 212
Apocynaceae
    Amsonia tomentosa 36
    Haplophyton crooksii 149
Apodanthera undulata 180
Apricot Globemallow 219
Aquilegia chrysantha var. *chrysantha* 203
Argemone polyanthemos 63
Aristida purpurea var. *longiseta* 109
Aristolochiaceae
    Aristolochia watsonii 136
Aristolochia watsonii 136
Arizona Blanket-Flower 157
Arizona Blue-Curls 127
Arizona Blue-Eyes 120
Arizona Fiesta Flower 125
Arizona Foldwing 74
Arizona Jewelflower 48
Arizona Lupine 92
Arizona Mariposa 57
Arizona Milkvetch 90
Arizona Poppy 227
Arizona Scarlet-Bugler 226
Arizona Tickseed 153
Arizona Yellow-Throat Gilia 111
Asclepiadaceae
    Asclepias albicans 150
    Asclepias nyctaginifolia 137
    Asclepias subulata 138
    Funastrum cynanchoides var. *hartwegii* 76
    Funastrum hirtellum 138
Asclepias
    albicans 150
    nyctaginifolia 137
    subulata 138

Aster
    Mojave 82
    Orcutt's Woody 81
    Spiny 39
Asteraceae
    Acourtia nana 76
    Acourtia wrightii 77
    Atrichoseris platyphylla 37
    Bahia absinthifolia 150
    Baileya multiradiata 151
    Baileya pauciradiata 152
    Bebbia juncea 152
    Calycoseris wrightii 38
    Chaenactis stevioides 39
    Chloracantha spinosa 39
    Cirsium neomexicanum 77
    Coreopsis californica var. *newberryi* 153
    Dimorphotheca sinuata 153
    Encelia farinosa 154
    Encelia frutescens var. *frutescens* 155
    Ericameria laricifolia 155
    Ericameria linearifolia 156
    Erigeron divergens 40
    Eriophyllum lanosum 40
    Eriophyllum pringlei 156
    Eriophyllum wallacei 157
    Gaillardia arizonica 157
    Geraea canescens 158
    Gutierrezia microcephala 159
    Helianthus annuus 159
    Helianthus ciliaris 160
    Helianthus petiolaris 160
    Heliomeris longifolia var. *annua* 161
    Heterotheca subaxillaris 162
    Hymenothrix wislizeni 162
    Hymenoxys odorata 163
    Isocoma pluriflora 164
    Lasthenia gracilis 164
    Machaeranthera canescens 78
    Machaeranthera pinnatifida 165
    Machaeranthera tanacetifolia 79
    Malacothrix fendleri 165

Malacothrix glabrata 166
Melampodium leucanthum 41
Monoptilon bellioides 41
Palafoxia arida var. *arida* 79
Pectis papposa 166
Perityle emoryi 42
Peucephyllum schottii 167
Porophyllum gracile 80
Psathyrotes ramosissima 168
Psilostrophe cooperi 169
Rafinesquia neomexicana 42
Senecio flaccidus var. *monoensis* 169
Stephanomeria exigua 80
Taraxacum officinale 170
Thymophylla pentachaeta var. *belenidium* 170
Trichoptilium incisum 171
Trixis californica 171
Uropappus lindleyi 172
Verbesina encelioides 173
Xylorhiza orcuttii 81
Xylorhiza tortifolia 82
Zinnia acerosa 43
Astragalus
    allochrous var. *playanus* 142
    arizonicus 90
    coccineus 216
    crotalariae 90
    lentiginosus var. *maricopae* 182
Atrichoseris platyphylla 37
Atriplex hymenelytra 141
Azul, Palo Verde 183

B

Bahia absinthifolia 150
Bahia, Silverleaf 150
Baileya
    multiradiata 151
    pauciradiata 152
Bajada Lupine 93
Banana Yucca 34
Barba de Chivato 68
Barrel Cactus
    Emoryi 214
    Southwestern 214
Bean Family. *See* Fabaceae
Bean, Slim-Jim 94
Beardtongue, Parry's 116
Beavertail Cactus 85
Bebbia juncea 152
Bee-Plant, Yellow 178
Bell, Desert 124
Bellflower Family. *See* Campanulaceae

Bells, Whispering 189
Bignoniaceae
    Chilopsis linearis ssp. *arcuata* 82
    Tecoma stans 173
Bill, Heron's 96
Bindweed, Field 52
Bird's-Foot Trefoil
    Broom 184
    Desert 186
    Greene's 184
Birthwort Family. *See* Aristolochiaceae
Bitterweed 163
Bixaceae
    Amoreuxia palmatifida 174
Blackfoot Daisy 41
Blackfoot, Plains 41
Black Mustard 175
Bladder Mallow, Curly 193
Bladderpod
    Gordon's 176
    Western White 48
Bladderpod Bush 178
Bladder Sage 126
Blanket-Flower, Arizona 157
Blazingstar
    Adonis 192
    Jones' 191
Blazing-Star
    Sand 190
    Silver 190
Blowball 170
Bluebells, Desert 124
Blue-Curls, Arizona 127
Blue-Eyed Scorpion-Weed 124
Blue-Eyes, Arizona 120
Blue Dicks 102
Blue Palo Verde 183
Bluestar, Woolly 36
Blueweed 160
Boerhavia coccinea 106
Borage Family. *See* Boraginaceae
Boraginaceae
    Amsinckia menziesii var. *intermedia* 174
    Cryptantha angustifolia 44
    Heliotropium curassavicum 44
    Tiquilia canescens var. *canescens* 83
    Tiquilia plicata 83
Bouvardia ternifolia 224
Bower, Texas Virgin's 68
Brassicaceae
    Brassica nigra 175
    Dimorphocarpa wislizenii 45

Dithyrea californica 46
Draba cuneifolio 46
Eruca vesicaria ssp. *sativa* 47
Erysimum capitatum 175
Lepidium fremontii var. *fremontii* 47
Lesquerella gordonii 176
Lesquerella purpurea 48
Lyrocarpa coulteri 139
Stanleya pinnata 176
Streptanthus carinatus ssp. *arizonicus* 48
Thysanocarpus curvipes 139
Brassica nigra 175
Brincadora 87
Bristly Calico 112
Brittle-Bush 154
Brittle-Bush, Button 155
Brittle Spineflower 145
Broad-Leaved Gilia 110
Broom Bird's-Foot Trefoil 184
Broom, California 185
Broomrape, Desert 107
Broomrape Family. *See* Orobanchaceae
Broom, Turpentine 131
Browneyes 60
Brownfoot 77
Brush, Turpentine 155
Buckhorn Cholla 215
Buckwheat
    Abert's Wild 65
    California 67
    Flat-Topped 66
Buckwheat Family. *See* Polygonaceae
Buen Día 195
Buffalo Bur 208
Buffalo Gourd 180
Bur, Buffalo 208
Bush-Beardtongue, Chaparral 204
Bush, Bladderpod 178
Bush, Fire-Cracker 224
Bush Pepperwort 47
Buttercup Family. *See* Ranunculaceae
Button Brittle-Bush 155

C

Cabeza de Viejo 85
Cactaceae
    Echinocereus fendleri var. *fasciculatus* 84
    Ferocactus emoryi 214
    Ferocactus wislizenii 214

Mammillaria grahamii var.
  grahamii 85
Opuntia acanthocarpa 215
Opuntia basilaris 85
Opuntia bigelovii 140
Opuntia echinocarpa 141
Opuntia engelmannii 86
Opuntia fulgida 87
Opuntia santa-rita 177
Opuntia spinosior 88
Peniocereus greggii var.
  transmontanus 49
Cactus
  Beavertail 85
  Emoryi Barrel 214
  Graham's Nipple 85
  Pink-Flower Hedgehog 84
  Southwestern Barrel 214
Cactus-Apple 86
Cactus Family. *See* Cactaceae
Caesalpinia virgata 182
Calabazilla 180
Calandrinia ciliata 113
Caliche Globemallow 220
Calico
  Bristly 112
  Desert 112
  Schott's 64
California Broom 185
California Buckwheat 67
California Evening Primrose 61
California Fagonia 117
California Goldfields 164
California Sage 126
California Spectacle-Pod 46
California Suncup 196
Calliandra eriophylla 91
Calochortus
  ambiguus 57
  kennedyi var. *kennedyi* 219
Caltrop Family. *See* Zygophyllaceae
Caltrop, Orange 227
Calycoseris wrightii 38
Camissonia
  brevipes ssp. *brevipes* 196
  californica 196
  cardiophylla 197
  claviformis ssp. *claviformis* 60
  refracta 61
Camote de Ratón 183
Campanulaceae
  Nemacladus glanduliferus 50
Camphorweed 162
Campo, Amapola del 198
Caña Agria 221

Canaigre 221
Cane Cholla 88
Canyon Morning Glory 121
Cape Marigold 153
Caper Family. *See* Capparaceae
Capparaceae
  Cleome lutea 178
  Isomeris arborea 178
  Polanisia dodecandra 51
  Wislizenia refracta ssp. *refracta*
    179
Carnation Family. *See*
  Caryophyllaceae
Caryophyllaceae
  Achyronychia cooperi 51
Castilleja
  chromosa 224
  exserta 114
  lanata 225
Catalina Mountain Phlox, Santa 65
Catalpa Family. *See* Bignoniaceae
Cat's Eye, Panamint 44
Cenizo, Palo 123
Century Plant, Desert 149
Cercidium floridum 183
Cereus, Desert Night-Blooming 49
Chaenactis stevioides 39
Chamaesaracha coronopus 69
Chamaesyce
  albomarginata 54
  florida 56
Chaparral Bush-Beardtongue 204
Chenopodiaceae
  Atriplex hymenelytra 141
Cherry
  Ivy-Leaf Ground 146
  Purple Ground 132
  Sharp-Leaf Ground 71
Chia 126
Chicória 170
Chicory, Desert 42
Chilcote 217
Chilopsis linearis ssp. *arcuata* 82
Chinchweed 166
Chinese Lantern 132
Chiricahua Milk-Spurge 56
Chivato, Barba de 68
Chloracantha spinosa 39
Cholla
  Buckhorn 215
  Cane 88
  Golden 141
  Jumping 87
  Silver 141
  Teddy-Bear 140
  Walkingstick 88

Chorizanthe
  brevicornu 145
  rigida 146
Chuparosa 152, 212, 213
Cirsium neomexicanum 77
Clammyweed 51
Claw
  Devil's 109
  Double 109
  Yellow Devil's 200
Clematis drummondii 68
Cleome lutea 178
Climbing Milkweed, Narrowleaf 76
Clover, Jackass 179
Cnidoscolus angustidens 55
Coachwhip 217
Cockroach Plant 149
Coffee Family. *See* Rubiaceae
Cola de Mico 44
Colorado Four O'Clock 106
Columbine, Golden 203
Common Frog-Fruit 72
Common Monkey-Flower 204
Common Sunflower 159
Convolvulaceae
  Convolvulus arvensis 52
  Evolvulus arizonicus 120
  Ipomoea barbatisepala 121
  Ipomoea coccinea var. *hederifolia*
    216
  Ipomoea nil 88
  Ipomoea ternifolia var. *leptoloma*
    89
Convolvulus arvensis 52
Copper Purslane 222
Coral-Bean, Western 217
Coreopsis californica var. *newberryi*
  153
Corona de Cristo 108
Corydalis aurea 188
Cotton, Thurber's 59
Coulter's Globemallow 220
Coulter's Lupine 121
Coulter's Lyre-Pod 139
Coulter's Wrinkle-Fruit 72
Coveria 102
Cowpen Daisy 173
Coyote, Mansanilla del 166
Coyote Melon 181
Crassulaceae
  Dudleya collomae 179
Creamcups 63
Crimson Monkeyflower 225
Crinklemat
  Fanleaf 83
  Wooly 83

Cristo, Corona de 108
Crossosoma bigelovii 53
Crossosomataceae
    Crossosoma bigelovii 53
Crownbeard, Golden 173
Crownpod Purslane 223
Cryptantha angustifolia 44
Cucaracha, Hierba de la 149
Cucurbita
    foetidissima 180
    palmata 181
Cucurbitaceae
    Apodanthera undulata 180
    Cucurbita foetidissima 180
    Cucurbita palmata 181
Cuernero 109
Cupfruit, White 38
Curly Bladder Mallow 193
Cuscutaceae
    Cuscuta umbellata 53
Cuscuta umbellata 53
Cutleaf Ironplant 165

D
Dagger, Spanish 35
Dainty Desert Hide*seed* 96
Daisillo 187
Daisy
    African 153
    Blackfoot 41
    Cowpen 173
    Tahoka 79
Dalea
    mollis 92
    neomexicana 56
Dandelion 170
Dandelion, Desert 166
Dasyochloa pulchella 145
Dátil 34
Datillo 35
Datura wrightii 70
Delphinium parishii 130
Desert Anemone 68
Desert-Beardtongue, Rosy 116
Desert Bell 124
Desert Bird's-Foot Trefoil 186
Desert Bluebells 124
Desert Broomrape 107
Desert Calico 112
Desert Century Plant 149
Desert Chicory 42
Desert Dandelion 166
Desert-Dandelion, Fendler's 165
Desert Evening Primrose, Yellow 198
Desert Five-Spot 102

Desert Globe Mallow 219
Desert Gold 158
Desert Golden-Poppy 199
Desert Hide*seed*, Dainty 96
Desert Holly 76, 141
Desert Honeysuckle 212
Desert Lily 58
Desert Lotus 186
Desert Marigold 151
Desert Mariposa 219
Desert-Mountain Manihot 142
Desert Night-Blooming Cereus 49
Desert Paintbrush 224
Desert Pincushion 39
Desert Rhubarb 221
Desert Rockdaisy 42
Desert Rock Nettle 190
Desert Rockpea 184
Desert Rose-Mallow 194
Desert Sand Verbena 104
Desert Senna 187
Desert Snow 64
Desertstar, Mojave 41
Desert Stingbush 190
Desert Stork's-Bill 96
Desert Sunflower 158
Desert Tobacco 71
Desert Trumpet 201
Desert-Trumpets, Golden 201
Desert Unicorn Plant 200
Desert Velvet 168
Desert Vine 192
Desert Willow 82
Desert Wishbone-Bush 60
Desert Woolstar 129
Desierto, Tomatillo del 207
Devil's Claw 109
Devil's Claw, Yellow 200
Devil's Lettuce 174
Devil's Spineflower 146
Devilweed, Mexican 39
Día, Buen 195
Dichelostemma capitatum 102
Dicks, Blue 102
Dicliptera resupinata 74
Dimorphocarpa wislizenii 45
Dimorphotheca sinuata 153
Dithyrea californica 46
Dock, Sand 221
Dodder Family. *See* Cuscutaceae
Dodder, Flat-Globe 53
Dogbane Family. *See* Apocynaceae
Dollarweed 59
Don Juan 207
Double Claw 109
Downy Prairie-Clover 56

Draba cuneifolio 46
Dudleya collomae 179
Dune Evening Primrose 62
Duster, Fairy 91
Dwarf White Honeysuckle 34

E
Easter-Bonnet, White 40
Eaton's Firecracker 226
Echinocereus fendleri var. *fasciculatus* 84
Ejotillo 178
Emmenanthe penduliflora var. *penduliflora* 189
Emoryi Barrel Cactus 214
Emory's Smokebush 94
Encelia
    farinosa 154
    frutescens var. *frutescens* 155
Engelmann's Prickly Pear 86
Epilobium canum ssp. *latifolium* 221
Eremalche rotundifolia 102
Eriastrum
    diffusum 128
    eremicum 129
Ericameria
    laricifolia 155
    linearifolia 156
Erigeron divergens 40
Eriogonum
    abertianum var. *abertianum* 65
    deflexum 66
    fasciculatum var. *polifolium* 67
    inflatum 201
Eriophyllum
    lanosum 40
    pringlei 156
    wallacei 157
Erodium
    cicutarium 95
    texanum 96
Eruca vesicaria ssp. *sativa* 47
Erysimum capitatum 175
Erythrina flabelliformis 217
Eschscholzia
    californica ssp. *mexicana* 198
    glyptosperma 199
    minutiflora 199
Escobita 114
Espanta Vaqueros 136
Eucnide urens 190
Eucrypta micrantha 96
Euphorbiaceae
    Chamaesyce albomarginata 54
    Chamaesyce florida 56
    Cnidoscolus angustidens 55
    Manihot angustiloba 142

Evening Primrose
    California 61
    Dune 62
    Yellow Desert 198
Evening Primrose Family. *See*
    Onagraceae
Evolvulus arizonicus 120
Eye, Panamint Cat's 44

F
Fabaceae
    Astragalus allochrous var.
        playanus 142
    Astragalus arizonicus 90
    Astragalus coccineus 216
    Astragalus crotalariae 90
    Astragalus lentiginosus var.
        maricopae 182
    Caesalpinia virgata 182
    Calliandra eriophylla 91
    Cercidium floridum 183
    Dalea mollis 92
    Dalea neomexicana 56
    Erythrina flabelliformis 217
    Hoffmanseggia glauca 183
    Lotus greenei 184
    Lotus rigidus 184
    Lotus scoparius var. *brevialatus*
        185
    Lotus strigosus var. *tomentellus*
        186
    Lupinus arizonicus 92
    Lupinus concinnus 93
    Lupinus sparsiflorus 121
    Marina parryi 122
    Mimosa dysocarpa 93
    Phaseolus filiformis 94
    Psorothamnus emoryi 94
    Psorothamnus schottii 122
    Psorothamnus spinosa 123
    Senna armata 186
    Senna covesii 187
    Senna hirsuta var. *glaberimma*
        188
Fagonia, California 117
Fagonia laevis 117
Fairy Duster 91
False Golden-Eye, Longleaf 161
False Prairie-Clover, Parry's 122
Fanleaf Crinklemat 83
Fanpetals, Spreading 195
Fendler's Desert-Dandelion 165
Fermina 192
Ferocactus
    emoryi 214
    wislizenii 214

Field Bindweed 52
Fiesta Flower, Arizona 125
Fig-Marigold Family. *See* Aizoaceae
Figwort Family. *See*
    Scrophulariaceae
Filaree 95
Fire-Cracker Bush 224
Firecracker, Eaton's 226
Fireweed, Rancher's 174
Five-Eyes, Green-Leaf 69
Five-Needle Pricklyleaf 170
Five-Spot, Desert 102
Flameflower, Orange 202
Flat-Globe Dodder 53
Flat-Topped Buckwheat 66
Flat-Topped Skeleton-Weed 66
Flax Family. *See* Linaceae
Flax, Meadow 128
Fleabane, Spreading 40
Flor de Tierra 107
Flower, Arizona Fiesta 125
Flower, Ghost 205
Flower, Mexican Passion 143
Flower, Onyx 51
Flower, Scarlet Fruit Passion 108
Fluffgrass 145
Foldwing, Arizona 74
Fountain Grass 110
Fouquieriaceae
    Fouquieria splendens 217
Fouquieria splendens 217
Fournwort, Hairy 148
Four O'Clock
    Colorado 106
    Showy 106
    Trailing 105
Four O'Clock Family. *See*
    Nyctaginaceae
Fringepod 139
Frog-Fruit, Common 72
Frostmat 51
Fruit Passion Flower, Scarlet 108
Fumariaceae
    Corydalis aurea 188
Fumitory Family. *See* Fumariaceae
Funastrum
    cynanchoides var. *hartwegii* 76
    hirtellum 138

G
Gaillardia arizonica 157
Garden Rocket 47
Gato, Uña de 200
Gatuño 93
Geraea canescens 158

Geraniaceae
    Erodium cicutarium 95
    Erodium texanum 96
Geranium Family. *See* Geraniaceae
Ghost Flower 205
Ghost, Gravel 37
Gila Live-Forever 179
Gilia
    Arizona Yellow-Throat 111
    Broad-Leaved 110
    Rock 111
Gilia
    flavocincta ssp. *flavocincta* 111
    scopulorum 111
Girasol 159
Gland-Leaf Milkwort 113
Globe-Amaranth, Sonoran 36
Globemallow
    Apricot 219
    Caliche 220
    Coulter's 220
Globe Mallow, Desert 219
Glory
    Canyon Morning 121
    Ivy Morning 88
    Three-Leaved Morning 89
    Orchard Morning 52
Goat Head 209
Gold, Desert 158
Goldenbush, Interior 156
Golden Cholla 141
Golden Columbine 203
Golden Crownbeard 173
Golden Desert-Trumpets 201
Golden-Eye, Longleaf False 161
Goldenhills 154
Golden-Poppy
    Desert 199
    Pygmy 199
Golden Prince's Plume 176
Goldenrod, Rayless 164
Golden Suncup 196
Goldfields, California 164
Gold Poppy
    Little 199
    Mexican 198
Golondrina 54
Gomphrena sonorae 36
Goodding's Vervain 117
Goosefoot Family. *See*
    Chenopodiaceae
Gordon's Bladderpod 176
Gossypium thurberi 59
Gourd, Buffalo 180
Graham's Nipple Cactus 85

Grass Family. *See* Poaceae
Grass, Fountain 110
Gravel Ghost 37
Greene's Bird's-Foot Trefoil 184
Green-Leaf Five-Eyes 69
Ground Cherry
    Ivy-Leaf 146
    Purple 132
    Sharp-Leaf 71
Ground-Cherry, Yellow 207
Guinagua 201
Gutierrezia microcephala 159

H

Hairy Fournwort 148
Hairy Prairie-Clover 92
Halfmoon Milkvetch 142
Haplophyton crooksii 149
Head, Goat 209
Heartleaf Suncup 197
Heather, Purple 100
Hedgehog Cactus, Pink-Flower 84
Hedge-Nettle, Scarlet 218
Helianthus
    annuus 159
    ciliaris 160
    petiolaris 160
Heliomeris longifolia var. *annua* 161
Heliotropium curassavicum 44
Herissantia crispa 193
Heron's Bill 96
Hesperocallis undulata 58
Heterotheca subaxillaris 162
Hibiscus
    coulteri 194
    denudatus 103
Hibiscus, Rock 103
Hideseed, Dainty Desert 96
Hierba Amarilla 151
Hierba de la Cucaracha 149
Hierba de la Hormiga 105
Hierba de la Virgen Maria 72
Hoary Tansey-Aster 78
Hoffmanseggia glauca 183
Hog Potato 183
Hogweed, Little 202
Hojasen 187
Holdback, Wand 182
Holly, Desert 76, 141
Honeysuckle
    Desert 212
    Dwarf White 34
Honeysweet, Woolly 136
Hormiga, Hierba de la 105
Horse-Nettle, White 133
Horsfordia alata 103

Hummingbird-Bush 213
Hummingbird Trumpet 221
Hydrophyllaceae
    Emmenanthe penduliflora var.
        penduliflora 189
    Eucrypta micrantha 96
    Nama demissum 97
    Nama hispidum 98
    Phacelia campanularia 124
    Phacelia crenulata var. *ambigua*
        99
    Phacelia distans 124
    Phacelia pedicellata 99
    Pholistoma auritum var.
        arizonicum 125
Hymenothrix wislizeni 162
Hymenoxys odorata 163

I

Incienso 154
Indian-Mallow, Yellow 193
Indian Paintbrush, Woolly 225
Indian-Root 136
Indianwheat, Woolly 144
Interior Goldenbush 156
Ipomoea
    barbatisepala 121
    coccinea var. *hederifolia* 216
    nil 88
    ternifolia var. *leptoloma* 89
Ipomopsis longiflora ssp. *australis* 129
Ironplant, Cutleaf 165
Isocoma pluriflora 164
Isomeris arborea 178
Ivy-Leaf Ground Cherry 146
Ivy Morning Glory 88

J

Jackass Clover 179
Janusia gracilis 192
Janusia, Slender 192
Jewelflower, Arizona 48
Jimmy-Weed 164
Jones' Blazingstar 191
Juan, Don 207
Jumping Cholla 87
Junco 152
Justicia californica 213

K

Kallstroemia grandiflora 227
Keckiella antirrhinoides var.
    microphylla 204
Krameriaceae
    Krameria erecta 100
Krameria erecta 100

L

Lacepod 139
Lacy Tansey-Aster 165
Lamiaceae
    Salazaria mexicana 126
    Salvia columbariae 126
    Stachys coccinea 218
    Trichostema arizonicum 127
Langloisia setosissima ssp. *setosissima*
    112
Lantern, Chinese 132
Larkspur, Parish's 130
Lasthenia gracilis 164
Laxflower 152
Lennoaceae
    Pholisma arenarium 101
Lennoa Family. *See* Lennoaceae
Lepidium fremontii var. *fremontii* 47
Lesquerella
    gordonii 176
    purpurea 48
Lettuce, Devil's 174
Liliaceae
    Calochortus ambiguus 57
    Calochortus kennedyi var.
        kennedyi 219
    Dichelostemma capitatum 102
    Hesperocallis undulata 58
Lily, Desert 58
Lily Family. *See* Liliaceae
Linaceae
    Linum pratense 128
Linanthus
    aureus ssp. *aureus* 201
    demissus 64
Linum pratense 128
Lipstick-Tree Family. *See* Bixaceae
Little Gold Poppy 199
Little Hogweed 202
Live-Forever, Gila 179
Lizard's-Tail Family. *See* Saururaceae
Loasaceae
    Eucnide urens 190
    Mentzelia involucrata 190
    Mentzelia jonesii 191
    Mentzelia multiflora 192
Loasa Family. *See* Loasaceae
Loeseliastrum
    mathewsii 112
    schottii 64
Longleaf False Golden-Eye 161
Lotus
    greenei 184
    rigidus 184
    scoparius var. *brevialatus* 185
    strigosus var. *tomentellus* 186

Lotus, Desert 186
Lupine
  Arizona 92
  Bajada 93
  Coulter's 121
Lupinus
  arizonicus 92
  concinnus 93
  sparsiflorus 121
Lyre-Pod, Coulter's 139
Lyrocarpa coulteri 139

M

Machaeranthera
  canescens 78
  pinnatifida 165
  tanacetifolia 79
Maids, Red 113
Malacothrix
  fendleri 165
  glabrata 166
Mala Mujer 55, 208
Mallow
  Alkali 59
  Curly Bladder 193
  Pink Velvet 103
Mallow Family. *See* Malvaceae
Malpighiaceae
  Janusia gracilis 192
Malpighia Family. *See*
  Malpighiaceae
Malvaceae
  Abutilon malacum 193
  Eremalche rotundifolia 102
  Gossypium thurberi 59
    Herissantia crispa 193
    Hibiscus coulteri 194
    Hibiscus denudatus 103
    Horsfordia alata 103
    Malvella leprosa 59
    Sida abutifolia 195
    Sphaeralcea ambigua 219
    Sphaeralcea coulteri 220
    Sphaeralcea laxa 220
  Malvella leprosa 59
Mammillaria grahamii var. *grahamii*
  85
Manihot angustiloba 142
Manihot, Desert-Mountain 142
Mansanilla del Coyote 166
Mansa, Yerba 69
Maria, Hierba de la Virgen 72
Maricopa Milkvetch 182
Marigold
  Cape 153
  Desert 151

Marina parryi 122
Mariposa
  Arizona 57
  Desert 219
Maurandella antirrhiniflora 115
Meadow Flax 128
Melampodium leucanthum 41
Melon, Coyote 181
Melon-Loco 180
Menodora, Rough 195
Menodora scabra 195
Mentzelia
  involucrata 190
  jonesii 191
  multiflora 192
Mesquitilla 91
Mexican Devilweed 39
Mexican Gold Poppy 198
Mexican Passion Flower 143
Mexican Yellowshow 174
Mexico Thistle, New 77
Mezcal 149
Mico, Cola de 44
Milk-Spurge, Chiricahua 56
Milkvetch
  Arizona 90
  Halfmoon 142
  Maricopa 182
  Salton 90
  Scarlet 216
Milkweed
  Mojave 137
  Narrowleaf Climbing 76
  Rush 138
  White-Stem 150
Milkweed Family. *See*
  Asclepiadaceae
Milkwort Family. *See* Polygalaceae
Milkwort, Gland-Leaf 113
Mimbre 82
Mimosa dysocarpa 93
Mimosa, Velvet-Pod 93
Mimulus
  bigelovii 115
  cardinalis 225
  guttatus 204
Miniature Woolstar 128
Mint Family. *See* Lamiaceae
Mirabilis
  laevis var. *villosa* 60
  multiflora 106
Mirasol 159
Mohavea confertiflora 205
Mojave Aster 82
Mojave Desertstar 41
Mojave Milkweed 137

Mojave Yucca 35
Monkeyflower
  Crimson 225
  Yellow-Throat 115
Monkey-Flower
  Common 204
  Seep 204
  Yellow 204
Monoptilon bellioides 41
Morada 97, 98
Morning Glory
  Canyon 121
  Ivy 88
  Orchard 52
  Three-Leaved 89
Morning Glory Family. *See*
  Convolvulaceae
Mountain Phlox, Santa Catalina 65
Mujer, Mala 55, 208
Mustard, Black 175
Mustard Family. *See* Brassicaceae

N

Nama
  demissum 97
  hispidum 98
Narrowleaf Climbing Milkweed 76
Narrowleaf Suncup 61
Needles, Spanish 79
Nemacladus glanduliferus 50
Neogaerrhinum filipes 206
Nettle, Desert Rock 190
New Mexico Thistle 77
Nicotiana
  glauca 207
  obtusifolia var. *obtusifolia* 71
Night-Blooming Cereus, Desert 49
Nightshade Family. *See* Solanaceae
Nightshade, Silver-Leaf 133
Nipple Cactus, Graham's 85
Noche, Reina de la 49
Nopal 86
Notch-Leaf Scorpion-Weed 99
Nuttallanthus texanus 131
Nyctaginaceae
  Abronia villosa 104
  Allionia incarnata 105
  Boerhavia coccinea 106
  Mirabilis laevis var. *villosa* 60
  Mirabilis multiflora 106

O

O'Clock
  Colorado Four 106
  Showy Four 106
  Trailing Four 105

Ocotillo 217
Ocotillo Family. *See* Fouquieriaceae
Odora 80
Oenothera
    californica ssp. *avita* 61
    deltoides ssp. *deltoides* 62
    primiveris ssp. *primiveris* 198
Oleaceae
    Menodora scabra 195
Olive Family. *See* Oleaceae
Onagraceae
    Camissonia brevipes ssp. *brevipes*
      196
    Camissonia californica 196
    Camissonia cardiophylla 197
    Camissonia claviformis ssp.
      claviformis 60
    Camissonia refracta 61
    Epilobium canum ssp. *latifolium*
      221
    Oenothera californica ssp. *avita*
      61
    Oenothera deltoides ssp. *deltoides*
      62
    Oenothera primiveris ssp.
      primiveris 198
Onyx Flower 51
Opuntia
    acanthocarpa 215
    basilaris 85
    bigelovii 140
    echinocarpa 141
    engelmannii 86
    fulgida 87
    santa-rita 177
    spinosior 88
Orange Caltrop 227
Orange Flameflower 202
Orchard Morning Glory 52
Orcutt's Woody Aster 81
Oreja del Perro 83
Orobanchaceae
    Orobanche cooperi ssp. *latiloba*
      107
Orobanche cooperi ssp. *latiloba* 107
Owl's-Clover, Purple 114

P

Paintbrush
    Desert 224
    Woolly Indian 225
Palafoxia arida var. *arida* 79
Paleface 103
Paleflower Skyrocket 129
Palmilla 35

Palo Cenizo 123
Palo Verde Azul 183
Palo Verde, Blue 183
Panamint Cat's Eye 44
Papaveraceae
    Argemone polyanthemos 63
    Eschscholzia californica ssp.
      mexicana 198
    Eschscholzia glyptosperma 199
    Eschscholzia minutiflora 199
    Platystemon californicus 63
Paperflower, White-Stem 169
Parachute Plant 37
Parish's Larkspur 130
Parralena 170
Parry's Beardtongue 116
Parry's False Prairie-Clover 122
Passiflora
    foetida 108
    mexicana 143
Passifloraceae
    Passiflora foetida 108
    Passiflora mexicana 143
Passion Flower
    Mexican 143
    Scarlet Fruit 108
Passion-Flower Family. *See*
    Passifloraceae
Pear, Engelmann's Prickly 86
Pectis papposa 166
Pedaliaceae
    Proboscidea althaeifolia 200
    Proboscidea parviflora 109
Peniocereus greggii var. *transmontanus*
    49
Pennisetum setaceum 110
Penstemon
    eatoni ssp. *exsertus* 226
    parryi 116
    pseudospectabilis 116
    subulatus 226
Pepperwort, Bush 47
Perityle emoryi 42
Perro, Oreja del 83
Petunia, Violet Wild 74
Peucephyllum schottii 167
Phacelia
    campanularia 124
    crenulata var. *ambigua* 99
    distans 124
    pedicellata 99
Phaseolus filiformis 94
Phlox Family. *See* Polemoniaceae
Phlox, Santa Catalina Mountain 65
Phlox tenuifolia 65

Pholisma arenarium 101
Pholistoma auritum var. *arizonicum*
    215
Phyla nodiflora 72
Physalis
    acutifolia 71
    crassifolia 207
    hederaefolia 146
Pigmy-Cedar 167
Pignut 183
Pima Ratany 100
Pincushion, Desert 39
Pink-Flower Hedgehog Cactus 84
Pink Velvet Mallow 103
Pinstalk Scorpionweed 99
Pipevine, Southwestern 136
Plains Blackfoot 41
Plains Sunflower 160
Plantaginaceae
    Plantago patagonica 144
Plantago patagonica 144
Plantain Family. *See* Plantaginaceae
Plantain, Woolly 144
Plant, Cockroach 149
Plant, Desert Century 149
Plant, Desert Unicorn 200
Plant, Parachute 37
Plant, Quail 44
Plant, Unicorn 109
Platystemon californicus 63
Plume, Golden Prince's 176
Plumilla 171
Poaceae
    Aristida purpurea var. *longiseta*
      109
    Dasyochloa pulchella 145
    Pennisetum setaceum 110
Poison Rubberweed 163
Polanisia dodecandra 51
Polemoniaceae
    Aliciella latifolia 110
    Eriastrum diffusum 128
    Eriastrum eremicum 129
    Gilia flavocincta ssp. *flavocincta*
      111
    Gilia scopulorum 111
    Ipomopsis longiflora ssp. *australis*
      129
    Langloisia setosissima ssp.
      setosissima 112
    Linanthus aureus ssp. *aureus* 201
    Linanthus demissus 64
    Loeseliastrum mathewsii 112
    Loeseliastrum schottii 64
    Phlox tenuifolia 65

Polygalaceae
  Polygala macradenia 113
Polygala macradenia 113
Polygonaceae
  Chorizanthe brevicornu 145
  Chorizanthe rigida 146
  Eriogonum abertianum var.
    abertianum 65
  Eriogonum deflexum 66
  Eriogonum fasciculatum var.
    polifolium 67
  Eriogonum inflatum 201
  Polygonum lapathifolium 67
  Rumex hymenosepalus 221
Polygonum lapathifolium 67
Poppy
  Little Gold 199
  Mexican Gold 198
  White Prickly 63
Poppy, Arizona 227
Poppy Family. *See* Papaveraceae
Pop-Ups, Purple 101
Poreleaf, Slender 80
Porophyllum gracile 80
Portulaca
  oleracea 202
  suffrutescens 222
  umbraticola var. *coronata* 223
Portulacaceae
  Calandrinia ciliata 113
  Portulaca oleracea 202
  Portulaca suffrutescens 222
  Portulaca umbraticola var.
    coronata 223
  Talinum aurantiacum 202
Potato, Hog 183
Prairie-Clover
  Downy 56
  Hairy 92
  Parry's False 122
Pricklyleaf, Five-Needle 170
Prickly Pear, Engelmann's 86
Pricklypear, Santa Rita 177
Prickly Poppy, White 63
Primrose
  California Evening 61
  Dune Evening 62
  Yellow Desert Evening 198
Prince's Plume, Golden 176
Pringle's Woolly-Daisy 156
Proboscidea
  althaeifolia 200
  parviflora 109
Psathyrotes ramosissima 168
Psilostrophe cooperi 169

Psorothamnus
  emoryi 94
  schottii 122
  spinosa 123
Puncture Vine 209
Purple Ground Cherry 132
Purple Heather 100
Purplemat 97
Purple Owl's-Clover 114
Purple Pop-Ups 101
Purple Three-Awn 109
Purslane 202
Purslane
  Copper 222
  Crownpod 223
Purslane Family. *See* Portulacaceae
Pygmy Golden-Poppy 199

Q
Quail Plant 44
Queen-of-the-Night 49
Quincula lobata 132

R
Rafinesquia neomexicana 42
Ragged Rockflower 53
Ragwort, Smooth Threadleaf 169
Rancher's Fireweed 174
Range Ratany 100
Ranunculaceae
  Anemone tuberosa var. *tuberosa*
    68
  Aquilegia chrysantha var.
    chrysantha 203
  Clematis drummondii 68
  Delphinium parishii 130
Ratany
  Pima 100
  Range 100
Ratany Family. *See* Krameriaceae
Ratón, Camote de 183
Rattlesnake Weed 54
Rayless Goldenrod 164
Red Maids 113
Redstar 216
Redstem Stork's-Bill 95
Red Three-Awn 109
Redtip Threadstem 50
Reina de la Noche 49
Rhubarb, Desert 221
Rita Pricklypear, Santa 177
Rockdaisy, Desert 42
Rocket
  Garden 47
  Salad 47

Rockflower Family. *See*
  Crossosomataceae
Rockflower, Ragged 53
Rock Gilia 111
Rock Hibiscus 103
Rock Nettle, Desert 190
Rockpea, Desert 184
Romero 167
Rose-Mallow, Desert 194
Rosy Desert-Beardtongue 116
Rough Menodora 195
Roving Sailor 115
Rubberweed, Poison 163
Rubiaceae
  Bouvardia ternifolia 224
Rue Family. *See* Rutaceae
Ruellia nudiflora 74
Rumex hymenosepalus 221
Rush Milkweed 138
Rutaceae
  Thamnosma montana 131

S
Sacred Thorn-Apple 70
Sage
  Bladder 126
  California 126
Sailor, Roving 115
Salad Rocket 47
Salazaria mexicana 126
Salton Milkvetch 90
Salvia columbariae 126
Sandbells 98
Sand Blazing-Star 190
Sand Dock 221
Sandmat 51
Sandmat, White-Margin 54
Sand Verbena, Desert 104
Santa Catalina Mountain Phlox 65
Santa Rita Pricklypear 177
Saururaceae
  Anemopsis californica 69
Scarlet-Bugler, Arizona 226
Scarlet Fruit Passion Flower 108
Scarlet Hedge-Nettle 218
Scarlet Milkvetch 216
Scarlet Spiderling 106
Schott's Calico 64
Schott's Smokebush 122
Scorpionweed, Pinstalk 99
Scorpion-Weed
  Blue-Eyed 124
  Notch-Leaf 99
Scrambled-Eggs 188

Scrophulariaceae
Castilleja chromosa 224
Castilleja exserta 114
Castilleja lanata 225
Keckiella antirrhinoides var.
microphylla 204
Maurandella antirrhiniflora 115
Mimulus bigelovii 115
Mimulus cardinalis 225
Mimulus guttatus 204
Mohavea confertiflora 205
Neogaerrhinum filipes 206
Nuttallanthus texanus 131
Penstemon eatoni ssp. exsertus
226
Penstemon parryi 116
Penstemon pseudospectabilis 116
Penstemon subulatus 226
Sea-Purslane, Western 75
Seep Monkey-Flower 204
Senecio flaccidus var. monoensis 169
Senna
Desert 187
Slim-Pod 188
Spiny 186
Senna
armata 186
covesii 187
hirsuta var. glaberimma 188
Sesame Family. See Pedaliaceae
Sesuvium verrucosum 75
Sharp-Leaf Ground Cherry 71
Showy Four O'Clock 106
Sida abutifolia 195
Silver Blazing-Star 190
Silver Cholla 141
Silverleaf Bahia 150
Silver-Leaf Nightshade 133
Silverpuffs 172
Siphonoglossa longiflora 34
Skeleton-Weed, Flat-Topped 66
Skyrocket, Paleflower 129
Slender Janusia 192
Slender Poreleaf 80
Slim-Jim Bean 94
Slim-Pod Senna 188
Small-Head Snakeweed 159
Smokebush
Emory's 94
Schott's 122
Smoketree 123
Smooth Threadleaf Ragwort 169
Smooth Twinevine 138
Snakeroot 136
Snakeweed
Small-Head 159
Sticky 159

Snapdragon
Violet Twining 115
Yellow Twining 206
Snow, Desert 64
Soaptree Yucca 35
Solanaceae
Chamaesaracha coronopus 69
Datura wrightii 70
Nicotiana glauca 207
Nicotiana obtusifolia var.
obtusifolia 71
Physalis acutifolia 71
Physalis crassifolia 207
Physalis hederaefolia 146
Quincula lobata 132
Solanum elaeagnifolium 133
Solanum rostratum 208
Solanum
elaeagnifolium 133
rostratum 208
Sonoran Globe-Amaranth 36
Southwestern Barrel Cactus 214
Southwestern Pipevine 136
Southwestern Spectacle-Pod 45
Spanish Dagger 35
Spanish Needles 79
Spectacle-Pod
California 46
Southwestern 45
Sphaeralcea
ambigua 219
coulteri 220
laxa 220
Spiderling, Scarlet 106
Spineflower
Brittle 145
Devil's 146
Spiny Aster 39
Spiny-Herb 146
Spiny Senna 186
Spreading Fanpetals 195
Spreading Fleabane 40
Spurge Family. See Euphorbiaceae
Squash Family. See Cucurbitaceae
Stachys coccinea 218
Stanleya pinnata 176
Star-Glory 216
Stephanomeria exigua 80
Sticky Snakeweed 159
Stingbush, Desert 190
Stonecrop Family. See Crassulaceae
Stork's-Bill
Desert 96
Redstem 95
Streptanthus carinatus ssp. arizonicus
48

Suncup
California 196
Golden 196
Heartleaf 197
Narrowleaf 61
Sunflower
Common 159
Desert 158
Plains 160
Sunflower Family. See Asteraceae
Sweetbush 152

T
Tabaco Amarillo 207
Tackstem, White 38
Tahoka Daisy 79
Talinum aurantiacum 202
Tangle, Turkey 72
Tansey-Aster 79
Tansey-Aster
Hoary 78
Lacy 165
Taraxacum officinale 170
Tecoma stans 173
Teddy-Bear Cholla 140
Tetraclea coulteri 72
Tetramerium nervosum 148
Texas Toadflax 131
Texas Virgin's Bower 68
Thamnosma montana 131
Thimblehead, Yellow 162
Thistle, New Mexico 77
Thorn-Apple, Sacred 70
Threadleaf Ragwort, Smooth 169
Threadstem, Redtip 50
Three-Awn
Purple 109
Red 109
Threefold, American 171
Three-Leaved Morning Glory 89
Thurber's Cotton 59
Thymophylla pentachaeta var.
belenidium 170
Thysanocarpus curvipes 139
Tickseed, Arizona 153
Tidestromia lanuginosa 136
Tierra, Flor de 107
Tiquilia
canescens var. canescens 83
plicata 83
Toadflax, Texas 131
Tobacco
Desert 71
Tree 207
Tobacco Weed 37
Toboso 209

Toloache 70
Tomatillo del Desierto 207
Torito 209
Trailing Four O'Clock 105
Trailing Windmills 105
Tree Tobacco 207
Trefoil
    Broom Bird's-Foot 184
    Desert Bird's-Foot 186
    Greene's Bird's-Foot 184
Tribulus terrestris 209
Trichoptilium incisum 171
Trichostema arizonicum 127
Trixis 171
Trixis californica 171
Trompetilla 224
Trumpetbush, Yellow 173
Trumpet, Desert 201
Trumpet, Hummingbird 221
Turkey Tangle 72
Turpentine Broom 131
Turpentine Brush 155
Turtleback 168
Twinberry 195
Twinevine, Smooth 138
Twining Snapdragon
    Violet 115
    Yellow 206

U

Uña de Gato 200
Unicorn Plant 109
Unicorn Plant, Desert 200
Uropappus lindleyi 172

V

Vaqueros, Espanta 136
Velvet, Desert 168
Velvet Mallow, Pink 103
Velvet-Pod Mimosa 93
Venado, Yerba del 80
Verbenaceae
    Phyla nodiflora 72
    Tetraclea coulteri 72
    Verbena gooddingii 117
Verbena, Desert Sand 104
Verbena gooddingii 117
Verbesina encelioides 173
Verde Azul, Palo 183
Verde, Blue Palo 183
Verdolaga 202
Vervain Family. *See* Verbenaceae
Vervain, Goodding's 117

Viejo, Cabeza de 85
Vine, Desert 192
Vine, Puncture 209
Violet Twining Snapdragon 115
Violet Wild Petunia 74
Virgen Maria, Hierba de la 72
Virgin's Bower, Texas 68

W

Walkingstick Cholla 88
Wallflower, Western 175
Wand Holdback 182
Waterleaf Family. *See*
    Hydrophyllaceae
Wedge-Leaf Whitlow-Grass 46
Weed, Rattlesnake 54
Weed, Tobacco 37
Western Coral-Bean 217
Western Sea-Purslane 75
Western Wallflower 175
Whispering Bells 189
White Bladderpod, Western 48
White Cupfruit 38
White Easter-Bonnet 40
White Honeysuckle, Dwarf 34
White Horse-Nettle 133
White-Margin Sandmat 54
White-Plume Wire-Lettuce 80
White Prickly Poppy 63
White-Stem Milkweed 150
White-Stem Paperflower 169
White Tackstem 38
White Zinnia 43
Whitlow-Grass, Wedge-Leaf 46
Wild Buckwheat, Abert's 65
Wild-Hyacinth 102
Wild Petunia, Violet 74
Willow, Desert 82
Willowweed 67
Windmills, Trailing 105
Wire-Lettuce, White-Plume 80
Wishbone-Bush, Desert 60
Wislizenia refracta ssp. *refracta* 179
Woody Aster, Orcutt's 81
Woolly Bluestar 36
Woolly-Daisy
    Pringle's 156
    Yellow 157
Woolly Honeysweet 136
Woolly Indian Paintbrush 225
Woolly Indianwheat 144
Woolly Plantain 144

Woolstar
    Desert 129
    Miniature 128
Wooly Crinklemat 83
Wrinkle-Fruit, Coulter's 72

X

Xylorhiza
    orcuttii 81
    tortifolia 82

Y

Yamate 150
Yellow Bee-Plant 178
Yellow Desert Evening Primrose
    198
Yellow Devil's Claw 200
Yellowdome 171
Yellow Ground-Cherry 207
Yellowhead 171
Yellow Indian-Mallow 193
Yellow Monkey-Flower 204
Yellowshow, Mexican 174
Yellow Thimblehead 162
Yellow-Throat Gilia, Arizona 111
Yellow-Throat Monkeyflower 115
Yellow Trumpetbush 173
Yellow Twining Snapdragon 206
Yellow Woolly-Daisy 157
Yerba Mansa 69
Yerba del Venado 80
Yucca
    Banana 34
    Mojave 35
    Soaptree 35
Yucca
    baccata 34
    elata 35
    schidigera 35

Z

Zauschneria 221
Zinnia acerosa 43
Zinnia, White 43
Zygophyllaceae
    Fagonia laevis 117
    Kallstroemia grandiflora 227
    Tribulus terrestris 209

$\mathcal{A}$BOUT THE AUTHOR

Richard Spellenberg is Professor Emeritus of Biology at New Mexico State University in Las Cruces, New Mexico. He obtained a doctoral degree in botany from the University of Washington in 1968, after which he moved to N.M.S.U., where he has since taught. He has studied plants in western North America during his career, particularly those of the desert American Southwest, contributing to numerous technical works on the classification of native plants. In addition he has contributed to several books on wildflowers and ecology.